THE RUSSET COAT

The oldest known engraving of the cottage in Alloway, Ayrshire, where Burns
was born. From McBain's 'Burns' Cottage' Glasgow 1904

(*By courtesy of the Mitchell Library, Glasgow*)

THE RUSSET COAT

A CRITICAL STUDY OF BURNS' POETRY AND OF ITS BACKGROUND

by

CHRISTINA KEITH

*M.A. (Oxon), M.A. (Cantab), M.A. (Edinb).
Scholar of Newnham College, Cambridge.
Sometime Fellow and Tutor of St. Hilda's
College, Oxford. Awarded Special Prize for
Gaelic at the National Mod, Dunoon*

'The star that rules my luckless lot
'Has fated me the russet coat
'An' damned my fortune to the groat
   'But in requit
'Has blest me with a random shot
   'O' countra wit'
   Burns—*Ep. to J. Smith*

London

Robert Hale Limited

63 Old Brompton Road S.W.7

FIRST PUBLISHED 1956

Printed in Great Britain by
The Camelot Press Ltd., London and Southampton

CONTENTS

SECTION I

SECTION II

SECTION III

LIST OF ILLUSTRATIONS

CHAPTER I

THE BACKGROUND OF BURNS:
EIGHTEENTH-CENTURY SCOTLAND

THE EIGHTEENTH CENTURY, into which Burns had the amazing good fortune to be born, was Scotland's Golden Age, when everywhere her latent talents were unfolding, and the sun rose towards the high meridian of her literary achievement. Not only that—it was the bright breathing-space between two centuries of religious intolerance—in different ways, both equally repellent. With the close of the nightmare seventeenth century, the Killing Times were over. No longer did the Edinburgh crowds mill round the gallows in the Grass-market for a sight of the latest Covenanter sent there 'to glorify God'. No longer were the dragoons out riding the Ayrshire mosses after hunted men. The era of the Covenant was over.... And the nineteenth century of materialism and Disruption, rending the land from the Solway to the Pentland with legalistic disputes, had not yet begun so that, in this Golden Age, Scotland had a breathing-space to think, for once, of other things than religion. It was this lighter mental atmosphere, already by Burns' birth in 1759 well-established over the whole realm, that made his literary achievement possible.... For this was the century of Boswell and Hume, of the raciest biography and the most original philosophy, of the revolutionary economics of queer Adam Smith,—the century too of the captivating old songs, 'John cum kiss me now', 'Guidwife, count the lawin' ', 'De'il tak' the wars'—of the merry Scots country dances, alike in a village barn or in a fashionable Edinburgh oyster-cellar—the century of the finest claret and the best law— of the infinite variety on the road from His Grace's magnificent chaise and four with its postillions and powdered footmen, to the blue-clad beggar with his badge—of chapmen like Patrick Walker

with the most breath-taking broadsheets in their pack—of the
first ships on the Clyde—of the beautiful old Edinburgh silver
and the spacious Regency squares—of surgery and medicine
such as carried Edinburgh's name far over the Seven Seas—of a
New Town with the most brilliant talk in Europe—before the
blighting nineteenth century fell, hushing all laughter on the
Sabbath and silencing all talk but what bore on the Free Kirk or
the Established, and strangling all thought, like an iron curtain
between living things and the sun. The eighteenth century was
Scotland's Golden Age.

For even at its outset, the atmosphere was lightened. The heavy
air that had hung thick round the Laigh Parliament House in
Edinburgh, where dripped the thumbscrew and the boot still
red with the blood of tortured Covenanters—that heavy air was
blown to the four airts. And if it were a quarrel nearly as violent
as the religious strife itself that now dispelled it, it may well be
that nothing less could have cleared that foul air. But in the
raging contentions over the famous—or infamous—Treaty of
Union of 1707, torture, arraignment, persecution itself were alike
swept into the limbo of the forgotten past, to disappear for ever
from contemporary Scottish thought. The atmosphere had
lightened. . . . Tho' it was a tornado that cleared the air. Not since
Bannockburn—and that was 1314—had Scotland been so conscious of her national identity, as now in 1707. And conscious
of it, only, it would appear, at the moment of losing it, for
henceforth her destinies were to be merged in those of the
larger kingdom to the South. Fury at such monstrous annihilation
—for it seemed no less to the man in the street—stung the country
wide awake, intensifying and sharpening those elements in the
national character that, by long disuse, had been growing blunted
or even indistinguishable. But now they were pin-pointed.
Never had men been so Scotch before. In the redoubtable thistle,
reposing on Queen Anne's bosom on that last Scots coin struck
on the eve of the Union, every prickle stuck out. . . . From the
point of view of our poet, this process is of great importance. For
the facets of Scots individuality were now being chiselled sharp
and clear so that men in Aberdeen—the cool and uncovenanted
Aberdeen—could realise their kinship with—say—dour Pres-
byterians in Edinburgh or simple country folk as in Thomas

Boston's remote parish of Ettrick, or worldly merchants stepping it high on the Trongate of Glasgow. Nationality now transcended parochialisms. All were Scots now. A public was thus being created that would recognise Burns to be not now a merely local figure, but of an appeal throughout Scotland. He was indeed the first Scots writer to be of national significance. . . . More than that, his subjects also were being prepared for him. For, had Burns come to Ayrshire in the seventeenth century, he would have found only folk like the pious John Brown of Priesthill, whom Clavers' dragoons shot down, or the fanatic Peden the Prophet skulking in dens and caves, or the ardent young Richard Cameron, the Red Rebel of Airdsmoss, all of them men fired to utter sincerity by one idea and so, incapable of being satirised. But, with this tide of nationalism spreading—even as the flood-tide of religion ebbed—other sorts came now into view—the tinkers on the road, the topers in the howffs, Holy Willie in his pew in Mauchline Kirk. And, unlike their seventeenth-century predecessors, these were universals—folk to be found as readily anywhere else. Thus, by the middle of the eighteenth century, the public and the material were alike ready for the satirist's pen. . . . But, by then, other changes too had taken place. For, after the Union with its bitterness had unified the country, as nothing else could have done, came a major event that extended, as it were, that country's cultural frontiers. In 1715 Jacobite Scotland rose for James the Old Chevalier. And Jacobite Scotland was largely, if not entirely, Scotland north of the Highland Line—country Aberdeenshire, in fact ('The Standard on the Braes o' Mar') under Mar himself, the Gordons of Huntly and the Earl Marischal. Here then, for the first time, a Gaelic-speaking area in the Highlands aligned itself with Southern Scotland, if only on behalf of such a sorry personage as 'Mr. Melancholy', heir to the long line of Stuart kings at Holyrood. But tho' it was only country Aberdeenshire so far—and the more distant areas of the Highlands and Islands remained in the '15 totally unaffected —it was still the first direct infusion of different blood and different traditions into the make-up of Scottish nationality. After the '15, Scotland no longer consisted merely of the cities, the Lowlands and a strip of the East Coast with its ancient towns of Arbroath—Montrose—Dundee. After the '15, if you spoke of

Scotland, you had to think of the Hinterland too, that vague, mountainous, unpredictable region of which the wilds of Aberdeenshire were but the gateway—those menacing fastnesses behind the mists—the Bens and over the trackless moors—those also were now equally Scotland. The horizon of the nation had widened, as throughout the eighteenth century it was to widen still more. . . . But the process came too late for Burns. Of East Coast blood himself (the most practical blood in Scotland) and born in agricultural Ayrshire, he never assimilated this new, strange element in the national character. For him · Scotland was always—the beggars, the topers, the churchgoers of the Lowlands and the girls you met with them, the woods and burns they walked beside. It was left for Scott, nurtured from boyhood on Border romance (at Smailholm Tower, on Tweedside, or riding the mosses at Carter Fell) to seize on and interpret the kindred spirit of the Highlands and relate it to the national character, as one component part of it. But for Burns neither Highland Ben nor Border Peel, tho' he visited both in his journeyings, held any meaning. He was stone-cold to both. It is this limitation of outlook that has to be considered when one comes to assess his personality and his title to speak for all Scotland. . . . And after the '15 came the '45, a Rising on a much grander scale and involving, especially after Culloden, the whole of the Highlands as far North as John o' Groats, as far West as Barra. With the Prince hiding in moor and cave or threading his way between the Outer Isles, and the English redcoats hot after him, not a Highlander now but was conscious of the antithesis between Scots and English. Not a Highlander but knew he was part of Scotland now. The lines from Holyrood now ran straight out to Benbecula and reached to far Strathnaver. Edinburgh at long last was the nerve-centre of the whole kingdom. What the hated Union had begun in 1707, the White Rose and its aftermath completed in the '45. For the first time, the whole of geographical Scotland was one united nation. . . . If rather a dull one. It was a good thing Burns didn't come in the first half of the eighteenth century, for there would have been no brilliant capital to welcome him. With no persecutions truly, Edinburgh in the early 1700's had now no pageantry either. With the last Scots Parliament sitting in 1707, the ancients in the dark Closes off the High Street might well talk of the magnificence they had once seen at that very Close-mouth when, year by year, the gorgeous procession of the Riding of the Parliament would sweep through the Canongate from royal Holyrood—Commissioners of the Burghs and Shires, periwigged Judges and their train, peers of Scotland in scarlet and ermine on their gaily caparisoned horses with their lacqueys in gold and silver coats, resplendent Bishops and the two Archbishops in brilliant vestments, trumpeters and heralds and pursuivants, the Sword of State, the Sceptre and the Crown— with the lawn sleeves of the Bishop of Edinburgh reaching out from a window high above, to bless them all as they passed. The Riding of the Parliament! Back into Scotland's remotest history it ran—the jingling of the bridles, the blast of the trumpets rousing the long-dead centuries. But all that was over. With the stroke of the pen in 1707 finished and done with. No need to crouch in the Closes now, or listen for a phantom bridle jingling up the causeway. Nothing in scarlet and ermine would ever pass that way again. . . . So, the political Scotland over and done with, it had to be a social Scotland now. New lights were riding on the horizon now. And, with the lighter air, new interests were springing up. You could sing a song now. And it needn't be one of those 'Gude and Godlie Ballates' either that the Kirk had tried to impose. But older songs than those. And bolder. Jollier songs altogether, like those in 'Cockelbie's Sow' that uproarious old poem of the fifteenth century, or in 'The Complaynt of Scotland' of 1549, when Mary Queen of Scots was but a child of six, and Scotland still carefree. Gay songs of Robin Hood or Johnny Armstrong, the Border reiver, or wild songs of 'The Red Harlaw'. Some, it is true, had got lost in the interval, but snatches of others still survived, enough to show that even in the worst shadow of the Reformation, someone must still have been humming them beneath his breath. . . . And now, old Scots songs became the rage. Old Scots poems too. What with the weary Kirk and that black Geneva gown, it was many a long day since Scotland had had her fill of either. But she took it now. In 1706, on the eve of the hated Union, Watson's Collection (the first of many) came out, of *Comic and Serious Scots Poems*. Here you could read the famous 'Christis Kirk on the Green' of King James I, that delectable poem of villagers on high holiday, or Sempill's popular mock-elegy 'The Piper of Kilbarchan', or Montgomerie's notable allegory 'The Cherrie and the Slae', a dull poem perhaps but with a ravishing metre. Burns pored over all three. . . . By 1724 there was more. Allan Ramsay the poet gathered all the old songs he could find into his *Tea-Table Miscellany* that Edinburgh devoured. The very cosiness of its title emphasises the difference between the comfortable eighteenth century and the bad old days of the Covenanters. Was not Edinburgh sitting at her tea-table now, instead of glowering up at a scaffold? But Scotland couldn't have enough of her old songs. By the mid-century there was a flood of them. *The Lark* ('my constant vademecum', Burns) in 1740 held nearly 500 of them—Scots and English too—with a glossary to help you out with the old Scots words. And 'The Charmer' came out after that, with more, and 'The Linnet', 'The Thrush', 'The Robin'—the whole country was singing. From castle to cot, the songs went everywhere. Most important of all, they were in Burns' pocket as, a lad of sixteen, he guided his plough, and in his head—ringing by day and by night.

And the songs weren't the only let-up either. There were books and plays. By 1725 you could borrow a book that was not ecclesiastical from Allan Ramsay's pleasant library in the High Street, and by 1736—wonder of wonders!—you could even see a play. The Drama was coming back! Tho' it was only the inoffensive and now well-known *Gentle Shepherd*, and the modest hall which showed it, had incontinently—under the fury of the Kirk—to shut up shop, but—Edinburgh had seen it! And with the turn of the century in 1759 the spark had become a fire. Here was the whole town crowding to the new Theatre Royal to see that wild success *Douglas*—the play that turned every Scottish head that saw it. A Scotsman—and a minister of the Kirk, at that!—John Home, had written it, and here—in open defiance of the fuming Edinburgh Presbytery—here was another, the most distinguished cleric in Scotland, the unsnubbable 'Jupiter' Carlyle, actually leaning out of his box 'neath the gay Canongate candles, to applaud it. The spark had become a fire! By 1781 you might call it a furnace. The immortal Mrs. Siddons was playing in town. And the General Assembly itself—that august Parliament of the Kirk—had perforce to rearrange its sessions (or there mightn't have been a Geneva gown present!) so as not to clash

with her performances. Truly the wheel had come full circle—
since the long shadows by the gallows in the Grassmarket.

EXCURSUS ON DRAMA

Tho' it wasn't as surprising as all that. For Scotland has always
been, in her way, a dramatic nation. Not, of course, in the way of
great tragedy, which is fundamentally alien to her temper,—
for even her great novelists fail in tragic themes, Scott's *Bride of
Lammermoor* and Stevenson's ambitious *Weir of Hermiston* alike
falling flat. But in the drama of low life, Scotland, like Holland,
finds herself. Here, like Holland (also afflicted with a stern Reformation and also finding relief from it in a similar way, in the
alehouse studies of Jan Steen)—here, like Holland then, she excels.
Give her a pot-house scene or the rollicking merriment of the
road, and no one can do it better. In this sphere, the nation's
dramatic history has been continuous. It began, as far as can be
traced, in the early fourteenth century with the *Tale of Rauf
Colzear*, a collier who, entertaining an unknown foreigner,
knocks him about in the wildest horse-play—only to discover on
his return visit, coals and all, to Paris, that it is Charlemagne, the
King himself, he has been buffeting about—a situation fraught
with the authentic appeal of its descendant, the Pantomime
Transformation Scene. *Cockelbie's Sow* too has just as lively
vignettes, with a harlot feasting her jovial friends on the proceeds
of the sow's sale—for a threepenny bit! While, all through the
(still un-Reformed) fourteenth and fifteenth centuries went on the
immensely popular miracle-plays and pageants,—presenting
Bible-stories of the most sensational kind (by choice)—like
Daniel in the lions' den, or Herodias dancing for John the
Baptist's head, with the head actually being struck off. You
couldn't have it too thrilling! It was in the towns, naturally,
you'd see most of this play-acting. Here is the city of Aberdeen,
in 1445, performing in the open air 'the secret drama of the Halie
Blude' (Holy Blood)—and in the next century the City of
Edinburgh's official welcome to Marie of Guise (mother of Mary
Queen of Scots)[1] takes the form of a pageant and a play. A few

[1] For this information I am indebted to Moffat's *The Bible in Scotland*,
pp. 30-2.

years later, on Good Friday morning in Stirling, they put on 'a drama against the Papists' by a certain Friar Kyllour before King James V himself. And you might have thought the Reformation, that stopped so many interesting things, would have put a stop to this fun too. But at first it did not. For here, on a July day in 1571 (eleven years after Scotland had been 'converted') is no less a personage than John Knox himself listening to a play at the University of St. Andrews. It wasn't a mild play either, for he saw '*The Castle of Edinburgh*, according to Mr. Knox's doctrine, being besieged and taken, and the captain, with one or two with him, hanged in effigy'. So writes the engaging James Melville, himself a young St. Andrews' student at the time. Even six years later at Perth, play-acting was still rampant. They were staging the Corpus Christi play,—that 'idolatrous and superstitious fancy' as it was now called—on a June day in the open. Now, however, the Kirk had had time to get going and the rash players were threatened with her excommunication. . . . Aligned with these Bible stories is the famous *Christis Kirk on the Green* (a wild success for three centuries and the direct spiritual ancestor of Burns' Holy Fair) where the jollification takes in the whole village and is as rough and riotous as either Rauf Colzear or Cockelbie's Sow. It is not till the eve of Flodden, in the flush of the Renaissance, that sophistication comes in, with the Court poet Dunbar and his incredible 'Twa Mariit Wemen and the Wedo' on that summer midnight over the roses and the wine—a dramatic interlude as outspoken as anything in the Heptameron of La Reine Margot, its contemporary in France—. Sophisticated too is, a little later, Lyndesay's drama of the *Three Estates*. And with that—like a thunderbolt—in the sixteenth century, descends the terrible Reformation. But even then, the dramatic instinct is not wholly quenched. Oddly enough, John Knox himself is the best witness to it, in those parts of his *History* like the brilliant dialogues between himself and the Queen—in his realistic account of Cardinal Beaton's murder—in his eyewitness tale of the sacking of St. Giles—all of them good 'theatre'. Nor, in the dreary Killing Time that followed, did drama utterly die. Driven underground, it is true, but here is Patrick Walker the chapman, up and down the road. And if you buy his broadsheets, as they did like wildfire alike on Edinburgh streets and lonely Galloway moors, you'll

get every kind of a thrill that you could ask of the tensest drama—
the thud of the dragoons riding across the mosses after John
Brown, the jingle of Clavers' bridle and the curt order to shoot,
the wild eyes of Peden the Prophet, as he sat in mortal danger, at
your ingle-cheek. But now, in the Golden eighteenth century
drama was free again. And down in country Ayrshire Burns was
to write his 'Jolly Beggars' and later, at Ellisland, his exhilarating
'Tam o' Shanter'. Sudden and unheralded as these two pieces
may appear, there is in reality nothing of suddenness about them.
Like the 'small white rose of Scotland' itself, their roots strike
deep and far—sunk profoundly in the nation's past. . . . And
after Burns' day, the drama of low life still went on. In the strait-
laced nineteenth century, it is true, it was again driven underground—but now, Neil Munro's Para Handy stories, Joe Corrie's
tense 'one-act'ers, the Repertory Theatres in Glasgow—Perth
—Dundee,—the Drama Festivals over the whole land, are one
and all in the tradition. Scotland's dramatic instinct, over the
centuries has been continuous.

EIGHTEENTH-CENTURY SCOTLAND'S BOOKS

But if the theatre, in the late eighteenth century, was making
the most notable come-back, it was by no means the only one.
Scotland itself was crackling with life—intellect stirring in all
directions. Tho' it was, unexpectedly enough, from the Highlands that the first sheet-lightning broke, with the publication of
Macpherson's famous Ossian in 1762. Ossian indeed carried
Scotland's name to every library table in Europe, and to every
literary salon—starting the rage for sentiment that was to last
for half a century and issue in Goethe's Werther and Scott's own
early work, Lenore. Were the Highlands—it was the universal
query now—really as Ossian showed them, misty mountains and
mournful heroines—tears and laments and phantom heroes? No
one knew but it made you weep to think they were. If hard-
headed folk like Mme. de Staël in worldly Paris (not to speak of
Napoleon later) choked with sobs over Ossian's plaints, no
wonder that inexperienced young Robert Burns in stolid Ayrshire didn't quite know what to make of this queer Highlander.
Over Henry Mackenzie's Man of Feeling (published nearly ten

years later in 1771) 'a book I prize next to the Bible' he was clearer.
It, at any rate, was Scotch of the brand he knew and written by a
plain Edinburgh man. Nothing here about mountains or mist,
tho' plenty still about tears. Burns, untaught by wider reading
(for 'prizing the Bible' didn't mean reading it. It was not until
his accident in Edinburgh in 1787 that he took to that, getting as
far as Joshua) and inexperienced in the great masters, lapped its
easy pathos up. And while the mawkish sentiment of both these
prize best-sellers must have been bad for any young poet—
accounting, later on, for such things as the fulsomeness of 'Edina'
and the worst sentimental patches of 'The Cottar'—they probably
did him no more harm than that. For, reflecting at the mature
age of twenty-eight in his autobiographical letter to Moore, on
the books that had given him the most pleasure, of all he'd ever
read, Burns singles out an astonishing couple—(1) an obscure
Life of Hannibal, author unnamed and (2) the *History of Sir
William Wallace* (himself an Ayrshire man) in a bowdlerised
version, then current, of Blind Harry—from which it can safely
be assumed that Robin's was not a bookish mind. Unimpression-
able with regard to scenery, he was just as unreceptive to the
written word. When he came to his life-work, the songs, he had
fortunately shaken off both Ossian and Mackenzie. . . . Tho'
there were books then being written in his Scotland, that were
well worth reading. Edinburgh knew them all. Apart from the
two best-sellers, there was the Glasgow-born novelist Smollett
whose latest work *Humphrey Clinker* (1771) brought his Southern
readers to the beauties of Loch Lomond and later, if somewhat
less flatteringly, up Edinburgh's own historic High Street. In
Theology, if you liked it—and Edinburgh did!—there was a
new and broad-minded kind purveyed by the admirable Dr.
Blair of the High Kirk, author of those *Sermons* that even George
III wished to read. In History there was Robertson, Principal of
the University, for the first time bringing the *History of Scotland*
in pleasant, and still readable narrative to Londoners that had
never looked at a Scots historian before. In Philosophy—ah!
here Scotland had once again a native-born son, David Hume, as
completely at home in Paris as her sons like Duns Scotus had been
in older days. Even more so, perhaps. For Hume not only wrote
his *Treatise of Human Nature* that the Sorbonne studied, but knew

Paris's fashionable world too in his friendship with a delightful French Marquise—and moved, as to the manner born, among the candles and music of Versailles. And in a quiet corner of the Canongate, sat shy Adam Smith whose epoch-making *Wealth of Nations* in 1776 had just introduced the world to the new and portentous subject of Economics. It was a society bred on books like these—the books Burns never read—that was being prepared to welcome him, as no Edinburgh society before or since would have welcomed a raw Ayrshire poet. For what would the fanatic seventeenth century have done to the brazen author of 'The Holy Fair', or the narrow Disruption nineteenth confronted with the blasphemy of 'Holy Willie's Prayer'? But the broad-minded eighteenth, at a first glance in 1786, asked him—straight from the plough—to dine with the cream of their own intellectual company, and unhesitatingly set the cachet of immortality—then in their gift—to the hitherto provincial *Kilmarnock Edition* so that, when in 1787 the first *Edinburgh Edition* of his poems came out, London (that had left the *Kilmarnock* unheeded) printed it at once, with Dublin—Philadelphia—New York—following suit. It was eighteenth-century Edinburgh 'made' Burns.

EIGHTEENTH-CENTURY EDINBURGH

The Capital that welcomed him, the Edinburgh that had been growing up now from 1769 on, was the city that is still the delight of Europe—that New Town of those splendid streets and squares, with their spacious, uncrowded magnificence and their long, alluring vistas carrying the eye far over the Forth into the distant mountains of the North. Robert Adam was at work, planning the elegance and perfect proportions of Charlotte Square: in the drawing-rooms of Moray Place—but a stone's-throw away— there were again mantelpieces and ceilings of a delicacy and curious carving that recalled the art of the sixteenth century in town-houses such as that of Marie of Guise, the Queen-Regent, in the old, dark Edinburgh High Street. . . . And by the close of the eighteenth century, Raeburn was painting men like the Highland chief, The MacNab, in full—and no longer forbidden —Highland dress, or the eminent Sir John Sinclair, Founder of the Board of Agriculture, or the homely and wise Dr. Adam,

B

Rector of the High School, or the sinister hanging Judge, Lord
Braxfield—even as young Allan Ramsay earlier painted the fine
Scots ladies in their delicate satins and pearly lace, with roses as
exquisitely poised on hair or bosom as ever was the Pompadour's
—so that the eye to-day can picture the people who moved in
those drawing-rooms or walked in those pleasant squares. A
wonderful Edinburgh—and a brilliant Scotland!

For if Edinburgh in the second half of the eighteenth century
seethed with intellectual life, it wasn't only Edinburgh, but
country Scotland as well. Boswell, touring it with Dr. Johnson in
1773, has left it on record that in the rudest country inn, as at
Glenmoriston, he'd come across books like *The Spectator* (which
you would never nowadays in any Scots inn at all!). In Dun-
vegan, over in lonely Skye, on every window-sill the Doctor
could finger a classical tome. In the ministers' manses he saw the
walls lined with authors of the standing of Bossuet or Massillon.
And the very rustics knew their Latin. While in the wilds of the
excessively practical Nor'-East he came upon eccentrics like Lord
Monboddo arguing with almost Oxford learning about the
Homeric problem or the Origin of Man. And if you think
Boswell is carefully choosing his evidence, you've only to look at
Sir John Sinclair's *First Statistical Account*, published, it is true, at
the close of the eighteenth century in 1798, but written of an
era at least ten years earlier, to find Boswell's account elaborated
in detail. Not a parish in rural Scotland but was alive with interest
in the Arts. The brilliance of the Capital was reflected in a
thousand facets in village and hamlet and town. Never had
Scotland been so well-educated before. Never has she been so
well-educated since. It was on to a stage like this, before an
audience as many-sided and as gifted that Burns came forward in
the second half of the eighteenth century to make his trials.

BURNS AGAINST HIS LITERARY BACKGROUND

Educated he was, if only self-educated, but without the discipline of Church learning which Knox, for example, a trained
priest, had had. With it, or because of it, Knox was able to write
that long and fascinating *History of the Reformation*. Without it,
Burns, never having had the advantage of any mental discipline

whatsoever, can write nothing long at all. His interest soon flags—his répertoire a series of occasional pieces. By contrast, again, with Knox, who had seen and lived in other countries, Burns, who had done neither, is, in outlook, provincial. He sees nothing but Ayrshire. By contrast, further, with Fergusson, his immediate predecessor (and to some extent, model) who had had a University education, Burns' outlook is illiterate. For while Fergusson, with his University behind him, is sensible of his own ignorance and will write only of what he knows, 'The Leith Races', 'The Farmer's Ingle', Burns, without any University standard, is totally unaware of it. Never once does it dawn on him there is anything more to know, so that he will write with equal confidence an epigram on a translation of Martial (whom he did not know) and a poem on Hallowe'en (which he did). . . . And when one comes to the perennial stuff of poetry—things like the Charlemagne legend, or the even more famous story of King Arthur and the Round Table, that had embroidered and enriched the fabric of all European literatures (Scots literature among them) from the fifteenth century on—all that is but a blank page to Burns. He knows nothing of it. Nor of that wealth of classical mythology that, with a single word, can light torches of poetic fire to illumine and glorify the surrounding scene. Yet Dunbar before him has the trick of it, and the modern Scots Renaissance School ('Babylon blaws doun in stour'—Wm. Soutar) after him. But Burns? No: alone of Scots poets, he claims no link with the immemorial background of European poetic thought. He alone knows no Muses. His poetry, therefore, rings no bells. There is a thinness about it that, if you come to it from any other poet, strikes you at once. It is all on the surface. That is all that Robin sees. And sometimes—you will say—a very good surface too. But in the Edinburgh of Hume's *Treatises* and Robertson's *History* and Adam Smith's *Wealth of Nations*—even of Smollett's *Humphrey Clinker*—they looked for something more. And Edinburgh opinion—even kindly Edinburgh opinion—was quick to notice that the young man from Ayrshire was over-sure of himself. A clever tongue—and ideas—but he made no allowances at all, in this exceptionally gifted Capital, for anybody else having either. It is a shallowness that is apparent also, if inevitably, in his work. . . . For, apart from Ossian and

Mackenzie, Burns had read little. Fergusson and Allan Ramsay, to be sure—some Shenstone, Pope, Sterne—Thomson's *Winter* —Beattie—nearly all of them his own contemporaries, or near-contemporaries. Yet it is not from these, but from writers of an earlier age, breathing a different air and looking at life from a different angle, that a man broadens his mind. But to these, Burns, not being a bookish person, was allergic. So that, without the breadth of mind this kind of education gives, he came to believe —for all his window-dressing of the brotherhood of Man (borrowed from the contemporary slogans of the French Revolution) that Virtue resided only in the class he knew. 'The birkie ca'd a lord' never had a trace of it. And Robin becomes— to his own disaster—Scotland's first class-conscious poet. . . . And, as it is assuredly from the Past, its standards and its art, that a man acquires a knowledge of Beauty, Burns, being thus insensitive to the Past (for his mental interest, like his physical, took in only what was nearest to him, as the mouse, the mountain daisy, the girl just then on the doorstep)—Burns therefore never attained to this, for a poet, most vital knowledge. So that he writes, as readily, abominations like 'the tenebrific scene', as gems like

> 'whiles glitter'd to the nightly rays
> 'wi bickerin', dancin' dazzle'.

He has no aesthetic criterion. . . . His appeal to the ear also traverses but the range of everyday things—the only things that interested him—like the hisses in the 'Holy Fair', the reel in 'Tam o' Shanter', the staggering lines in 'Death and Dr. Hornbook'. A witchery potent, no doubt, and at times both instant and compelling—but a witchery of the street. For he cannot lift you, like Milton or Tennyson, those masters of verbal harmonies, into the sonorous music of the spheres. . . . And being thus insensitive to the past, it further follows there is little appeal in Burns' work to the imagination. When the Kirk (the only traditional institution to which he responded) is behind him, her imagery does indeed colour his thought, which elsewhere is but plain statement, unrelieved by literary figures of any kind. . . . In the main, then, his appeal—ironically enough, like that of the Kirk he hated—is neither to the imagination nor to the ear, but to the intellect. But, luckily for him, Scotland has always been a country that looked to the intellect for enjoyment. Even from the time of Barbour, author of the earliest known Scots poem 'The Brus', emphasis falls largely on the intellect, for Barbour was not only Archdeacon of Aberdeen, but an Oxford scholar too. And the galaxy of poets at the Renaissance Court of James IV were not only poets, but men of learning as well—Henryson, author of the delightful pastoral 'Robin and Makyn' but also a learned Benedictine at Dunfermline Abbey, Dunbar of 'The Golden Targe' an Oxford man again and as a Franciscan, trained in the Church's lore, Gavin Douglas, first European translator of Virgil's *Aeneid*. Even when the writer is not himself of much learning, the appeal is still the same, as in Davie Lyndesay's 'Three Estates', making a direct bid to the intellect, in its powerful political satire. To this traditional bias in favour of the intellect rather than the senses, the Reformation only added strength, for Knox, author, it is true, of the famous *History*, is even better known as the planner of Scotland's austere and highbrow modern education. In the seventeenth century, the great Samuel Rutherfurd of the magnificent *Letters* and the rebellious *Lex Rex*—the foremost author of his time in Scotland—was to be found in the Chair of Latin in Edinburgh University and later as Principal of St. Mary's College, St. Andrews. While in the eighteenth Hume—Boswell—Adam Smith—were all of them definitely preoccupied with learning. And if Burns, who now took up their mantle, was Scotland's first unlearned writer, the appeal of his work was nevertheless—paradoxically enough—the same as theirs, and in line with his country's long tradition. As firmly as Knox himself, Burns aimed at the intellect. Tho', being as he was, without the ancient learning, he—more than any of his predecessors—was thrown on his own resources to do it.

These were, however, considerable. He was possessed of a native wit, keen and sharp, that made him see through shams, and a tongue, the match of it, to pillory them. And not having the learning of his forebears to trick out and adorn the wit, he must needs polish that wit itself till, sharp as a surgeon's knife, it cut right through to the bone. You might miss a point of Dunbar's for the aureate gods and goddesses nearly smothering it. Nobody in this world ever missed a point of Burns's. With nothing to shade it, it is diamond-clear. . . . And having great natural parts, he did not transmogrify the rural life he saw around him, into such stylised woodenness as Ramsay's 'Gentle Shepherd'. He looked directly at his world and drew from that. Moreover, the Cottar, tho' clearly drawn from life, is not a transcript either, but an artistic whole. Burns could create. . . . He had, further, an imagination that,—since it could not feed on the famous mythology of the past—had perforce to feed on something within its own range, as—the superstitions of the Kirk, the twa dogs, the mountain daisy. Within that range, it is both original and sincere and can move an audience as it will. When, however, it is flung beyond that range and faced with the historic past or the glorious present of Edinburgh, it fails dismally, as in the artificial 'Edina' which moves nobody. The quality, indeed, of Burns' imagination is sharply realist. For while Scott at the mouth of an old Close in the High Street would see the centuries roll back in vivid and romantic cavalcade, Burns—at the same point—never saw anything but a tavern, and a chair to carry him to Clarinda. And no visitor, great or small, of all the millions that, down the ages, have paused o'er the city, ever saw less of Edinburgh's beauty. Robin, indeed, looked through it blankly, as he did through Highland Ben and Border Peel. For him they had, all three, no existence. . . . And he had, finally, a gift that only came to him late in life, after much trial and error—an artistic skill that became, in his best songs, well-nigh impeccable. Here, with a self-criticism as remarkable as it is unexpected, in a man of his hot blood, he pruned and cut, cut and pruned, till only the rounded bud remained—the glowing heart of the song, crystal-clear and brief as the rose itself. And the song, with the certainty of an eagle's wing, carried the emotion he desired, straight to the listener's heart. . . . With these gifts and these deficiencies, Burns had really no choice in the form his work took. Apart from the epistle (which has more the character of versified prose, but to which he gave a new life by making it the vehicle of his own rich personality) there are only two literary forms that demand no background and no mental breadth for their successful practice —the satire and the song. With the wit, and the tongue—you can write satire. From Rome down, who wrote it first, it needs only these and concentration upon its immediate object. The song, again, is all the better for no background and demands the same kinds of heat and concentration as the satire, but in a positive— not negative—direction. To the song, then, and the satire, by his very limitations, Burns was, of necessity, driven. Of these forms and of these only, he made a complete success.

So that, on the momentous November evening in 1786 when, an unknown young man of twenty-seven, he first rode into Edinburgh, he was not as empty-handed as he seemed. He had, indeed, considerable assets. Already to his credit stood the *Kilmarnock Edition*. And in the *Kilmarnock* was 'The Cottar's Saturday Night' that he himself considered his best work, and for satires, that scathing 'Holy Fair' and for epistles, some of the best he was ever to write, like that gay one to James Smith

> 'And large, before Enjoyment's gale,
> 'Let's tak' the tide'—

And for songs, that 'Corn-Rigs' (the only good one) that would ensure him a place, if not at the head, at least among the first half-dozen of his country's lyrists. And, for humour, the incomparable 'Address to the De'il'. Up his sleeve (written, but not published) there was the blistering 'Holy Willie's Prayer', that most perfect example of satire in our tongue, and the highly original cantata of 'The Jolly Beggars'. All in all, Burns came to Edinburgh with a full quiver. Had he never written another word, he would still take his place, on his satires, as a classic of English literature. . . . Apart from his poetic achievement, Burns came to Edinburgh in the prime of manhood, with his mind razor-sharp to the characters of those around him. Had he not proved it, with the beggars in Poosie Nansie's, with the ministers and their audiences in Mauchline Kirk, pin-pointed one and all in his ruthless satire? With an eye too, to the excellences of family life. The Cottar, if over-sentimentalised, is still a recognisable picture of a well-known original. . . . And with a fund of humour for all things, high and low. Burns, that is, was now in the full tide of mastery of his craft. . . . Yet, after Edinburgh, he wrote no more satires, few of these salty epistles even, so full of urbane wisdom —nothing of low life to compare with 'The Jolly Beggars', nor of good life to set alongside 'The Cottar'. At twenty-seven, the full flood of his genius seems arrested—dammed up. That wit,

diamond-clear, razor-sharp, found nothing, it seems, further to
cut. . . . What, then, happened to Burns in Edinburgh? It was not
lack of recognition. For Edinburgh—brilliant, sophisticated
Edinburgh—it is a matter of history now—took the young poet
straightway to her arms, if not to her heart. Within a fortnight
of his arrival, every door was opened to him. And it is likewise
admitted that this tumultuous reception did not sweep him, raw
as he was, off his feet. He moved through the elegant drawing-
rooms, sat at wine with the learned and the travelled and the
polished and talked with them as if he were sitting and talking
in his rightful place, where he had always been, where he should
be. And yet—found nothing to write of! But by his second visit
in 1787 it had got about that the clever young Ayrshire satirist
was keeping a memorandum-book, with the characters of his
entertainers shatteringly—and amusingly, if you took it that way
—hit off to the life. And the epigram on the dignified Lord
Advocate ending

> 'His argument he tint it
>
> .   .   .   .   .
>
> But what his common sense came short,
> He eked out wi' law, man'

or that on the eloquence of the Dean (the extremely popular
Henry Erskine)

> 'Like wind-driven hail it did assail,
> 'Or torrents owre a lin, man:
> 'The Bench sae wise lift up their eyes,
> 'Hauf-wauken'd wi' the din, man'

tho' neither was at the time published, may well explain why
brilliant Edinburgh, on second thoughts, had appreciably cooled
off. A formidable pen! But the epigrams, clever as they were,
were not satire. Edinburgh might enjoy them—or fear them—
but the world at large, to whom the Lord Advocate and the
Dean were but names—could not savour them to the full.
Whereas folk like Holy Willie or the preachers at Mauchline
Fair, unlike the Dean, had a universal audience, for hypocrites
are kent folk to all the world. How then came it that Burns wrote
no more satire? . . . But for satire you have to know your victims

—so to speak,—inside out, as Horace knew the bore of the Via Sacra on his daily walks through the lively Forum, and the travellers he would meet on the way to the coast. As Burns did too, who had lived all his life with Holy Willie at his elbow and seen Holy Fairs times without number. Whereas the men he met now at the fine Edinburgh tables, with the candle-light falling softly on polished silver and fragile cut crystal, were men he met only there—mere voices to him. They talked—or listened—but what they did to-morrow, or what they were really thinking now? Who could tell? How could any man tell? For there was an impenetrable armour of sophistication—polish—conventionality —whatever it was—about them, that kept you at arm's length and effectually prevented you from ever really knowing. Burns would plunge with a forthright Jacobin swordthrust, and the Lord Advocate, or his like, merely lifting an eyebrow, would riposte. You couldn't even make them angry. So that satire faded out. Unlike Daddy Auld, these men never gave themselves away. So that you could only hate them—those 'elegant patricians'. And hatred filling all your mind because of the too too vivid contrast, seen now at close quarters, between what they had and what you hadn't, stifled all the laughter and the mockery that alone made Horatian satire (Burns's kind) possible. It was, perhaps, inevitable that the brilliant Have-Not, meeting the brilliant Have's, should react like this. And the hatred lasted, after Edinburgh—long after Edinburgh—till it issued in fierce thunderbolts like 'A Man's a Man for a' that'. So maybe the fine Edinburgh tables had done their work after all. . . . For the conditions for satire were gone for ever.

But if the New Town, all unconsciously, killed something in Burns, the Old Town made amends. Over there in the High Street, in the dark, crowded Closes, with the winter dusk ancient Edinburgh of the dead-and-gone centuries seemed to come alive again. And as Burns moved out from his Lawnmarket lodging into the black street, an old song would greet his ear, 'De'il tak' the wars', or, in lighter vein, 'Saw ye my dearie, my Eppie Macnab?', or that universal favourite 'John, cum kiss me now'. From the Anchor Close? Or the Advocate's? Or even the aristocratic Canongate? From any or from all of them, for everybody was singing the old songs here. Robin knew them too, from *The*

Lark that he had pored over, as a boy in Ayrshire, but here in Edinburgh you could hear them every night—in every Close—and from all sorts of people. A periwigged Judge, perhaps, like Lord Hailes, a connoisseur in all these old songs—or a sedan-chair would come past, with the brightest eyes in Scotland flashing out at you from it—the Duchess of Gordon?—and she knew them too—or Mr. Creech (the famous bookseller)'s printer, that convivial William Smellie, founder of the Crochallan Fencibles, that riotous club that met in the Anchor Close—and the coarser the old song here, the more to the taste of the Crochallans. Burns knew that too. Or, best of all, in Libberton's Wynd, down the Cowgate way, in the dark recesses of Johnnie Dowie's Howff—far ben, in that innermost stifling cellar they called 'the Coffin'—two men would be sitting, that had all the Scots songs at their finger-tips. Here Burns would drift in oftenest, as if pulled by a magnet, for one of the two was the now famous William Herd, that poor Edinburgh clerk who had been writing down every odd scrap of old Scots song—every random line still floating in the air—all his working life, and who, like as not, had the treasure-trove with him there. The other was noteworthy too—that James Johnson on whose little music-shop in Lady Stair's Close, Burns could look down from his window in the Lawnmarket. Johnson had the authentic passion too. Songs by Scotsmen were what Johnson wanted, whether in the vernacular or no. Herd would have naught but songs in the braid Scots. Over the good Edinburgh ale and the guttering candles in Johnnie Dowie's, Burns would listen to Herd and Johnson. It was surely Destiny herself brought these two within his ken—the two of all then alive in broad Scotland, who could help him most in the work he had to do. And when the clock of St. Giles' beat out twelve, and Dowie's doors shut—as shut they aye did on the stroke—and Burns made home, under the midnight stars, to the Lawnmarket again,—the High Street, as he passed down it, would be still aglow with life—fiddles scraping and laughter pealing and the tap-tap of dancing feet. Reels and strathspeys down every Close—and as a stray cellar-door would open, you could see the lighted room within, and the whirl of gay brocade and the gallants' fine coats.. And ever and on, the quick beat of the reels—the slower strathspeys. Slow them both down a beat or two, and you could set a song to them. A Scots song. And Robin knew all the tunes. Were they not, every one in that *Caledonian Pocket Companion* he'd studied all his life? . . . Night after night in Johnnie Dowie's, talking with Herd—night after night with those reels and strathspeys ringing in his head. Down in Ayrshire as a boy he'd liked the Scots songs himself, but up in the New Town the vogue had been all for the English. Tho' maybe Herd was right. Maybe the Scots ones were better— 'We're a' kissed sleepin', 'Guidwife, count the lawin'! You couldn't get better than these. Like his own 'Corn-rigs were bonnie', that he'd put in the *Kilmarnock*. And most unlike his own 'From thee, Eliza, I must go', that he had also put. . . . Those old Scots songs. Was there anything else that could charm you—hold you—fill your whole mind like them? 'There is a certain something in the old Scotch songs, a wild happiness of thought and expression', Burns is writing from Edinburgh in the winter of 1787. 'An engraver (Johnson) in this town has set about collecting and publishing all the Scotch songs with the music, that can be found . . . I have been absolutely crazed about it, collecting old stanzas . . .' Absolutely crazed about it! To the two over the ale in Dowie's howff there was nothing in the whole world but just Scots songs. And to that third man now, making home under the midnight stars, to the fiddles scraping out the fey old tunes in every dark Close—to that third man now too. From then on, to his last breath in 1796, nothing in the world for Robert Burns either but Scots songs. It was eighteenth-century Edinburgh, the Old Town and the brilliant New, that together 'made' Burns.

CHAPTER II

THE KILMARNOCK BURNS—
'I rhyme for fun'

'WHO ARE YOU, Mr. Burns?' So, the *Edinburgh Magazine*
breathlessly in October 1786, over the slim, blue boards of the
Kilmarnock—newly out. 'Who are you, Mr. Burns? At what
University have you been educated?' For there was no doubt,
even at the first perusal, that the *Kilmarnock* was to make history.
There hadn't been anything like it in Scotland before. Not quite
like—tho' of course, when you looked closer, there were shadows
behind it. As of Fergusson's 'Farmer's Ingle', for example, behind
'The Cottar's Saturday Night', or his 'Leith Races' behind 'The
Holy Fair'. But then, nobody read Fergusson much now and
Edinburgh herself had only read him because Fergusson, after all,
was an Edinburgh man. Whereas this 'Cottar' and the rest of it—
to judge from the reviews—were being read everywhere, over
the whole breadth of the land. The *Kilmarnock* was something
new. . . . It was not, however, for all its Ayrshire origin, rustic.
The *Edinburgh Magazine* had jumped to that, with its pertinent
question about Burns' University. For the *Kilmarnock*, in much
the same way as Adam Smith or Hume (University men both)
made you think. . . . It was a limited edition (600 copies only, of
which 350 had already been bespoken by subscribers known to the
poet)—published at some risk by the printer, John Wilson of
Kilmarnock, on July 31st 1786, when Burns was now twenty-
seven years of age. It was also the poet's first appearance in print
—tho' much of his work, including the wildly profane 'Holy
Willie's Prayer' (which he finally never did print) and songs of the
level of 'Mary Morison' had already been circulating in MSS.
among the farms and howffs of Ayrshire. But the *Kilmarnock*
was a venture of a different sort. Here Burns, for the first time,
was appealing to a public that did not know him and whom he
did not know. He must, therefore, be cautious. Nobody thought
so more than Wilson, the printer—as anxious as himself—
who pointed out that a title like 'Scotch Drink'—the proposed

opening poem of the *Kilmarnock*—was hardly likely to ingratiate the new author with the severer—and larger—section of the community. Could the poet not think of something else? Hastily Robin put the finishing touches to 'The Twa Dogs'. That should rope them in, all sorts. For the love of dogs—what with the many famous Scottish breeds, from Dandie Dinmonts to the Cairns and collies at every shepherd's heels—ran through all classes and ages, as it still does in Scotland. The 'Twa Dogs' would surely do? . . . Robin's own doubt had been about the songs. Those Scots songs he knew—from *The Lark* and other collections—were of a broad outspokenness little likely to appeal to the strait-laced. And if his own extremely proper 'Cottar's Saturday Night' was to be the bait to sell the *Kilmarnock*—as it certainly was—it would never do to include with it, anything that might put prospective purchasers clean off. Yet his own songs were mostly unlike the current proper ones either—say, those of Allan Ramsay. Robin's were warmer—a deal warmer. Did the gentry like warmth? Burns had never been out of Ayrshire and had been in a drawing-room only once—that of kindly Mrs. Stewart of Stair. He did not know. But songs he had written. He'd better put some in. Those he did put in—three at the tail-end of the volume—were, on the whole, an unfortunate choice. Two of them in high English—the first 'Now westlin winds and slaughtering guns' introducing an interminable list of birds, with clichés like 'Avaunt, away' and 'vernal showers' and 'the fluttering, gory pinion' (neither the buyers of the *Kilmarnock*, of whatever brand, nor later addicts, spend much time on 'The Westlin Winds')—the second 'From thee, Eliza, I must go', just a blank, bald statement of fact with 'boundless oceans', 'a boding voice', and 'cruel Fates'—phrases cut straight from the textbooks—plastering it together, until it stops dead—without one hint of genuine feeling from first to last. Nobody, from this abysmal pair, could ever guess that their author, within a brief eight years from then, was to make his name immortal, just on the writing of songs. The third, however, in Scots (for the most part) was altogether different.

       'It was upon a Lammas night
       'When corn rigs are bonie'—

and whether it is the moonlight, or the familiar Scots background, or the fact that it celebrates Burns' own favourite adventure

> 'I kissed her owre and owre again
> 'Amang the rigs o' barley'—

there is no doubt that this third song goes with a tremendous swing. The poet was only twenty-three when he wrote it—yet, looking back towards the end of his life, when he knew all there was to be known about the writing of Scots songs, he considered he'd never done anything better than its last verse—

> 'I hae been blythe wi' comrades dear,
> 'I hae been merry drinking
> 'I hae been joyfu' gath'rin gear,
> 'I hae been happy thinking.
> 'But a' the pleasures e'er I saw
> 'Tho' three times doubled fairly
> 'That happy night was worth them a'
> 'Amang the rigs o' barley.
> 'Corn rigs an' barley rigs,
> 'An' corn rigs are bonie,
> 'I'll ne'er forget that happy night
> 'Amang the rigs wi' Annie.'

But if you read the list of the *Kilmarnock* contents for the first time to-day, what strikes you more than anything, is the extraordinarily doleful nature of the titles. You have only got to Item 6, out of a total of forty-five, before you come on 'The Death and Dying Words of Poor Mailie' (whoever that may be) and by the time you've reached No. 16, it's a steady downpour of such items 'The Lament', 'Despondency, an Ode', 'Man was Made to Mourn', 'Winter, a Dirge', 'A Prayer in Prospect of Death', 'To Ruin', 'The Farewell', concluding, for good measure, with a shower of epitaphs,—among them, the poet's own. Who, you might wonder, was going to take this funereal stuff home for light reading? . . . But, if that is one's reaction to-day, it's not how it struck folk in the eighteenth century. By no means. The eighteenth century, as far as its poetry was concerned, luxuriated in gloom. Had it not been brought up on Ossian? Burns couldn't have laid the misery on too thick for it. The gloomier, indeed, the better. Was there not the poet Blair—cousin of the great Dr. Blair, of the High Kirk—whose most famous poem, and a highly belauded one, at that, was entitled 'The Grave'? And the eminent Dugald Buchanan, greatest of the Gaelic religious poets and a life-long Edinburgh resident, whose masterpiece 'The Skull' ('As I sat by the grave, At the brink of its cave—Lo! a featureless skull on the ground', etc.) or whose sensational 'Day of Judgment', opening with the crack of doom, as the Archangel Michael sounds the Last Trump and the whole world totters to total ruin—had entranced literary Edinburgh since their publication there in 1768? That's the sort of title sold like wildfire in Mr. Creech's crowded bookshop in the High Street. For this is the century that buried itself (to the consternation of later writers like R.L.S.) under the grim skull and crossbones and all the ghoulish emblems of mortality flaunted with relish on their tombstones in the Old Greyfriars. Gloom was the fashion. Tho' it hadn't been in the first half of the century, when the kindly Allan Ramsay published his *Evergreen* collection of Scots songs in 1724. He'd found life a cheerful business—there's hardly a tear in one of them. But by the time Fergusson gets to it in 1772, Ossian had been out for a good ten years and Fergusson's list fairly drips with them. The very first item to confront you in it is 'Elegy on the Death of Mr. David Gregory',—Elegy again for Item III, with several more en route until the climax 'Ode to Horror', 'Ode to Disappointment', 'A Dirge'—and poor young Fergusson only twenty-four. In the *Kilmarnock's* tearful list, therefore,—as the printer must have noted with satisfaction—young Burns had nicely hit off the taste of the time. As the many reviews of it, Scots and English, corroborate, for not one of them as much as mentions the dismal character of the fare. Here Burns knew what he was about. . . . Tho', did he, in that title on the flyleaf 'Poems Chiefly in the Scottish Dialect'? That hit you in the eye. They might speak Scots in Ayrshire—indeed the poet, in his preface, declared it was his 'native language'—but where else? On the Bench at Parliament House, no doubt, where My Lords, the 'Auld Fifteen', well-known to be eccentric, would toss it about—a lingo as auld-farrant as the auld Scots Law that was written in it—but you wouldn't hear Scots in the fashionable Canongate, where Adam

Smith had his friends in for supper, and precious little in Creech's, where you bought your books, and not a word—you could be positive—in the famous sermons of Dr. Blair, the best preacher in Edinburgh, or in the merry talk of Dr. (Jupiter) Carlyle of Inveresk, over the punch with his cosmopolitan friends like Ambassador Murray Keith. Even John Home's great play *Douglas* that had raised the roof of the Edinburgh of '59, hadn't a word of Scots in it from beginning to end. True, by 1772, poor Fergusson was introducing some (there were but nine in Scots) alongside his English poems—'Poems' he called them, 'in the Scottish dialect'. But here was this young man from Ayrshire now going much further. 'Poems *Chiefly* in the Scottish Dialect'. What chance had he? Who was going to read them? . . . The reviews on this point were crushing. 'We much regret' says the *Monthly Review* of December 1786, 'that these poems are written in some measure in an unknown tongue . . . being composed in the Scottish dialect, which contains many words altogether unknown to an English reader', with the unhappy consequence, prophesies the *Monthly Review*, 'this work, therefore, can only be fully relished by the natives of that part of the country where it was produced'. Burns was to be limited to Ayrshire! And Henry Mackenzie (of *The Man of Feeling*)—the voice that now swayed all Edinburgh opinion—put it just as plainly in *The Lounger* of the same month 'Even in Scotland the provincial dialect which Ramsay and he have used, is now read with a difficulty which greatly damps the pleasure of the reader: in England it cannot be read at all.' Back to Ayrshire again! 'Tho' some of his productions', conceded Mackenzie with commendable penetration, 'are almost English', while the *New London Magazine* of the same date, naturally enough—as coming from England—echoes the wail, 'It is to be regretted that the Scottish dialect, in which these poems are written, must obscure their native beauties . . . and render the same unintelligible to an English reader'. Nobody, native or foreign, like Burns's Scots. . . . But they liked the rest. Oh! they liked the rest! It wasn't remarkable that Ayrshire and Galloway bought up the *Kilmarnock* (with such fury that, within a month, the edition was exhausted and there wasn't even a copy left for the poet's own home at Mossgiel)—for Ayrshire and Galloway could read every word of it and had read most already in MSS.

—but the *Kilmarnock*, Scottish dialect and all, travelled further. There was a public waiting for it—in Edinburgh—in Aberdeen —all over Scotland. For there were only two poems in it where the dialect really hampered you—'Hallowe'en' (for which Burns supplied a glossary) and 'The Farmer's Salutation to his Auld Mare Maggie', and it wouldn't have mattered much if you skipped both. For, tho' they are of the small group (seventeen out of the *Kilmarnock's* forty-five) that still have a living interest, they are neither of them in the front rank. But what the contemporary critics really liked the best, was not—astonishingly enough—those carefully chosen dirges, elegies, epitaphs, etc.— but rather, something that was entirely new. . . . There was fun in the *Kilmarnock*! 'Those (poems) of the humorous kind are the best', decided the *Edinburgh Magazine*. The *Monthly Review* seemed to have read nothing else. 'These poems are chiefly in the comic strain.' Something to laugh at, in the *Kilmarnock*! After Blair's 'Grave' and Buchanan's 'Last Judgment' buy it up. You'll get a laugh here. Something Scots poetry hadn't had for three sorry centuries! Something Scotland herself hadn't had! A laugh in the *Kilmarnock*! And here was Henry Mackenzie—Edinburgh's own voice—after a brief three months' acquaintance with this totally unknown kind of poetry in a dialect of which he disapproved—pronouncing what was to prove the uncontradicted verdict of Time itself. 'If I am not greatly deceived . . . a genius of no ordinary rank.' Edinburgh had said it! . . . Tho', South of the Border, they weren't so sure. Satire and fun Burns could certainly do. That 'Address to the De'il' now, and 'The Holy Fair'. And these wouldn't grow stale either. Did the Devil ever grow stale? Or—for that matter—the Flesh? But, of course, 'The Cottar's Saturday Night' was really the plum. And as for those songs— songs, did you say?—'The love-poems', hooted the *English Review* in derision in 1787, with Shakespeare and Donne and the long line of the singing Cavaliers no doubt in mind, 'The love-poems are execrable!'

What, then, was in the *Kilmarnock*? Discarding the dross of the dirges, etc., and the two high English songs and the dull Mailie poems about a sheep (of no appeal to-day, if they ever had any) there is still a small residuum, if not of pure gold, at least of gold in the alloy. . . . The first poem, 'The Twa Dogs', gives you a line

c

on the poet's mind. Argumentative—Burns was nothing, if not a debater—and with that colouring of politics that was to deepen later and develop. Here Caesar, the rich man's dog, argues with Luath, the poor man's, over whether it's better to be rich than poor—a question that is never out-of-date. Burns, however, answers it as few Scots poets before him—or, indeed, after him— have answered it. It is better, he holds, to be poor—thus elaborating, as he often does, Fergusson's hint in the Edinburgh poet's 'Ode to the Gowdspink,

> '. . . wae's heart! we aften find
> 'The brawest drest want peace of mind
> 'While he that gangs wi' ragged coat
> 'Is weil contentit wi' his lot'.—

Yet, from the hard-up fifteenth-century Court poet Dunbar grousing openly 'My painful purs so prickis me', as he begs for a benefice, to Jamie Thomson of *The Seasons* with hardly a bawbee, fawning before possible patrons as recently as 1726, Scots poetry had generally taken the opposite view. Not so Burns, tho' speaking in that age of privilege, the eighteenth century, when the rich still held all the cards. Poverty, says Robin (and who knew better?) has its points—the fireside welcome of weans and wife, the day's darg o'er—the foaming glass ('whyles') with a friend or two, when you talked of 'Kirk and State affairs, wi' kindling fury in your breasts'—the sound sleep o' nights. As against that, what had the rich? 'Their days insipid, dull and tasteless' with no work to do, 'their nights unquiet, lang and restless'. It was a thunderingly new point of view! Burns struck the prevailing taste of his day, like an ice-cold shower-bath—bracing and invigorating. For the *Kilmarnock*, just as surely as Ossian, turned a corner in literature. And one of the lesser, if incidental, benefits it conferred, was that it killed Ossian. For, after the direct speech and the clear thought of the *Kilmarnock*, there could be no more sentimental vapouring. There must have been many an eighteenth-century gasp over 'The Twa Dogs'. . . . 'Scotch Drink' that the printer had queried, has, nevertheless, not the punch you may be looking for. For whisky had not yet established itself instead of ale, as the national favourite (in Sheriff Nicolson's definitive collection of Highland Proverbs there is but one mention of whisky in all the 4000 odd) and Burns, in any case, still knew little of it. Mighty thin stuff his 'Scotch Drink' must have seemed to the practised claret-topers too in Edinburgh, like old five-bottle Lord Newton, for, as early as v. 3, Burns abandons whisky for praise of the domestic scone and the prosaic porridge, summing up with whisky sandwiched in—a most lamentable position where its force is certainly lost!—between the triumphant scone and the usual clamour for 'a rowth o' rhyme'. You'd hardly know the whisky was in it. . . . The two political poems, 'The Author's Earnest Cry and Prayer' (on the hackneyed theme of Scotland's wrongs) and 'The Dream' (a birthday greeting to the King) are of interest only as they show Burns, if unconsciously, in the true Scots tradition, of commenting outspokenly on current politics— a practice dating from the fourteenth-century Barbour with his impassioned 'Oh Freedom is a Noble thing' after the joyful Bannockburn, through Dunbar with his well-known 'The Thrissle and the Rose', on King James IV's fateful marriage that was to unite the two crowns, to Davie Lyndesay's 'Satyre of the Thrie Estates', attacking the whole set-up of the realm. Burns' political pieces are as outspoken as Lyndesay, but, being purely topical, have long since faded. . . . There remain the poems of a living literary interest, like 'Hallowe'en'. Here Burns starts from scratch, allowing himself the unchecked use of the Ayrshire vernacular. Critics have indeed found precedents for the poem (and no poet was keener on precedents than Burns, or charier of moving without them) in Fergusson's little-known 'Hallow Fair', or the even lesser-known 'Hallowe'en' of *Ruddiman's Magazine* of 1780. But, if Burns borrowed anything from these, it was only the title. His 'Hallowe'en' is all his own—a companion-picture to 'The Cottar' of Ayrshire country life—but this time of Ayrshire gone gay. A curious picture too—with only one verse in it to haunt you—the look of the 'burnie' under the moon

'Whyles glitter'd to the nightly rays
'Wi' bickerin', dancin' dazzle'

—for the rest, a long monotonous account, in merciless detail, of country practices interesting him, but not you! Yet 'Hallowe'en', as a historical document for the poet's own mind, is of first-rate importance. For here Burns, off his guard in the vernacular and without a thought of playing up to any 'English' audience, reflects as in a mirror, the Ayrshire he knew. Reflects it too with enormous gusto (every third word is a verb!) and with no criticism at all. It is just the absence of criticism, plus the piling of statement upon statement, that makes of the poem the deadly monotonous thing it is. As such, it is the rawest of all Burns' works. For in its complement, 'The Cottar', he does realise the importance of allowing the reader periods of rest by the alternation of thought and action,—thought in the high English, the congenial action in the braid Scots. But in Hallowe'en, from first to last, there is no rest. And you glimpse Ayrshire just as Burns saw it—a place thick with elves and fairies and with the 'Foul Thief' himself (the Devil) lurking behind every stone fence. But this is the authentic countryside of the Scottish seventeenth century, as depicted in that renowned work of the minister of Aberfoyle, Rev. Robert Kirk, *The Secret Commonwealth of Elves, Fauns and Fairies*, published in 1691—or in Mr. George Sinclair's yet more fearsome *Satan's Invisible World Discovered* of 1685— the seventeenth-century Scotland lingering on in rural Ayrshire, home-country of those religious primitives, the Covenanters. Or as the historians of the Kirk, Wodrow or Kirkton, show it up, with demons, witches and devils on their every other page. Wodrow indeed will point you out Satan himself in actual presence administering the Communion in such a diabolical place as an Episcopalian chapel. It is this demon-haunted countryside that reappears now in 'Hallowe'en'. It is the countryside Burns believed in. To him, as to every other ploughman in Ayrshire, these presences were not imaginary, but of a most vivid and actual realism. So that 'Hallowe'en' in this, reaches out to and interprets the much greater and more brilliantly written 'Tam o' Shanter' of 1790, otherwise a poem sui generis in Burns' life. The imagination revealed in both poems is of precisely the same quality, revolving round witches, fairies, ghosts, the Devil—a communal imagination, not one personal to the poet. That 'Tam o' Shanter' is a work of art, while 'Hallowe'en' is not, is due to two other factors—the first, the maturing of the poet's selective powers, unexercised in Hallowe'en,—the other, the open presence in 'Tam o' Shanter' of the Devil, that richly imaginative conception dominating the poem and not, as in 'Hallowe'en', lurking in the background. Between them, these two lift 'Tam o' Shanter' to a level impossible to the raw 'Hallowe'en'. But there is no more personal invention in the one than in the other. And it is significant that both alike were written in the heart of the countryside, when Burns was immersed in rusticity and its beliefs. He found no Devil in enlightened Edinburgh or—for that matter—fairies either. It is from the picture it gives of Burns' own mind, ranging thus freely in the uninhibited vernacular, that 'Hallowe'en' is of supreme importance.

Over 'The Cottar's Saturday Night' the companion-picture and obvious 'set piece' of the *Kilmarnock*, opinion has varied. The taste of the time approved it, the *English Review* of February 1787 thinking it 'without exception, the best poem in the collection', as did Burns' well-known Scots correspondent, the difficile Mrs. Dunlop. And in 1809 no less a critic than the acute Jeffrey of the redoubtable *Edinburgh Review* adds his praise. 'The Cottar' 'with its exquisite description . . . is perhaps the finest example of Burns' supreme quality of pathos'. But the taste changed. 'Doomed to popularity from the first' groans Henley, Burns' *Centenary* editor and a poet himself, tearing up 'The Cottar'. And modern criticism, in general, has followed suit. . . . And it is true enough that 'The Cottar' makes nearly every conceivable mistake—half of it in English—and such English!—like 'life's sequestered scene', and 'this melancholy vale', and 'Anticipation forward points the view', and 'the milk-white thorn'—clichés, every one of them. With the rest of it in kailyard Scots, 'his wee bit ingle, blinkin' bonnilee', 'her sair-won penny fee' and 'the big Ha'-Bible'—all oozing sentiment at every word. Then the metre —the voluptuous Spenserian stanza reminiscent of an ethereal Fairy Queen and of Jamie Thomson's languorous and lovely 'Castle of Indolence', but degenerating in Burns' hands into banalities like 'To help her parents dear, if they in hardship be'. Then—there is the unctuous moralising about the wickedness of the rake who might seduce young Jenny (and this from our Robin!) or on the vanity of religions other than Calvinism, with their 'pompous strain and sacerdotal stole' and how much the Almighty must prefer 'well-pleas'd, the language (Calvinist) of the soul', and a final ecstatic contemplation of ourselves the 'hardy sons of rustic toil'

'Certes, in fair Virtue's heavenly round
'The cottage leaves the palace far behind'—

on which complacent note, 'The Cottar' ends. . . . Every conceivable mistake, you would say, in tone, in metre and in
language—and yet 'The Cottar' is read to-day, when no one looks
at 'Poor Mailie', and read the world over, when an exile wishes to
conjure up Scotland. For conjure it up 'The Cottar' will un-
failingly do. Its very faults are our own. The sentimentality that
drips from it, is the same that takes us out for all the lost causes.
And that final note 'Oorsel's an' wha's lek' us' is unmistakably
Scots. From a different angle and never darkened by a doubt, it
has made us the world's best colonisers. 'The Cottar's' faults are
our own. . . . But so too are its good points. No poem in the
English language breathes such an atmosphere of respectability.
And we like respectability. Davie Deans himself, that stern
Covenanter, in Scott's *Heart of Midlothian*, might have sat for the
portrait of 'The Cottar', for here Scott and Burns see identically
into the pattern of Scots family life. Yet Scott was a middle-aged
man, with several novels to his credit, before he could achieve the
full round of Davie Deans—Burns at 'The Cottar' but an inexperienced twenty-seven. And were there nothing else in the
Kilmarnock to justify Henry Mackenzie—that 'Man of Feeling'
who launched Burns in Edinburgh with his dictum 'A genius of
no ordinary rank' (*The Lounger*, December 1786)—the characterisation of 'The Cottar's Saturday Night' alone would do it. For
only a master-hand—the hand that had shown itself already
(altho' unbeknown to the public) in 'The Jolly Beggars' also—
could have brought it off. That admirable line 'The father mixes
a' wi' admonition due' with one stroke brings the typical Scots
parent to life, and then the deliberation over the Scripture
reading,—'He wales a portion wi' judicious care' is another
Rembrandt-like touch, where every word tells. Nor is the
perspective less excellent—'The Cottar' in the foreground and the
'guidwife with her needle' slightly in the shadow but 'garrulous'
for the supper—the supper itself a model of accurate observation
—Jenny and her shy young man etched in, with a stroke or two.
With consummate skill—almost as if they had grown there—
Burns puts the whole family across. . . . And even the language

—so wrong from the critic's point of view—has a rightness of its own, for the dignified English is the habitual language of family worship, while the vernacular comes in with the supper. And right or wrong, Burns is only doing here what Scott and Stevenson—without any condemnation—do regularly later in family scenes,—mixing their English and their Scots. It is in his infelicitous choice of words, not in the principle he adopts, that Burns goes astray.... And so persuasive is the drawing, so fine the art, it's not till you've laid 'The Cottar' down, that a doubt arises 'Can this be really Saturday night in Ayrshire?' In the eighteenth century—without a glass at all? And at that, a memory of the lurid Kirk Session records, of Poosie Nansie's over the way, of the smugglers at Ardrossan—disturbs you. But Boswell, an Ayrshire man too, saw Scotland in very much the same way, when touring it up and down, not so many years before. Nobody (but Boswell) got drunk in Boswell's Scotland either. You didn't, in the houses. In the oyster-cellars in Edinburgh—yes—or in Poosie Nansie's at Mauchline, of course. But at your own fireside? No. So 'The Cottar' in this respect, is not misdrawn. Burns knew his Ayrshire. And Ayrshire the poem definitely is. A glance at Fergusson's 'Farmer's Ingle', Burns' model, makes this clear. For, after supper in the 'Farmer's Ingle',—written by an Edinburgh man—it is to 'couthie cracks' the family settle down. Not so in Calvinist Ayrshire. Here, on the contrary, the great central scene, to which all the rest leads up, is—after supper—Family Worship. The dividing line between the Capital and rural Scotland could not be more clearly drawn.... And there is a further point of Art in the poem. Unlike the scenes in Gray's 'Elegy', for example, to which it owes much, the picture here is not static. It develops, keeping the interest alive. Opening with its wild November blasts over the bare field—the miry beasts unyoking —the Cottar collecting spade, mattock, hoe—all is busy action, each new detail adding to the sense of toil and inclemency. Against that, is set in the succeeding verses the peace of the bright fireside with wife and weans—the contrast telling out. 'The Cottar' begins well. It goes on well too (apart from the moralising!) with movement and action thrown into relief by the pauses to look around, until the end when—a contrast again—come bed and sleep and rest, giving that quiet close so beloved of the

Greeks. 'The Cottar' ends well too. And it is by the action, and
not by the poet's intrusion, that the characters, point by point,
are revealed. The staging and production of 'The Cottar',
in fine, show superb art so that the incongruities, the jolts and
mishandling of the metre, the ungainly diction, fade into the
background, and you rise from the reading of it with a sense—as
unexpected as it is delightful—of complete enjoyment.

But the poems contemporary taste liked best, from one end of
Britain to another, were—as has been said—the poems that gave
you a laugh. Laughter in Scotland had—publicly, at least,—been
the rarest of all emotions. It had not figured in Scots literature for
two centuries—not, perhaps, since the fifteenth century when
there weren't, as yet, any sanctified (Scotland not having had her
Reformation) and you could let yourself go and no bother over
things like Dunbar's wicked 'Twa Mariit Wemen and the
Wedo'. And lately, laughter hadn't been so common in England
either, tho' the Restoration dramatists of a century ago had raised
it often enough. But not lately—what with the mordant Pope and
the serious Cowper. And now, here were two poems 'The Holy
Fair', and 'The Address to the De'il' that set the whole world
laughing. . . . Of 'The Holy Fair', we are not perhaps, close
enough to the original it lampoons to savour the full tang of the
satire. Twentieth-century Scotland has never seen those enormous rural gatherings (3000 or more, it has been credibly com-
puted) for 'The Sacrament', so that Burns' poem to-day has lost
something of its effectiveness. We have nothing to contrast it
with and so it stands on its own merits—a pleasant, rather mild,
satire to us on the whole. It did not seem that to the eighteenth
century that first read it. And whatever the more sophisticated
towns thought of it, it must have electrified the simpler countryside. That the omnipotent Kirk, whose thunders were louder than
Scotland had ever heard from Rome—that the tyrant, from
whose anathema there was no appeal, should be derided and
laughed at, in this, her central ceremony—and that by a delin-
quent she had more than once chastised on her own doorstep!
It was not only unprecedented. It was unthinkable! For, ever
since the Revolution Settlement of 1689—close on 100 years
ago now—and to some extent, before that—the Kirk had held
the realm in thrall, with not a voice bold enough to be raised

against her, with her elders—that Scottish Gestapo—spying into every man's life, and her preachers flaying you with the fear of Hell—and now, now at last, here blew in a breath of fresh air with a bubble of mocking laughter at the whole preposterous set-up!

'We will get famous laughin'
'At them this day'

promised Fun herself in the opening verses. Laughter! . . . But, to recapture the original thrill of 'The Holy Fair' as it burst on fettered Scotland, one should dip into some of the theologians of that dreary century of Presbyterian supremacy and absorb the mental atmosphere generated by the Kirk. The *Memoirs* of Thomas Boston (floruit about 1712) for example, author of the famous *Fourfold State*, so long a fireside book in Scotland, will throw a light on the outlook of one of the Kirk's thinkers. Thomas, under a perpetual cloud of dread, found his every step dogged by a malign and interfering Providence, on the alert to catch him out at the slightest slip. And the dice were loaded. Providence *would* catch him out. Or the *Memorabilia Domestica*, that classic account of Kirk life in Scotland of the Rev. Donald Sage, minister of Resolis in Ross-shire, provides evidence over three generations, his own at Resolis, his father's pastorate at Kildonan in Sutherland, his grandfather's at Loch Carron in ·Wester Ross—between the three covering the best part of two centuries. Or—for the half century after Burns, the Rev. Alexander Auld, of Olrig, Caithness, in his *Ministers and Men in the Far North* will show a Scotland as yet untouched by the moral scourge of the *Kilmarnock*. All these (and others like them) have the same ferocious theology to expound, which they do, not only without a vestige of criticism, but even with a certain smug approval. And why not? Had they not, after all, transferred the thunder? It did not fall upon them but upon their flock. For, the more you reviled your fearful flock, the more 'faithful' a pastor Calvinism adjudged you to be. Even the tremendous power of the Keys once denounced as the illicit prerogative of Rome, was now hurled, almost at random, by a power-drunk Kirk. ('Power' Lord Acton warns in his famous aphorism, 'tends to corrupt. Absolute power corrupts absolutely.' The Kirk for long now had had absolute power.) The Kirk Session Records e.g. of Kilwinning in seventeenth-century Ayrshire note its use without comment as an everyday affair. And Mr. Auld in the Far North has the same tale to tell. Cross an irate minister and you would see. Flatten him out in an argument, if you were a mere woman—as did this poor creature at Watten (but it might have happened anywhere), in 1816, it is true (but it might have happened earlier). Here, however, is Mr. Auld's story—

MINISTER (Rev. Alex. Gunn, that light of his generation and famed for his Christian piety far and wide). What is the Lord's Supper?

OLD WOMAN. I cannot repeat the answer, but I know all about it well enough.

MINISTER. The heart is deceitful.

OLD WOMAN. Yes—the hearts of the wicked, but I have a good heart.

MINISTER. There is none that doeth good—no—not one.

OLD WOMAN. But there are many good people.

MINISTER. If you continue of that mind, I must withdraw from you the privilege of which this question speaks, and if you go to Eternity as you are, you will perish.[1]

(*Ministers and Men of the Far North.*)

[1] Here is the sentence of the 'Greater Excommunication' as it was pronounced in Thurso in 1709 for the crime of murder 'As by the word of God and the law of nations, the heinous guilt of murder and the shedding of innocent blood, renders the murderers liable to the highest capital punishment (in this case they had escaped) so, by the Acts of the General Assembly of this Church, such as are guilty of atrocious, horrid murder are appointed to be excommunicated from the society of the faithful and to be delivered over to Satan, for the punishment of the flesh, that the soul may be saved in the day of the Lord. And the presbytery finding that Wm. Sinclair did barbarously, feloniously and deliberately murder the body of Lawrence Calder late bailie of Thurso, by shooting him with a pistol in the back . . . therefore the presbytery, after solemn prayer to God for counsel and direction and being moved with zeal for the glory of God, the uttermost detestation of the foresaid villany, for the purging the Lord's house and church of all such rotten, wretched and corrupt members, did and hereby do, according to the power committed to them by the Lord Jesus Christ, the great King and Head of this Church, Excommunicate and deliver over to Satan the fore-named Wm. Sinclair—obtesting and entreating all and sundry to whose ears this dreadful sentence shall come, to look on them as heathens and infidels, who, by their horrid wickedness have cut off themselves from the

When Christianity of that pattern was being purveyed by the Kirk, it was time and more than time, that Burns should arrive. And 'The Holy Fair', with laughter, that potent solvent of all pretentiousness, was set to explode it. . . . As this is the most subtly constructed of all Burns' poems, it may be worth while to analyse it. The poem begins all innocence 'Upon a simmer Sunday morn'—hisses (simmer Sunday) recurring throughout the verse until the final 'Fu' sweet that day' in the bob. The metre is the disarmingly simple one of eight short rhyming lines and a bob—tailing back to the old fifteenth-century 'Christ's Kirk on the Green', but simplified from it, to give an air of utter natural-ness, as if the whole thing ran on wheels—unpremeditated and artless. But the hisses are there. And you hear them. For in this poem, as in one or two of his others, Burns manages to get the sound of his words to echo their sense—thereby doubling the effect, when the appeal to the ear reinforces the appeal to the intellect. And the hisses go on—till, with the appearance of the three ribald sisters (v. 5) they crash out.

> 'An' this is Superstition here
> 'An' that's Hypocrisy—'

By v. 10, when we are now gathered in the tent, every line seethes with them, up to the triumphant climax—

> 'On this hand sits a chosen swatch
> 'Wi' screw'd-up, grace-proud faces.'

But, in v. 18, when the scene shifts to the change-house, with the happy liquor flowing, there isn't a hiss at all, nor in v. 26 when the folk go home

> 'Wi faith an' hope an' love[1] an' drink
> 'They're a' in famous tune
> 'For crack that day'—

mystical body of Christ Jesus, and are hereby Declaratively cut off, in His name, from the privileges and benefits of His house . . . and finally these are to give warning that none receipt, entertain or harbour the foresaid murderers, or have any unnecessary correspondence with them, as they would not come under the same guilt and be in God's account, found liable to the same sentence.' (Calder, *History of Caithness*, p. 195.)

[1] The almost blasphemous parody of St. Paul's trinity.

tho' with the final verse, the hisses are back

'How monie hearts this day converts
'O' sinners an' o' lasses.'

and 'The Holy Fair' ends on a hiss 'Some ither day', the metre thus, like a pianist to a singer, playing up to the main theme throughout and loud-pedalling its points. Tho' Burns at times uses this device again, this is his longest and most spectacular use of it. . . . The plan of the 'Holy Fair' is the same as 'The Cottar's'—a day from morn till eve, with action and contrast developing it. So, in the first nine verses we have the summer morn, the jolly crowds gathering, farmers, youngsters in their 'braw braid claith', the lasses in their silks and scarlets, the good country fare—every happy touch building up an atmosphere of gaiety and contentment, with innocent Fun trotting along beside them. The sky only darkens with the hail of hisses (v. 10) bringing them into the tent, and their first contact with the Kirk. With the ironical opening line of the service—the grand old psalm— 'O Happy is the man an' blest' (the bitterest parody in the poem) Hypocrisy clearly takes over, and into this now clouded atmosphere rises the first minister 'wi' tidings o' damnation', whereupon Superstition now, the third sister, is with us. To denounce as Superstition this the orthodox teaching of the Kirk was an extraordinarily bold act on Burns's part. And with that, the whole poem seethes with turmoil—the din of the pulpit, the brawl of the change-house, pint-stoups clattering, 'the Lord's ain trumpet' blaring 'o' Hell, whare devils dwell'—the roar of the ministers—the snoring of the congregation—what a contrast to the innocent happiness before the Kirk came in! . . . But this poem too, like 'The Cottar', is to end in quiet, so the old folk are now brought into the foreground—the guidwife with her kebbuck sitting douce at the fire, the auld guidman 'about the grace' (the only touch of real piety in the poem) when the homely food, in pointed contrast to the Divine, restores peace and happiness. With a final glimpse of Youth happy again, now the Kirk's well out of it. . . . Apart from the blistering portraits of the ministers, pilloried for all time in just a line or two and with more than Hogarthian skill, the real sting of the satire is implicit and lies in the whole setting—in the ironic contrast between what the

Kirk does—ruining peace and driving men to drink, as Burns the realist saw it—and what it claims to do, bringing them to salvation. And then the whole proceedings (like the so guileless metre) have a show of such utter and complete naturalness. This is just a Holy Fair like thousands of others they'd known in Scotland (they and their fathers before them)—with everything, the crowds, the girls' scarlet, the change-house, the ministers bawling, the love-making—everything down to the smallest detail exactly as everyone knew it to happen, so that the utter normality of it all, together with the simplicity (so cunningly calculated) of the metre, between them carry over the one point in the whole poem that wasn't in any way normal—the mocking laughter and make it seem natural too. For, under this compulsion, now wasn't it? The one point, anyhow, that to the milling crowds long familiar with the scene, was utterly and completely new. For, in this Holy Fair, as not in all the others, you bubbled with laughter—irrepressible, hilarious laughter from first to last, instead of—well, what did the ministers really think you should have felt about it? Reverence, perhaps, was it? . . . But the laughter rocked and eddied like a stone thrown into a stagnant pool, in ever-widening circles—from Ayrshire out to Edinburgh —far over the Border——. A thunderbolt to the indignant and unsuspecting Kirk, Burns' 'Holy Fair' was undoubtedly the big noise of the Kilmarnock.

Tho' the second poem, 'The Address to the De'il' was a close runner-up. It was not so remarkable, however, that this work was a success, for there has never been a dull poem yet written on the Devil, nor a bad one either. He is the making, as all men know, of Milton's magnificent *Paradise Lost*—and to Burns he was a veritable gift. For the Devil,—that brilliantly picturesque personality created and cherished by the Kirk—and Burns the poet with no imagination at all, but with immense resources of wit and humour—together form the perfect combination. Between them, there was nothing they couldn't put over. And whether the Kirk, in this, owes more to Burns for immortalising her creation, or Burns to the Kirk for this ideal subject, is hard to say. And it wasn't only that the one was a perfect complement to the other, but Destiny here too—as so often in Burns' career—had brought the two together at the right moment. For the Devil, in early

Scots poetry,—as in Dunbar's 'Dance of the Seven Deadly Sins'—
had been a mere skeleton. The Catholic Church, indeed, had but
little use for him. But the Kirk had filled the skeleton out. Denied
by her Reformers all access to the saints ('Popish', weren't they?)
she had perforce to turn in the only direction left open to her.
And the Devil, from the flaming pages of Davie Lyndesay, in the
artless *Diary* of James Melville, through the vituperations of
Knox and the fulminating Covenanting sermons of the seventeenth century, had by now acquired a substance and a vitality—
a range of terrific attributes—that made him out and away the
best-known character to every Scots man, woman, and child—
without a rival in broad Scotland. Not the remotest hamlet but
had heard of him. He was more real than your next-door neigh-
bour, far more real than the King upon his throne, nearer to you
far than the august Creator. . . . As for what he did to you, here is
the eloquent and famous Samuel Rutherfurd, Scotland's greatest
divine, in a letter to a friend (Letter 180, p. 334) in 1637 particular-
ising on it, 'To feel the smoke of Hell's fire in the throat . . . to
stand beside a river of fire and brimstone, broader than the earth,
and to think to be bound hand and foot and casten into the midst
of it quick (i.e. alive) and then to have God locking the prison
door, never to be opened for all Eternity!' When the most learned
scholar in Scotland (and Mr. Samuel, Principal of St. Mary's
College (St. Andrews' University) was undoubtedly that)
believed such doctrines, what must its hold on the ignorant
have been, and the potency of its terrors 'I dreamt ae night I saw
Auld Nick', shivered poor Fergusson, in that slow, spondaic
line. . . . You could tell too, in every detail, what the Devil looked
like—the black, flapping wings, the horns, the cloven hoof—
where he lived—in that glowing furnace ninety times hotter
that any Daniel ever knew. What he did—burning you, burning
you, to all Eternity, if so be the lot, casual as the dice (for wasn't
there Predestination and what could anybody do about it?)
had fallen on luckless you. . . . Worse still, if worse could be, the
Devil—unlike mere humans—wasn't chained in his Hell. He went
roving, as Job knew. You might meet him on any dark night,
round a sudden corner, at your elbow, within an inch of your
face and always, always, as poor Thomas Boston was so well
aware, catching you out. And every sermon in Scotland—

sweeping the good news of the Gospel into a vast oblivion—just told you more and more about the Devil. By Burns' time there wasn't a better publicised or more dreaded personage within the four corners of the realm, or one that had gripped the imagination of the whole land in more hair-raising terror. He had you—in this world *and* the next! . . . And it was at that point this exotic creature, now in all the shimmering aura of his fantastic plumage, came up against the cool sanity and ironic gaze of Scotland's arch-satirist. Burns had heard of the Devil all his life—in Mauchline Kirk as in the Alloway but and ben, but it was the Devil of the Alloway but and ben, as seen in 'Hallowe'en' and 'Tam o' Shanter', that he believed in most. That was more likely work for a devil to do, like a mischievous Jack o' Lantern, to be haunting the countryside. As for this other—this portentous fellow in the 'lowin' heugh'—he was just incredible. 'Spairgin' brunstane' as a non-stop job? Now, really! . . . And a surprised, not to say stupified Scotland, over the opening lines of 'The Address to the De'il' found her breath taken away. 'O Thou whatever title suit Thee.' (Good enough, for gods, as is well-known, whether Jewish or classical, have their preference. Does not Horace himself say 'Matutine pater, seu Jane libentius audis', addressing one?) But in the very next line, duly cataloguing the titles, if there isn't that disrespectful 'Auld Hornie', first, with 'Clootie' grinning at you from the other end, and 'Satan'—the only dignified title—lost in the middle! And then for his office—that awe-inspiring doctrine of eternal punishment is here resolved into nothing more than 'spairgin' brunstane from a lowin' heugh'! And more and worse, as you went along. So that, by v. 20, no wonder Burns was saying

'An' now, Auld Cloots, I ken ye're thinkin'
'A certain Bardie's rantin', drinkin'—

for, drunk or sober, no one in Scotland had ever yet spoken like that *to* the Prince of Darkness before. Let alone, *of* him! Shades of the haunted Samuel Rutherfurd or the poor, scared Thomas Boston! For here was somebody who obviously wasn't afraid of him, somebody who even laughed at him, 'lowin' heugh' an' all —somebody who actually seemed—not to believe in him! . . . And with that, like a gorgeously coloured and perfectly rounded soap-bubble, at the first breath from outside, the whole elaborate

phantasmagoria faded out—the age-long spell was broken. As
Burns freed Scotland from the tyranny of the Kirk, so now he
released her from the hold of the Devil. For once you had laughed
at the Devil—and there were, to be sure, laughable points—
you couldn't be afraid of him again. Tho', from the point of view
of literature, there may have been a compensating loss. This richly
imaginative figure, so carefully built up over two grim centuries
of the Kirk, was gone and gone for ever. The Devil would make
no more poems or books for Scotland again. And indeed, after
Burns, he has disappeared, almost totally, from literature with one
last, brilliant appearance in R. L. Stevenson's 'Thrawn Janet',
where it is the Devil and the atmosphere of terror he creates, that
makes 'Thrawn Janet' the little masterpiece it is. But, the Devil
gone, there has been nothing to replace him. To this day, Scots
poetry feels the blank. . . . Like 'The Holy Fair', 'The Address to
the De'il' is in the vernacular which, indeed, with a true instinct,
Burns chose for all his satires. You could say things straight from
the shoulder more easily in the language you knew best, and be
sure they hit home. Also, in the everyday tongue it was easier to
make folk laugh. So, the 'braid Scots' it was, with an odd lapse
when, talking of Eden (à propos of Satan's disastrous visit there)
and Adam and Eve—

> An' all the soul of love they shared
> 'The raptured hour,
> 'Sweet on the fragrant, flow'ry swaird
> 'In shady bower'

the poem cascades into the worst eighteenth-century clichés, 'The
raptured hour', 'The flow'ry sward'. For the curious truth is that
love is the last subject on which Burns learned to write well, and
the very thought of it, at this stage, sends him distractedly to his
high English, with such resulting baldness as 'From thee, Eliza,
I must go' (the deplorable love-song of the *Kilmarnock*) or the
stiff affectation of 'Oh Mary, at thy window be, It is the wish'd, the
trysted hour', which is all he can manage in 'Mary Morison'. Yet,
love apart, he can use the English well enough, as in this sudden,
charming vignette

> 'Or where auld ruined castles gray
> 'Nod to the moon'—

And the Devil too, was not as embarrassing a subject as love.
The tone throughout, in regard to him, is one of frank camarad-
erie, typically youthful. Experience, alas! was to alter both these
attitudes diametrically, and before the last hard milestone in
Burns' life was reached, he can write of love with the easy freedom of 'A Red, Red Rose', and of the Devil with a kind of
reproachful anguish—

> 'Oh Nick, oh Nick, it isna fair
> 'First showing us the tempting ware
> 'Bright wines and bonnie lasses rare
>   'To put us daft
> 'Syne weave unseen thy spider snare
>   'O' hell's damned waft.'
>   ('Epistle to Col. De Peyster', 1795.)

But into the 'Address to the De'il' there falls as yet, no shadow of
misgiving. . . . The very metre, the old, gay one of the Trouba-
dours—that carries the verve and snap of its French origin still
intriguingly with it—lifts the thought lightly along, making the
points inevitably as the poet makes them. It was a metre Burns
had used before, for his 'Scotch Drink' and that he was to use
again and again e.g. for most of those tart and pithy Epistles that
are the charm of the *Kilmarnock*—and indeed, for nearly anything
that struck him. It is easily his favourite, partly, no doubt, because
its qualities are so like his own that it almost never let him down.
As a metre too, it had many advantages. You couldn't be dead
serious in it (a point for a satirist), for that gay French origin would
always defeat you. But as witty as you liked. And not too 'poetic'
either. That blunt fourth line brought you back with a jolt to
earth. Like most of his other metres (for Burns invented none) he
found it in the much-studied Watson (Part I, 1706), where
Sempill's famous mock-elegy, 'The Piper of Kilbarchan' goes
careering along to it. But it was an old metre in Scots literature,
from Davie Lyndesay on, tho' no poet of them all used it with
Burns' skill. The Troubadour's metre, indeed, fitted him like a
glove. Gaiety, lightness, wit, the very quintessence of common
sense—French qualities every one of them—were what it had been
built and moulded to convey, and these were precisely Burns'
own. . . . An admirable metre. 'The Address to the De'il' would

D

run on it to perfection—especially once you'd grasped the idea. To write it then might not be as hard as you would think. Not with the idea. And the Calvinist sermons gave you that. The sermons you'd heard all your life. You just put down what you'd heard of the Devil—more or less as you heard it. At a slightly different angle, of course, like a rakish French hat. But there wasn't any need to invent. The Calvinist sermons did that for you. The angle and the Troubadour's metre would do the rest. As simple as that! . . . All but that face-to-face encounter in the last two verses, that Robin never could resist. And this time, as it meant a close-up talk with the Devil himself, it was something he certainly couldn't miss. What Burns had to say here, was new indeed. Never a Calvinist sermon had given him that. An audacious jest in the first verse about himself, and then the famous

> 'But fare-you-weel, Auld Nickie-Ben!
> 'O wad ye tak' a thought, an' men'
> 'Ye aiblins might—I dinna ken—
>   'Still hae a stake:
> 'I'm wae to think upo' yon den
>   'Ev'n for your sake!'

To the ministers gingerly edging their way through the *Kilmarnock* in the privacy of their own studies, that must have been the most staggering verse of all! . . . New indeed!

But if you would really know what Burns was like, it is to the Epistles you will turn. Ten of them in the *Kilmarnock*—and the most revealing things he ever wrote. You may begin by disliking him—for the indiscriminate adulation under which Burns has laboured for the past hundred years or so, is a distinct disability to a great writer, in itself creating a prejudice against him in the mind of a newcomer—but if so it's odds the Epistles will win you over. For that charm of personality that touched even the sophisticated Duchess of Gordon 'the only man I ever knew, who could sweep me off my feet', and that held the critical Maria Riddell entranced still irradiates the Epistles. . . . Few works of art, indeed, bring their author, faults and all, so close to the reader. It's the way the faults come over, of course—that vital human link insisted on by Aristotle—that makes Burns the living figure he now is for all Scotland. Not one of the ten Epistles is written to a woman. They show Burns as he would appear to men. So, mercifully, there's not one grain of sentiment in the Epistles. The very titles are plainness itself—'Epistle to James Smith', 'To a Mouse', 'To his Auld Mare, Maggie' (this, tho' nominally a 'salutation' may well be classed with the Epistles, as of the same character) and most of the rest, to folk one has never heard of—mere names now—'To J. Lapraik', 'To William Simpson'—. An unpromising bundle truly. Burns has set no bait here, to allure a possible public. But there's some work, like a Savile Row tailor-made, that needs no bait. And the Epistles are of that order. The eighteenth century was fond of Epistles. Ramsay and Fergusson had written them too, as also that Hamilton of Gilbertfield, whose modernised version of Blind Harry's Wallace, was the one Burns read. But none of the three had personality enough to make an Epistle live. Whereas those of Burns—vibrant with life—stand out still from the dulling pages of the *Kilmarnock* as if they were written yesterday. Like this one, for instance, to J. Smith. Only three verses on the luckless James, and all the rest, twenty-six of them, on R.B.—more or less the usual proportion when the writer is young. Here Burns is thinking aloud—for this is probably the earliest poem in the book—on the all-important question of whether he should or should not—publish the *Kilmarnock*. There were, indeed, 'pros' and 'cons'.

> 'The star that rules my luckless lot
> 'Has fated me the russet coat
> 'An' damned my fortune to the groat
>   'But in requit
> 'Has blest me with a random shot
>   'O' countra wit.'

And would the 'countra wit' be enough? For

> 'There's ither poets, much your betters
> 'Far seen in Greek, deep men o' letters'—

like the poet Gray, perhaps, whose highly didactic 'Elegy' Burns had studied. Whereas Robin's Muse was lighter—

> 'For me, an' aim I never fash;
>   'I rhyme for fun.'

Would it do? Ah well! anyway he had Youth.

> 'Just now we're living sound an' hale;
> 'Then top and maintop crowd the sail,
>> 'Heave Care o'erside!
> 'And large, before Enjoyment's gale
>> 'Let's tak the tide.'

With the girls, that 'Joy of Joys' to play about with. . . . But when you looked round, what easy lives, to be sure, some folks had and how they got on—while

> '—others, like your humble servan',
> '—nae rules nor roads observin'
> 'To right or left eternal swervin'
>> 'They zig-zag on.'

But what of it?

> 'Grant me but this, I ask no more
>> 'Ay rowth o' rhymes.'—

as he'd asked it in 'Scotch Drink' too, and as he asks it here again,

> 'But give me real, sterling wit,
>> 'And I'm content.'

And on a second glance at those 'douce folk that live by rule', 'Your hearts' he cries 'are just a standing pool, Your lives a dyke', and turns with relief to 'The hairum-scairum ram-stam boys, The rattling squad.'

This opening Epistle, that is, breathes the very air of Youth, if you will—but its uncertainty of itself too (How would he stand beside those others 'far seen in Greek'?) its imperious demand for a good time (Let's tak' the tide). But it also throws a searchlight on Burns' own mind—in particular on his attitude towards his art—'I rhyme for fun', which is a clear break with the didactic eighteenth century and heralds the romantic nineteenth just about to dawn. Byron too, unlike Dryden, was to rhyme for fun. . . . But yet, Burns's singling out of wit in preference to any other poetic quality, marks him as still of the eighteenth century, which adored wit—and raises the interesting question as to whether wit can—or does—make a great poet. A great writer, maybe, but a poet? . . .

And finally, young the whole set-up may be, but it's a very extraordinary youth that could find the phrases, so memorable and clear-cut, 'the hairum-scairum ram-stam boys';

> 'An' large, before Enjoyment's gale,
>   'Let's tak' the tide'—

to say exactly what it means. It is as a master of words, trenchant, brilliant, vivid—such as Scotland had not known since John Knox —that the youthful Burns comes before us here.

'The Mouse', 'The Mountain Daisy', and 'The Louse'— three of the humblest subjects ever addressed in literature— show him from a different point of view, as a poet of the incidental. The mouse, indeed, had appeared in poetry before, when Henryson, in the fifteenth century, had made a fable on her, 'The Town and Country Mouse'. But objectively, as poets were wont to do with the lower creation,—from a height—like Fergusson later in his 'Ode to the Gowdspink'. Burns broke that convention. He addresses the mouse close-up and as on his own level—

> 'Me, thy poor earth-born companion
>   'An' fellow-mortal'

and with a wide humanity (to which Wordsworth, that lofty patron of humble life, never attained) puts himself in the mouse's place,

> 'That wee bit heap o' leaves an' stibble
> 'Has cost thee mony a weary nibble!
> 'Now thou's turn'd out, for a' thy trouble
>   'But house or hald,
> 'To thole the winter's sleety dribble
>   'An' cranreuch cauld!'

Seen at that angle, life, for high or low, seems very much alike. 'The best-laid schemes o' mice an' men, Gang aft agley.' It is this power of universalising an incident—an imaginative quality seen at its height in 'The Jolly Beggars' which depends for its effect on little else—that makes 'To The Mouse' a living poem still. Resting on life itself, it does not grow out-of-date. . . . Tho' Burns was not always so successful in his sublimation of the lowly. 'The Mountain Daisy', for example, is a failure. It begins well enough, if rather reminiscent of 'To the Mouse', with its 'Wee, modest, crimson-tipped flower', but, after a line or two, the poet's invention flagged. He could get no further. And looking ahead you discern those familiar rocks—the eighteenth-century clichés like the 'artless maid', the 'simple Bard', 'Suffering Worth'—one worse than another. And there goes 'The Mountain Daisy' tailing off into emptiness and vacuity. Yet a daisy was surely a more poetic subject than a mouse? . . . But the truth is that, with things in motion ('The Cottar', 'The Holy Fair', 'Hallowe'en' had all progressed from one stage to another,—movement all through) Burns' mind could work. And the 'Mouse' —and for that matter, the 'Louse' too, his next subject—had plenty of movement in them. While the Mountain Daisy, alas! was completely and obstinately static, and she brings Burns to a standstill within a couple of verses. No more original thoughts —a dead stop! . . . The Louse, however—tho' never before or since rising to the dignity of literature—was lively enough, and the poem marches with it. Torrents of verbs—all of them verbs of action—rush the thought along, until, at the end,—as always, when Burns' mind is working well—he sees the incident in the conspectus of humanity—

'O wad some Power the giftie gie us
'To see oorsel's as ithers see us'—

But it is not the treatment only of such subjects that is original. The very choice of them implies a new outlook,—that no subject was so low that it might not be made into an artistic whole and thus, a thing of beauty. It all depended on the atmosphere—on the way you looked at it—the secret too of 'The Jolly Beggars'. This, of course, is the Impressionist's creed, appearing here for the first time in literature, and without a successor (for Wordsworth reverts to the objective 'Fergusson' method of treating his 'Idiot Boy') until some hundred years later in art, when the Glasgow School of Painting found the unprepossessing and smoky Bridgeton slums—fog, filth, chimney-pots and all—could, in the right atmosphere—and did—like Burns' 'Mouse'—also make an artistic whole. But it was Burns who found it first.

'To his Auld Mare, Maggie' shares with 'Hallowe'en' (the poem next to it in the *Kilmarnock*) the honour of having the finest

Lallans Burns ever wrote. With this topic he is completely at his ease—an old farm-horse such as he had known and worked with, all his life—and thought follows thought in brilliant and lightning-like rapidity, thro' mounting masses of verbs—almost as thickly packed with verbs as St. Paul's famous eulogium on charity, which is verbs all through. If the verb is, as the logicians say, the unit of thought, then no poem is more packed with thoughts—as certainly none has more verbs to the square inch—and all of them verbs of motion—

'How thou wad prance, an' snore an' skriegh

. . . . . .

'Thou never braing't, an' fetch't, an' fliskit'—

with this glowing picture at the core,

'When thou was corn't an' I was mellow
'We took the road aye like a swallow'

so that the poem races along to Burns' favourite, quiet ending when

Wi' tentie care I'll flit thy tether
'To some hain'd rig'.

Here is a Burns with no bitterness, unlike the poet of the satires —with no shadow of human misfortune breaking in to darken his theme, as it does in 'The Mouse'—a Burns, in short, completely happy. It is significant that only two subjects can put him in this mood, and so excite him as to drive the English clean out of his head. Neither of the two is a woman—for one was this old farm-horse and the other the ploys on Hallowe'en. Here then, in these two poems, is the Burns they saw on a good day at Mossgiel.

The 'Epistle to Davie' is, in some ways, the most interesting of them all. For here Burns experiments with a new metre—new to him—viz. the famous and highly original one of Montgomerie's 'Cherry and the Slae', that old Scots poem of the sixteenth century. The conventional metre of 'Christ's Kirk on the Green' (the octave with the bob) for 'The Holy Fair', the sparkling Troubadour's metre for 'The Address to the De'il—and now this, more complicated than either, for Davie who, being a poet himself, might appreciate its difficulty. For the metre—a fourteen-er, equable enough in the first ten lines, does some startling things in the last four—shooting off into a mad, intoxicating dance that leaves the reader gasping. It hadn't suited 'The Cherry and the Slae'—for which Montgomerie had invented it—for, in an allegory of Good and Evil, which is 'The Cherry and the Slae' —and dull at that—who ever wanted to dance madly at the end of every verse? Yet the metre would do it! . . . Burns was no more successful with it in his 'Epistle to Davie'. As long as he has Davie, the poet, more or less in mind, it goes, perhaps, none too badly. But alas! in v. 8—unluckily enough—he bethinks himself of Jean his wife, when—hey presto!—metre and theme crash precipitately to catastrophic ruin. And if anything can be worse than v. 9, with its high English and affectation, its pious thought to demoniac metre, it is v. 10 with phrases like 'a more endearing band', and 'the tenebrific scene'. v. 11 (happily the concluding one) recovers a little, with Robin returning to the Doric and reflecting complacently—Jean well out of mind!—on how skilfully he's managed the metre after all.

> 'The ready measure rins as fine
> 'As Phoebus an' the famous Nine
> 'Were glow'rin owre my pen'.

Not, perhaps, the reader's view, after the disastrous 'Jean' interlude. . . . For Burns' wife never did go with Burns' poetry. The only song she ever inspired ('O' A' the Airts') was written when she was miles—and months—away from him. And there's no doubt she ruins 'The Epistle to Davie'—she and the metre between them. The incongruity was too obvious. . . . Yet it was still a fascinating metre—tho' not, assuredly, one for Epistles and Burns only used it for that once again,—and this time, to a woman. His 'Second Epistle to Davie' (later than the *Kilmarnock*) is in the customary Troubadour metre, which gives the thought no trouble. . . . Yet, a fascinating metre, this of 'The Cherry and the Slae', none the less, and one in which Burns was yet to do some of his finest work. For it is Montgomerie's metre and none other— mastered, at last, to perfection—that was to carry 'The Jolly Beggars', for which it was clearly born,—to triumphant immortality.

The contents of 'The Epistle to Davie' show Burns thinking

along the lines of 'The Twa Dogs', but now a step further on—

> 'It's hardly in a body's power,
> 'To keep at times frae being sour
> 'To see how things are shared'—

It is probably the moderation, no less than the lucidity of those telling monosyllables,[1] that made them sink into his country's consciousness, to emerge with such dramatic effect some hundred years later, in the birth of the Labour Party in his own Ayrshire. Or of the companion picture that follows—

> 'To lie in kilns and barns at e'en
> 'When banes are crazed an' bluid is thin'—.

Yet in both Burns was no mere political tub-thumper. For he moves away almost at once from the material, into a sphere that is 'terra incognita' to Socialism. Mind, he proclaims, mind it is that can make you happy anywhere.

> 'Yet then content could mak' us blest
> 'E'en then, sometimes, we'd snatch a taste
> 'Of truest happiness.'

For even misfortunes, as he reads it, have their part to play in the larger pattern of human life.—

> 'They make us see the naked truth
> 'The real guid and ill'.

And lifting the material to the higher plane of the spiritual, he universalises, as is the way of his genius, what is incidental and particular—

> 'Tho' losses and crosses
> 'Be lessons right severe,
> 'There's wit there, ye'll get there
> 'Ye'll find nae other where.'

It is not only Sophocles, most thoughtful of the Greek dramatists,

---

[1] Burns, like the great Samuel Rutherfurd before him, gets his best effects from monosyllables, as 'Scots Wha Hae', 'For Auld Lang Syne', 'O' A' the Airts', etc. 'A Man's a Man for a' that' e.g. has 283 words in all, of which 243 are monosyllables.

who 'saw life steadily and saw it whole'. Burns also has the same viewpoint. . . . His 'To a Young Friend' goes even further. For here Burns, at his most original, actually raises his voice against the Scots national ideal of 'getting on'—that ideal derived from prolonged contemplation of such determined go-getters as the Old Testament heroes like Abraham and Jacob, and an ideal now well-established in the nation's marrow. Burns will have none of it.

> 'They wha fa' in Fortune's strife
> 'Their fate we shouldna censure
> 'For still th' important end of life
> 'They equally may answer'—

But that is not a philosophy to which any other Scots writer subscribes—Barrie in *A Window in Thrums*, in *What Every Woman Knows*—identifies without a qualm, the go-getter with the good man. George Douglas Brown, at the opposite pole from Barrie, is yet with him here. Worldly failure in *The House of the Green Shutters* is complete failure. Burns alone sees clearer.

. . . And then, that matter of the 'light o' love's? How far should a young man go? Or—should he go at all? Here Burns spoke from experience, tho' he was still only twenty-seven. And, unlike his thoughts on Socialism, which are continually on his pen, this is a subject to which he does not recur. His opinion, however, is not what, from his own career, one might expect—

> 'But never tempt th' illicit rove
> 'Tho' naething should divulge it;
> 'I waive the quantum of the sin
> 'The hazard of concealing
> 'But oh! it hardens a' within
> 'And petrifies the feeling'—

For while Time only deepened his sense of social injustice—of the unfairness between the 'Have's and the 'Have-not's,—so that it irked him at every turn—the very hardening process he notes here, effectively prevented him from ever seeing the 'light o' love's from this sensitive angle again. But, at the start of the road, he did see it. . . . And then, the absorbing topic of religion. The Kirk apart—and how he hated the Kirk!—should a young

man have religion? On this point Burns is clear. He certainly
should.

> 'The great Creator to revere
> 'Must sure beseem the creature'—

Tho' the 'reasons annexed'—as usually happens—do not attain
the same high level.

> 'When on Life we're tempest-driven
> 'A conscience but a canker,
> 'A correspondence fixed wi' Heaven
> 'Is sure a noble anchor.'

So much for the theories of life. . . . In the remaining Epistles, it
is Life in general—his own in particular—on which he meditates,
with an aptness and clear-sightedness that even suggest at times a
flash of La Rochefoucauld, who surveyed Life from older eyes
than Robin's. But Burns has something of the Frenchman's ripe
quality. Here are some of the flashes. How, for instance, did
Robin come to be a poet?

> 'Amaist as soon as I could spell
> 'I to the crambo-jingle fell
>   'Tho' rude and rough—
> 'Yet crooning to a body's sel
>   'Does weel eneugh.'
>   ('First Epistle to Lapraik', v. 8.)

Tho' when you looked at those others,—great names like Pope
and Steele and Beattie—was he a poet really?

> 'I am nae poet, in a sense
> 'But just a rhymer, like by chance
> 'An' hae to learning nae pretence—'
>   ('To Lapraik', v. 9.)

Ah! that learning! There was the rub. Why did the critics make
so much of it? For the folk you knew that did go to a University
(in Burns's case, at the time of the *Kilmarnock*, these would be
limited mostly to the ministers)

> 'They gang in stirks and come out asses
>   'Plain truth to speak'—

and in any case, how could learning help a man to write poetry?

> 'They think to climb Parnassus
> 'By dint o' Greek!'—

is his bitter cry. Well, since he couldn't have it,—and by the frequency of his reference to it, one senses his envy of it, as of something like claret, far out of his reach, rather than because there is something more to know (for Burns, as has been already said, has none of the scholar's consciousness of ignorance). Since then, he couldn't have it, he must turn his eyes to what he could have—

> 'Gie me ae spark o' Nature's fire
> 'That's a' the learning I desire
> 'That, tho' I drudge thro' dub an' mire
> 'At pleugh or cart
> 'My Muse, tho' hamely in attire
> 'May touch the heart'—

a prayer that Providence has surely answered. . . . And how well, after all, one can do without learning! Driven to write just what one thinks, as one thinks it, Burns writes this—

> 'But I shall scribble down some blether
> 'Just clean aff-loof'.
> ('Second Epistle to Lapraik.')

little dreaming of what a revolution he was inaugurating in the highly elaborated poetic diction of the eighteenth century— after the formal elegance of Pope and the prim correctness of Ramsay (and long before Wordsworth's 'new' theories of poetic diction in the famous Preface to the *Lyrical Ballads* of 1798). Yet, unlike Wordsworth in the bathos of the 'Idiot Boy', Burns is not vulgar. In his alliance of plain words and good sense, he looks forward, for an equal, to some forty years ahead, to the final cantos indeed of Byron's masterpiece, *Don Juan*. And Byron was at the end of his life (1824) before he came to *Don Juan*—Burns in the *Kilmarnock*, almost at the start. But Robin could make the Muse talk as she had never talked before (and very rarely since!) to ordinary men. . . . A glance at the folk that passed Burns by,

'the paughty feudal thane
'Wi ruffled sark an' glancing cane'
    ('2nd to Lapraik', v. 12.)

—at the really great that thrilled him,

'At Wallace' name, what Scottish blood
'But boils up in a spring-time flood!'
    ('To Wm. Simpson', v. 11.)

—at the weather he liked

'Ev'n winter bleak has charms to me
'When winds rave through the naked tree
'Or frosts on hills of Ochiltree
    'Are hoary gray,
'Or blinding drifts wild-furious flee
    'Dark'ning the day'
    ('To Wm. Simpson', v. 13.)

—or when you lay awake, nerve-racked, in the attic at Mossgiel

'An' winter howls, in gusty storms
    'The lang, dark night'
    ('To Wm. Simpson,' v. 14.)

—or again, on the fine days when the mood was on you

'The Muse, nae poet ever fand her
'Till by himsel' he learned to wander
'Adown some trottin' burn's meander
    'An' no think lang'
    ('To Wm. Simpson,' v. 15.)

for, lights and laughter of Poosie Nansie's notwithstanding, you had to be alone to compose—with something moving beside you, some 'trottin' burn'—moving—moving—before the words would come. . . . There was another side of life too, that the eighteenth century, high and low, old and young, knew better than we know it to-day. How could you help but know it when every Sunday, in every Kirk in broad Scotland, there stood the 'cutty stool', plumb beneath the pulpit? With Hypocrisy's sons, 'the lads in black' ('Epistle to Rankine') roaring there high above you? And they were the lads, and no mistake, to tell you all about it! When, Sunday after Sunday, sermon over, the offenders (the women, on occasion, in sackcloth and paper hat) were ceremoniously escorted to that same cutty stool—plain for all to see—while the minister, from the pulpit, meticulously expounded their offence. Not the veriest child but knew then what adultery meant. The Kirk, with an ignorance of psychology as astounding as it was deplorable, saw to that. Sunday after Sunday this sin, above all other sins, was burned into the imagination of the people. You hadn't a chance to forget it. It was the thrill you waited for, thro' the long drones of the sermon. The Kirk Session records—that damning testimony to the eighteenth-century religion—are full of it. With the whole mind of Youth thus deliberately polluted by those who should have been its guardians, it was no wonder that adultery figured, openly and prominently, in the talk of the countryside. Being the mainstay of the pulpit discourse, it could be no other than in the thoughts of the people. So that Burns' 'Epistle to John Rankine', besides being intelligible in its venereal slang, to a far wider audience than it is to-day, —would evoke then far less interest than it might do now and absolutely (as in fact it did) no comment at all. It would merely take its place as one of the many subjects on which talk was ordinary and free—a clever enough poem, no doubt, and amusing, but if you wanted something really shocking, something blazingly new—you would turn back to that extraordinary 'Epistle to Davie'

'It's hardly in a body's power
'To keep at times, frae being sour
'To see how things are shared'—

For who had ever said anything like that before? Or—even thought it? 'To see how things are shared'. . . . How then were they shared?' . . . Was Burns perhaps right? . . . And an eighteenth century, to whom adultery, however you dressed it, was but 'cauld kail in Aberdeen', sat up electrified over Burns' 'Epistle to Davie'.

And, as you closed the *Kilmarnock*, a picture or two would linger in your mind—of the cosy winter nights

'While winds frae aff Ben Lomond blaw
'An bar the doors wi' drivin' snaw
　　'An' hing us owre the ingle'—
　　　　('Epistle to Davie'.)

—a picture well understood in Edinburgh when the winter haar
crept in from the Firth of Forth and you sat snug in those high
lands in the Canongate over the claret and Montaigne, and a
picture already old in Scots literature, for Henryson the early
fifteenth-century poet of Dunfermline paints it too

'I mend the fyre and beikit me about
'Then tuik ane drink my spreitis to comfort
'And armit me weill fra the cauld thairout
'To cut the winter nicht and mak' it short
'I tuik ane quair an' left all uther sport'
　　　　　('Testament of Cresseid.')

—or of the good plain fare 'souple scones, the wale o' food'
('Scotch Drink'), the 'butter'd sowans' of Hallowe'en, the famous
Ayrshire cheeses of 'The Cottar' and 'The Holy Fair' (was it from
Fergusson, who fills the 'Farmer's Ingle' with it, that Burns had
learned to talk about food?).
—then a silhouette of the horizon o' nights

'Where auld ruined Castles gray
　　'Nod to the moon'
　　　(Add. to De'il.)

or a grim close-up in the daytime

'See crazy, weary joyless eild
　　Wi' wrinkled face,
'Comes hostin', hirplin' owre the field
　　'Wi creepin' pace.'
　　　　('Epistle to J. Smith.')

for in the eighteenth century, on a farm, you were old at forty:
a sudden gleam across your eyes

'An' wear thou this, she solemn said,
'And bound the holly round my head'
　　　　　('Vision.')

—the lure of the lonely burn

> 'Whiles glittered to the nightly rays
> 'Wi' bickerin', dancin' dazzle.'
>
> ('Hallowe'en.')

The delight of summer-time in Ayrshire

> 'The days when daisies deck the ground
> 'An' blackbirds whistle clear.'
>
> ('Epistle to Davie.')

and your part in it

> 'When sic as you an' I
> 'Wha drudge and drive thro' wet and dry
> 'Wi' never-ceasin' toil'
>
> ('Epistle to Davie.')

so that, the kindly Lallans forsaking you, and the hot blood rushing to your head, you burst out

> 'If I'm designed yon lordling's slave
> 'By Nature's law designed,
> 'Why was an independent wish
> 'E'er planted in my mind?'
>
> ('Man was Made to Mourn.')

—much as Rousseau had been thinking in the woods of Montmorency, over his 'Contrat Social'—
And finally the egregious, the Rabelaisian, the unforgettable picture of these ministers—

> 'Learn three-mile prayers an' half-mile graces
> 'Wi weel-spread looves an' lang, wry faces
> 'Grunt up the solemn, lengthen'd groan'—

that was the cream of the whole book. In truth the *Kilmarnock*, when you came to think of it, lit up most facets of the eighteenth century—its conventional tastes, of course, as in 'To Ruin', 'The Lament', 'Despondency'—the sort of thing those poets always did think about,—eighteenth-century poets, anyhow, whose minds ran in grooves like that. But then, there were other things

Bell's Wynd. Here was the Assembly Room where Old Edinburgh danced the night through, and Burns must often have heard the reels and strathspeys

(By courtesy of the Central Library, Edinburgh)

POEMS,

CHIEFLY IN THE

SCOTTISH DIALECT,

BY

ROBERT BURNS.

THE Simple Bard, unbroke by rules of Art,
He pours the wild effusions of the heart :
And if inspir'd, 'tis Nature's pow'rs inspire ;
Her's all the melting thrill, and her's the kindling fire.

ANONYMOUS.

KILMARNOCK:
PRINTED BY JOHN WILSON.

M,DCC,LXXXVI.

The title-page of the 'Kilmarnock' edition of Burns. Note how Burns presents himself here 'The Simple Bard, unbroke by rules of Art' that it lit up too—odd, rather bewitching things that were quite new, like

> 'It was upon a Lammas night
>   'When corn-rigs were bonnie.'

Had the *English Review* now, noticed that one, when it said 'the love-songs in the *Kilmarnock* were execrable'? For there were bits in this one

> 'I kiss'd her owre and owre again
>   'Amang the rigs o' barley'

or its gay ending

> 'Corn rigs an' barley rigs
>   'An' corn rigs are bonnie
> 'I'll ne'er forget that happy night
>   'Amang the rigs wi' Annie'—

bits that almost swept you off your feet! Unconventional, of course, but—with promise? If Mr. Burns were to try it again? . . . So that, when you heard the new poet was coming to Edinburgh, and there might be a chance of meeting him—with all these new ideas—that biting tongue—of hearing him talk—well, there wasn't another phrase for what you felt about it, but just his own 'It put me fidgin-fain to hear't'. . . . The *Kilmarnock* had unlocked every door. All Edinburgh awaited Burns.

E

BURNS AS A SATIRIST.
'The lads in black'

Satire as a literary form is the invention of the Romans, a people as practical and legal-minded as the Lowland Scots. It is from that type of mind that satire springs, when the contrast between appearance and reality strikes the clear-headed as ridiculous. Out flashes the satire. But the clear-headed are not the imaginative—for you cannot at once see clear and see deep—and it is noteworthy that neither Roman nor Scot achieved that most imaginative of all literary forms, high tragedy. While Athens, that did achieve it, wrote no satire. And England that achieved it also, wrote only satire that has dulled and become, except to scholars, unreadable. The gifts for satire and for tragedy are—it would appear—mutually exclusive. If you can write the one, you cannot write the other. For the satirist, beyond all other writers, has his feet planted firmly on solid earth. He may tread lightly, as did Horace, the first great master of the art, poking fun as he goes along,—or rage and stamp, as did Juvenal, attracting the mob by his exaggeration and his fury—but on the earth he walks. . . . And Burns, seldom lifting his eyes from the Ayrshire earth, discerned clearly enough what lay there—the Mouse, the Mountain Daisy, poor Mailie, the Corn Rigs—even while thrills like the splendour of Ailsa Craig or the lowering beauty of a sunset, inevitably escaped him. Yet, even in things like the Mouse he could see not only what was transient, but the link his subject had with the eternal.

'The best-laid schemes o' mice and men
'Gang aft agley'—

so that the pitfall, to which all satire is prone, of fading out with the contemporary, was unlikely to trap him. And no writer ever said what he meant, with a more complete lucidity. Burns was thus in some sort born for satire. . . . And satire was native to the

Lowland air. Kay up there in Edinburgh, caricaturing from his High Street window, throve on it. By registering the oddities of individuals down below, he caught the snap and the salt of the city's life. And the dry humour of the traditional stories blowing about, is the very raw material of satire. Like that one in Dean Ramsay's *Scottish Life and Character* of the old retainer replacing the Laird's wig despite its inebriated owner's protest that it wasn't his, with a curt 'There's nae wale o' wigs i' Galston Muir'. They saw clear in the South—there wasn't a mystic among them. . . . But, in the Highlands, of course, even before Ossian, nothing is clear. The mist perpetually shrouding the Bens made folk imaginative—the tempests thundering from peak to peak struck them with awe. You couldn't write satire in the Highlands. Nobody ever had. Not even in the ancient Erse, foaming with humour, or with wrath. But never with satire. And not even now in the eighteenth century when Highland poetry, asleep for centuries, had revived again. Buchanan might write gloomily about 'The Skull', and Alastair Mac Maighstir of the spell of the sea in his 'Birlinn of Clan Ranald'—Duncan Ban brought the high hills clear before you in his grand 'Ben Dorain', but of satire? None of the three. It's not the way a Highlander looks at things, and never has been. Abuse of one's enemies is common enough. Rob Donn can do it with the best of them. But abuse is not satire. . . . Of this peculiarly Lowland art, then, Burns was to be the master. They'd done it in the Lowlands long ago, of course. That celebrated 'Christ's Kirk on the Green' (Scotland's delight for centuries) with its extraordinary opening for such an occasion

'Was nevir in Scotland heard nor sene
'Sic dancing nor deray'—

perhaps led off. But Dunbar had done it too in his 'Twa Mariit Wemen and the Wedo', with its scathing arraignment of the lovelies, and then Lyndesay, bolder than either, in his 'Three Estates'. Tho' it is doubtful whether Burns had any of the three in mind, when he set pen to paper. 'Christ's Kirk on the Green', perhaps? For he had read it in Watson, and its metre and lay-out are at the back of 'The Holy Fair'. But for the rest, here and here alone he worked without models. There is no precedent for 'The Address to the De'il'—still less, for 'Holy Willie's Prayer'. In the satires, Burns is at his most original. . . . There are not many, less than a dozen and of varying quality. The two in the *Kilmarnock*, 'The Holy Fair' and 'The Address to the De'il' had been brilliant successes, but then—their subjects had been well chosen. 'The Holy Fair'—or Sacrament of the Kirk—in an age of little travel and less entertainment, was the one event of universal appeal in Scotland, commanding an audience as diverse as for a modern International, and with the preachers' points as hotly debated as ever a centre-forward's of to-day. And tho' the detail of it might die out,—as, in fact, it has—the essence would remain. The Holy Fair, that is, might fade. As long as the Kirk lasted, it wouldn't fade out. While the Devil, like Horace's bore on the Via Sacra, is timeless. The subjects were well chosen. . . . Their treatment too. The satirist who would live, must never lose his temper. For there is nothing so hard to read as yesterday's stale wrath. So,—much as Burns hated the preachers, and furiously as he detested their picture of eternal punishment, there isn't a trace of temper in either of the two Satires. They are carried along from start to finish on the one thing that ensures survival—that great preservative, alike in letters as in life—the stinging salt of humour. With, of course, an incomparable turn for words too, the 'grace-proud faces', Moodie 'speeling the holy door, wi' tidings o' damnation', the poet himself at the brink of the Pit, 'But faith, he'll turn a corner, jinkin', An' cheat you yet'. Diamonds of the first water, all of them. The *Kilmarnock* satires are secure. . . . The *Edinburgh Edition* of 1787 had three more, of which 'Death and Dr. Hornbook' the first, has an unusual interest, tho' not as a satire. It is, indeed, Burns' only example of a social satire (its occasion the exposure of a local village quack). But you turn to it now for something quite other. It is here Burns gives the first hint of that narrative skill, afterwards so conspicuous in 'Tam o' Shanter'. The scenery too is very like Tam's—midnight when

'The rising moon began to glow'r
'The distant Cumnock hills out-owre'—

(the couplet which gave rise to Ruskin's famous criticism about Burns' parochialism, that for him the moon must always rise o'er Cumnock hills) with a reveller here also returning home and encountering something fearsome on the road. The story is not,

however, told in Tam's racing octosyllables, but in the slow and
pawky Troubadour's metre—

> 'Some books are lies frae end to end'

it begins, all monosyllables, netting in those who tell them,
in a wide sweep—even the ministers. A 'rousing whid' at times,
from them. Then, with your mind full of world-wide lies, it
goes on,

> 'But this that I am gaun to tell
> 'Which lately on a night befell,
> 'Is just as true's the De'il's in Hell'

(all monosyllables but two) where the anticipation ('that I am
gaun') and the fact that this is to be a true story (every story is
better if it's true) and the hisses over the De'il showing it's going
to be sinister, together with the ironic metre putting a question-
mark to the whole, make a matchless beginning, combining all the
lures to catch a listener's ear. And the next verse keeps it up,

> 'The clachan yill had made me canty

(did ever ale flow more smoothly, word melting into word?)

>   'I was na fou, but just had plenty
> 3.   'I stacher'd whyles, but yet took tent ay
>   'To free the ditches
> 4. 'An' hillocks, stanes an' bushes kent ay
>   'Frae ghaists an' witches.'

where the endings of the lines 'plen-ty, tent-ay, kent-ay' give
the staggering effect that the words wish to convey. The totter-
ing steps in line 3 (but—yet—took—tent—ay) and the run in line
4 ('an' hillocks, stanes an' bushes') all the words running in to
each other and brought up short by 'kent-ay', call up the picture
with a wizard clearness. Then, in v. 6, again like Tam,

> 'I there wi' Something does foregather
> 'That pat me in an eerie swither'—

and it's not till v. 9 that the secret is out and you learn who the
'Something' is, Burns, with the true story-teller's art, keeping up
the suspense till then. And now follows an excellent dialogue, in
the very best braid Scots (quite up to the level of 'My Auld Mare

Maggie') between two old cronies (actually Death and the narrator) in phrases that Burns must have heard over and over again up at Mossgiel.

> 'We'll ease our shanks an' tak' a seat,
>> 'Come, gie's your news'. V. 11.
> 'Folk maun do something for their bread'. V. 12.
> 'Ye ken Jock Hornbook i' the clachan? V. 14.
> 'I drew my scythe in sic a fury
> 'I near-hand cowpit wi' my hurry.' V. 18.
> 'A' kinds o' boxes, mugs an' bottles
>> 'He's sure to hae.' V. 20.
> 'His braw calf-ward whare gowans grew
>> 'Sae white and bonie'. V. 23.
> 'That's just a swatch o' Hornbook's way'. V. 29.

You can almost hear them at it, leaning against the wall—so natural is the diction. The story ends well too.

> 'But just as he began to tell
> 'The auld kirk-hammer strak the bell
> 'Some wee-short-hour ayont the twal'

where the third line has the monosyllables that imitate the stroke of the bell, and do not run into one another. . . . The racy 'braid Scots', the vivid picture of the two old worthies at their crack, leave not a doubt that Burns, had he so chosen, was master of dramatic dialogue, at least in the vernacular. He could also do characterisation, as 'The Cottar' and 'Holy Willie' show,—'The Jolly Beggars' too—tho' all these it must be remembered, are elderly, well-developed characters already, much easier to draw than a youthful Hamlet or a Romeo. And indeed Burns has nowhere attempted to draw Youth. Nor—except for the drab and the carlin in 'The Jolly Beggars', who are only given songs— are there any women either in his gallery. True, the guidwife in 'The Cottar' mends the 'claes', and in 'The Holy Fair' she cuts the kebbuck, but both are indistinguishable in the half-light. Could he then have created a Juliet, or even a Jeanie Deans? The question is interesting, for it has been claimed (notably by the great French critic Angellier) that Burns, on the strength of his character-studies, ought to have written drama. Plays, however, require a

good deal more than just character and dialogue—however
excellent. If you have not an eye for a central situation from
which action must inevitably spring, you cannot—as Aristotle
long ago pointed out—write a play. For the essence of drama is
situation. And there is no sign whatever that Burns, any more than
Scott, had any eye for that. Indeed the situation in which both
these masters (here extraordinarily alike) place their characters
is very much the same and totally undramatic. In Burns, the
Cottar's family gather round a table—in 'The Holy Fair' a motley
crowd take the road from dawn to dusk, as Scott too sends them
off in *Rob Roy* or *Waverley*. In 'The Jolly Beggars', even in
an inn parlour where so much drama is usually born, he can do
nothing to bind them together in one common action. They
remain as separate at the end as at the beginning. . . . One has only
to look at Shakespeare to see the difference. *Lear* opens with the
division of his kingdom, which must have far-reaching and un-
foreseeable results, involving all the characters—*Macbeth*, when
the witches, meeting an unnerved Macbeth, create situations
from which fresh action must inevitably arise—*Othello*, where
the elopement does the same. But there was nothing dramatic in
Burns' make-up. A piercing eye for the folk around him—a
quick ear for the way they talked—but nothing more. He never
saw two consecutive scenes, as a dramatist must, in any of their
lives. His pictures thus have neither past nor future, and there is
no evidence that he could have made them anything else. His
genius, that is, is essentially undramatic. . . . The other two satires
in the *Edinburgh*,—'The Calf' and 'The Ordination', are little
more than clever skits, tilting again at the Kirk and adding to the
cumulative effect of Burns' attack on it. But there is too much of
the topical in them for them to have much interest to-day. 'The
Kirk's Alarm', however, published as a broadside in 1789, has
more stuff to it—. The jingle of its opening—

> 'Orthodox, orthodox
> 'Wha believe in John Knox'

would sell any broadside, even now. You can hear the windows
flung up, to a pedlar chanting that. It's partly the metre, of course.
Gay had used it in his *Beggar's Opera* of 1728, and the lively metre
sets the whole thing going—keeps it going too, with a swing

rather like that of a students' song. Verse after verse—it might be
'John Brown's Body'—and with no particular reason why it
should ever stop. Still, you do get your money's worth from some
of the verses. This one, for instance—

> 'To join faith and sense
> 'Upon onie pretence
> 'Was heretic, damnable error'.

That could hardly have been put more neatly, or carried greater
venom. And there's laughter for all time in the fifth verse

> 'Calvin's sons! Calvin's sons!
> 'Seize your spiritual guns,
> 'Ammunition you never can need.
> 'Your hearts are the stuff
> 'Will be pouther enough
> 'And your skulls are store-houses o' lead
> 'Calvin's sons
> 'Your skulls are store-houses o' lead.'

Wouldn't that raise the roof of a Saturday night in Poosie
Nansie's, or even on the Edinburgh High Street when the
Crochallans got going? The inimitable fun of it! And the rapier-
thrusts! . . . 'The Twa Herds', tho' not published till 1796, was
apparently the earliest satire Burns wrote, or so he says in a note
in a MSS. now in the British Museum. 'The Twa Herds' or 'The
Holy Tulzie' on a notorious local quarrel between two ministers.
The picture of the typical eighteenth-century Presbyterian minister
is perhaps the best thing in it—

> 'He fine a mangy sheep could scrub
> 'Or nobly swing the gospel club
> 'Or new-light herds could nicely drub
> 'And pay their skin,
> 'Or hing them owre the burning dub
> 'Or heave them in'.

For the rest, Pope—whom maybe Burns had in mind here—
could scarify with just as great precision. But Pope knew where
to stop. Whereas 'The Twa Herds', alas! do not. But, short or
long is now no matter. For 'The Herds' are dead as Pope's dunces
long since and all the wit in the world couldn't save them. For

here Burns, like Pope, is only hitting out at particular individuals, while the object of satire, if it is to live, must be something fundamental, something basic, in human nature. . . . And with 'Holy Willie's Prayer' Burns had found it. The distance between 'The Twa Herds' and 'Holy Willie' is almost the whole length of the measuring tape. And it's not that Burns had developed so much either, between the two—'Holy Willie' was written as early as 1785, the year before the *Kilmarnock*. It is rather that, while in 'The Twa Herds' his interest was comparatively mildly en-engaged, he saw 'Holy Willie', on the contrary, with every faculty of his genius at the stretch. And Holy Willie himself was not only a hypocrite,—that eternal element in him, which lifts him out of his provincial Ayrshire and makes him a subject for all time—. He was also—what brought out everything Burns had—Calvinism incarnate. So that 'Holy Willie's Prayer' is Burns at his supreme best. Even his *Centenary* editors, Henley and Henderson, usually so sparing of praise, let themselves go over this, 'this amazing achievement in satire—this matchless parody—so exquisite in detail—so overwhelming in effect'. And 'Holy Willie's Prayer' on any reading, first or four hundredth, deserves it all. There is no catching Burns out here. Every stroke hits home. But it shows the hold of the Presbyterian influence on the country in general that, tho' he circulated the satire in MSS. he never dared print it. It was not, in fact, published till three years after his death, when easygoing Glasgow, jovial with her Jamaica rum and philosophical Virginian tobacco, took a chance on it in 1799. Only as a leaflet, tho', 'printed for and sold by Stewart & Meikle' to give you a laugh after a hard morning in the Saut-market. Edinburgh wouldn't look at it. What—would—the omnipotent Kirk say? For there was more than fun here. Pro-fanity, or as near it as made no odds. . . . The satire has that air of perfect simplicity that masterpieces so often have. Thought following thought as if anybody could have written it. All in that gay Troubadour's metre, with its undertone of mockery. It is also written in character—Holy Willie himself speaking it—thus doubling its satirical effect. For Burns could draw characters —the Cottar, the Jolly Beggars, and now Holy Willie—when he'd known them all his life, and here he gets under Holy Willie's skin. Yet this power of dramatic characterisation is an exceptional and very rare one for a satirist. None of the other masters possess it. And it is this, together with his satirical gift, that raises 'Holy Willie's Prayer' to its supreme position. . . . But Burns knew more than Holy Willie. He knew also, and just as well, exactly the sort of thing that was said week in, week out, in the Presbyterian pulpits. Had he not parodied it already in 'The Address to the De'il', and 'The Holy Fair'? And now he was to parody it, not only in the opening lines or the middle, as in these—but throughout. Here it was to be blazing satire all the time—but objectively and without a word of rancour—and all so devastatingly like the original you could hardly tell the two apart. 'Holy Willie's Prayer', in fact, was the last and final nail in the eighteenth-century Scots Kirk. It was driven triumphantly home. . . . The 'Prayer' begins, not in the vernacular, too familiar for a prayer, but in the more distant and dignified tongue, used also in 'The Cottar' for family worship. 'O Thou that in the Heavens dost dwell', with only an occasional dialect form 'onie' and 'guid' to suggest the scene is Ayrshire. In English then—but not the heavy, sententious English of the pulpit. This 'Prayer' had to be intelligible and convey its meaning instantaneously and beyond possibility of question. For that Burns uses the clearest English at his command—an English so clear and so superlatively difficult of attainment that no Holy Willie could ever have acquired it. And as always when Robin is working at white heat (as later, for instance, in his best songs 'For Auld Lang Syne', 'The Red, Red Rose') the diction is largely monosyllabic. You can't mistake a monosyllable. It has the clarity of a pistol-shot. So equipped, then, Burns starts off on the cardinal theory of Predestination, expounded, as a child might understand it, in the first verse.

> 'O Thou that in the heavens dost dwell,
> 'Wha, as it pleases best thysel'
> 'Sends ane to Heaven an' ten to Hell
>   'A' for thy glory
> 'An' no for onie guid or ill
>   'They've done before Thee'.

Put like that, though, and stripped of its theological panaches, it made you think. By v. 3 we are on to the equally vital tenet of Original Sin—

'I, wha deserv'd most just damnation
'For broken laws
'Sax thousand years ere my creation
'Thro' Adam's cause'

—a juxtaposition that even Calvin could hardly have desired.
v. 4 takes up the choice and oft-preached Calvinist doctrine that
babes, dying unbaptised, go straight to Hell—a doctrine that
seems to have roused Burns' special ire, for, of its thirty-six words,
thirty-two are monosyllables.

'When from my mither's womb I fell
'Thou might hae plung'd me deep in Hell
'To gnash my gooms an' weep an' wail
'In burning lakes
'Whare damned devils roar an' yell
'Chain'd to their stakes.'

Then follow the peculiarly Calvinist sins—indeed the only
ones of which the Kirk was ever aware—those of wine and
women, with a prayer not unlike St. Augustine's, anent the
women—

'Maybe Thou lets this fleshly thorn
'Buffet Thy servant e'en an' morn

. . . . .

'If sae, Thy han' maun e'en be borne
'Until Thou lift it'.

Could Burns have heard of St. Augustine's similar entreaty
'Lord, give me chastity—but not yet'? Then a brief couplet in
v. 10 to ask a blessing (but only on the Lord's elect, the 'chosen
race'), with all the remaining lines and all the remaining verses
(five in all, until the last) packed with concentrated curses on
those who

'Set the warld in a roar
'O' laughin' at us'.

Here is one—

'Pass not in Thy mercy by them
'Nor hear their prayer
'But for Thy people's sake destroy them
'An' dinna spare.'

twenty-one words, of which seventeen are monosyllables. Even the Athanasian Creed, beside the energy of this, wants sap. . . . The final verse entreats for the speaker himself

'That I for grace an' gear may shine
'Excell'd by nane,'

—with the usual Calvinist bargain attached to it

'An' a' the glory shall be Thine
'Amen, Amen!'

And binding and crowning the whole, gleams throughout the character of the speaker, that living illustration and product of the doctrines he enunciates—his conceit as being one of the chosen, with its corollary, his Pharisaic outlook on those not chosen (these from the doctrine of election)—his complete lack of contrition for wrongdoing (from the doctrine of original sin, making him completely irresponsible for it)—his bias towards cursing (after the Calvinist emphasis on the Old Testament):— it is this character, so exquisitely delineated and so brilliantly pointed, that was one day to flame out, floodlighting the Kirk and all it stood for.

On the technical side, the poet's predilection for monosyllables to hurl home his meaning, recalls the great dramatists' use of them for the same purpose, e.g. Sophocles, at the crisis of the *Oedipus Tyrannus*, uses little else 1184-5

φύς τ' ἀφ' ὧν οὐ χρῆν, σὺν οἷστ'
οὐ χρῆν ὁμιλῶν, οὕς τέ μ' οὐκ ἔδει κτανών[1]

And Shakespeare too, e.g. in that tense scene (Act IV, Scene 3) before Desdemona is murdered.

EMILIA: I have laid those sheets you bade me on the bed.
DESDEMONA: All's one. Good faith, how foolish are our minds! If I do die before thee, prythee, shroud me
In one of those same sheets.

—or in *King Lear* (Act I, Scene 1) putting that momentous question, on which the whole tragedy hangs

'Which of you shall we say doth love us most?'

[1] Born of those I ought not, living with those I ought not
Killing those I should not.

The urgency of the monosyllable (as seen also in swearing, the expression of man's most violent mood) is the greatest of which language is capable. It was a true instinct which made Burns use it for 'Holy Willie's Prayer'.

But it was not to be supposed that so powerful a work, ridiculing every tenet of orthodox religion, should make much headway in a country like Scotland, thirled so long and so obstinately to the Presbyterian Kirk. Nor did it. The eminent Dr. Currie, Burns' first publisher, in 1800 would have none of it. His *Burns' Complete Works* appeared without it. Nor was Sir Walter Scott surprised, for tho' 'A piece of satire more exquisitely severe than any which Burns ever afterwards wrote', 'Holy Willie's Prayer' was undoubtedly 'too daringly profane to be received into Dr. Currie's Collection' (*Quarterly Review*, 1809). The great critic Jeffrey cut it dead too, for all that he'd thrown 'The Excursion' into a well-merited waste-paper basket, and been the first to greet the rising star of Byron. But even the *Edinburgh Review* missed the bus here. Burns fared no better in his own home-country, the strong-hold of Calvinism. That an Ayrshire man—Ayrshire being 'a part of Scotland formerly so remarkable for tenacious adherence to religious truth', should be guilty 'of such Socinian ribaldry' as 'Holy Willie's Prayer', appals the *Ayrshire Advertiser* as late as March 10, 1809, a good ten years after the Glasgow leaflet. Carlyle too, in his famous Essay, has not one word of the Prayer. And Lockhart, Burns' first notable biographer, in 1828 is moved to say, 'To a place among profane rhymers, the author of this terrible infliction (*sc.* 'Holy Willie's Prayer') has undoubtedly established his right' (Lockhart, *Life of Burns*, p. 51). . . . But even in Scotland genius will out. And the light was to come. And from the East again—as of old, from Edinburgh. 'In the case of Holy Willie' proclaims that eccentric Victorian, Professor Blackie, 'the lash was wisely and effectively wielded.' It was the herald of the dawn. And with Burns' *Centenary* editors in '96 'this amazing achievement in satire—this matchless parody', it was high day. The stey brae had been climbed. And a transported Scotland knew at last all she owed her son. . . . For indeed 'Holy Willie's Prayer' has almost every merit a satire can have. First and foremost, that of brevity, essential if one is to keep the temperature at white heat throughout. For a satire loses by being long. Even a satire as admirable as Byron's *Don Juan*—much more, Swift's *Gulliver's Travels*—has its off-moments, its flat patches, even its tedium. But when you allow yourself only sixteen verses, with every word pulling its weight, you can maintain a high tension of excitement throughout. Nobody has ever laid 'Holy Willie's Prayer' down half-through. Burns' charged monosyllables carry you breathlessly on. . . . And then its concentration. 'Holy Willie's Prayer' is packed with thought. There is no stuffing anywhere. The thought itself bears on ultimate matters of universal concern, fresh to each succeeding generation, so that, unlike Pope's dunces or Gulliver's little men, its theme will never grow out-of-date. Yet presented with such brilliant ease (only in Calvin himself has recondite theology been put so clearly) that you jump to it at once and pass on to savour, like sips of vintage wine, its pungency, its kick, its delectable irony, here distilled into every stinging word. . . . Simple words, simplicity being that quality which Burns, in later life, came to regard as the supreme merit of artistic writing. Yet simplicity has its dangers. Anything prosy, as in Wordsworth's 'We are Seven' would have shot the satire into precipitate ruin. But the associations of all Burns' simple words are here noble. . . . The crown of the poem is, no doubt, its end. For only there does the figure of Holy Willie, in the full round, stand at gaze. And in your rapture at this superb creation, all thought of Original Sin, babies in Hell, even the grand Predestination itself,—the whole subject-matter, in fine, of the satire—flies to the four winds. As, perhaps, it should not. For character-drawing is not the primary object of satire. But here is a figure to stand, if in the shadow, beside Sir John Falstaff himself. A figure like his to set unregenerate laughter rocking at the very sound of his name. Yet Shakespeare took a History-play or more, to create Falstaff—Burns but sixteen verses for his 'Holy Willie'. . . . And how much Burns owed the Kirk for him becomes clear enough when you turn to Robin's political satire, the best of which is the well-known 'Address of Beelzebub',—written when Lord Breadalbane tried to stop 500 Macdonalds from emigrating for a better living to Canada. Burns was not against emigration—and dead against Lord Breadalbane. So he spoke in the role of his favourite character, Beelzebub, where you might think he would speak well. But alas! without the goad of the Kirk behind him

Beelzebub gets nowhere. The brilliant imagery that lights up the religious satires, its flaming Hell with Clootie himself shovelling the fire and 'brunstane', the vivid and tremendous ecclesiastical doctrines—the whole imaginative content of the satires, it now appears, was the gift to Burns of the Kirk. Stripped of that, as of necessity he is now—for it is out of the picture here—he has only himself to rely on and 'The Address of Beelzebub' topples to street-level. It is, in fact, just a compound of rage and coarseness (of which last, there was to the end, a strong vein in Burns). With still, of course, the biting word. He was always master of that. But lines like these—

'They an' be damned! What right hae they (*sc.* the Highlanders.)
'To meat or sleep or light o' day
'Far less to riches, pow'r or freedom
'But what your Lordship likes to gie them'—

Lines like these (and they are the best of 'The Address') would have no doubt made him a first-class political pamphleteer (which he is),—but never—what he also is—the finest satirist in English literature. It is the great body of religious satires make him that,—those satires lashing the whole life of the Kirk, its ordinances in 'The Holy Fair', its set-up in 'The Kirk's Alarm', its ministers in 'The Calf', 'The Ordination', 'The Twa Herds', its beliefs in 'The Address to the De'il', its products in 'Holy Willie's Prayer'. For sustained and bitter invective launched with the ringing laugh of mockery, there is nothing to compare with them since Rabelais in the sixteenth century attacking the Décrétalistes of the Roman Church on much the same grounds. And indeed, in temperament and outlook—if not in the learning which he lacked—Burns has a great deal in common with the towering Rabelais. . . . And the closer one looks at the religious satires, the more one is struck with the immense debt Burns owed to religion in general. It was the Kirk and nothing else that lifted him here to his high place. For, hate her as he might, it was in the Kirk and her traditions, for good or ill, that his whole personality was steeped. Until the Edinburgh days, they were the very food of his mind —rankling in it, day in, day out—the yeast that fermented in the satires to a rich and pulsating life. And not in the satires alone. For while on the one hand he knew folk like Holy Willie, he knew also and just as intimately other folk like the Cottar, the 'auld guidman over the grace' in 'The Holy Fair'—those people that stood for that other and better side of Calvinism. And 'The Cottar's Saturday Night' also is part of Robin's debt, for its whole atmosphere is permeated with religion. . . . And, for the satires, it was just the principles Burns had imbibed from the Kirk, that made him so furious with the hypocrisy he now saw in it. It was just the Calvinist in him that cared. Everyday folk like Gavin Hamilton didn't care—still less, folk like the worldly Dr. Blair of the High Kirk in Edinburgh. That there were hypocrites in the Kirk, as elsewhere, was to them a fact of life. What of it? But to Burns Holy Willie, Black Russell and the like, stood in a different category altogether from, for example, the loose-living reprobates of the road. For the Jolly Beggars he has whole-hearted sympathy—for the reprobates of the Kirk he has none. That there should be hypocrites in the Kirk at all, was a fact he just couldn't thole. It sets his blood on fire. It goes to his head like wine and maddens him. And the great series of religious satires, like the lava from a volcano, pours forth as a result. But only someone with a passion for religion could have seen it that way. Only, perhaps, a Calvinist? And that sensitivity came to him from the Kirk, together with all the colour and splendour that flood the religious satires. For, as the political satires make all too plain, it is only on the Kirk's wings he can rise. Without her, he is earth of the earth. With her, he can scale the heavens. Under his whip and lash, it is true, she shuddered. But he is, nevertheless, her son. As truly as ever Holy Willie, as Daddy Auld or the rest of them. . . . So that to those who would point the accusing finger at the Scots Presbyterian Kirk of the eighteenth century for narrowness, bigotry, intolerance, Pharisaism even—these her unquestioned and alas! unquestionable sins—that Kirk has still one proud and sufficient answer. She produced Robert Burns.

Johnnie Dowie, the most famous tavern-keeper of Burns'
Edinburgh. From the Old Scots Magazine of 1806

(*see page 26*)

JOHN DOWIE'S TAVERN. (*From the Engraving in Hone's "Year Book"*).

Johnnie Dowie's Tavern. Burns' favourite haunt in Edinburgh, where he probably met Herd and Johnson. From 'Old and New Edinburgh'

(*see page 27*)

CHAPTER IV

'THE JOLLY BEGGARS.'
'I like the jads for a' that'

'I HAVE FORGOT THE Cantata you allude to' wrote Burns in 1793 in response to an enquiry from George Thomson, the editor of *Scotish Airs* for whom he was then making songs, 'as I kept no copy and indeed did not know that it was in existence'. He had sent it originally to Richmond, the friend with whom he stayed at Baxter's Close in the Lawnmarket, 'I have enclosed you a piece of rhyming ware for your perusal'. That was February 17, 1786, in the days before the *Kilmarnock*, but Richmond didn't pay much heed to it. Lost some of it, indeed. There had been a song for a sweep in it—he remembered later, when people began to ask about it—and a song for a sailor too (neither, alas! in 'The Jolly Beggars' as we have it now). Burns never published the Cantata, nor did anybody else want to, for some time after his death. Certainly not Currie, in his chaste *Burns' Complete Works* —Currie, as shocked at 'The Beggars' as he had been at that profane 'Holy Willie's Prayer'—until irrepressible Glasgow, hearing of it somehow (for there were many MSS. of it) announced in the *Glasgow Courier* of Thursday July 11, 1799: 'On Saturday first will be published, price 2*d.*, by Stewart & Meikle, "The Jolly Beggars", a cantata by Robert Burns, carefully printed from the author's own MSS.' And re-printed again and again after that, for hilarious Glasgow loved it,—for all that its subject, as Carlyle declared, was 'the lowest in nature'. . . . The subject, indeed, is a gathering for a carousal, on a wild winter's night at Poosie Nansie's in Mauchline, of some six strolling vagabonds— the sodger and his drab, a Merry Andrew or fool, the pickpocket carlin, the little fiddler and the 'caird' or tinker, with some others, mutes, like the fool's Grizzie and the fiddler's 'twa Deborahs', who do not have a part. The eighteenth century loved cantatas and Ramsay had written one too, the 'Merry Beggars', on which

F

Burns here had his eye. But Ramsay's six characters had been grander altogether—a poet, a lawyer, a soldier, a courtier, a fiddler—and a preacher! Burns took over the soldier and the fiddler, but picked his others from the road. The refuse of the road, you might say. Rags and tatters, drink and lust—the kind of thing you see in Hogarth's 'Rake's Progress' (but with the accent here more on the poverty)—and further back, in Shakespeare's *Henry IV*, with Bardolph, Nym and Poins along o' Doll Tearsheet in the Eastcheap tavern over the flagons of sack. For Shakespeare knew the road as well as Burns. . . . It wasn't the road we'd know now—what with the Welfare State an' a' that. Alive with beggars was the road then—the more respectable ones like Scott's Edie Ochiltree important with their blue gown and badge (Scotland licensed her beggars then), the old soldiers (who didn't have pensions and clumped along on their wooden legs), the tinkers (mending your pots and pans), the crazed auld wives with nowhere to go like Madge Wildfire in Scott's *Heart of Midlothian*, a piper or two after Culloden off to the wars like John o' Lorn, or home from them—down-and-outs certainly, but down-and-outs with character—not an inexperienced young face among them. A rowth of material here for those who could see it and who, like Burns, could portray character. On the road by Kilmarnock and Irvine, up and down a Tarbolton street, out from Ayr to Alloway, many a night in Poosie Nansie's, he'd seen the pack of them. It was no sudden flash, as of passing a lighted window and hearing the roar of revelry within, that set him to his 'Jolly Beggars', tho' that might well have been the match that fired the train. But the beggars, like the Cottar, he'd known all his life. They were part of the furniture of his mind, so that there is no chance stroke,—nothing uncertain—about their presentation. Unlike the city-bred Ramsay's wooden figures,—a line or two and Burns' beggars come alive before us. . . . But life, after all, only lit the match. The powder came from the old songs Burns had read, with beggars roving up and down in them, or from Gay's *Beggar's Opera* (1728) that he'd studied also, and from those alluring broadsides, King James V's 'Gaberlunzie Man', or— where Burns undoubtedly got his title—King James's 'Jolly Beggar'. But the King, like his race, had a flair for romance and his 'Jolly Beggar' has a haunting lilt with it.

'There was a jolly beggar and a-begging he was boun'
'And he took up his quarters into a land 'art toun

. . . . .

'And we'll gang nae mair a-roving, a-roving in the night
'And we'll gang nae mair a-roving, let the moon shine ne'er sae
    bright.'

A romance that Byron leapt to ('We'll go no more a-roving, by
the light of the moon') but that Burns, the realist, turned down.
For Burns' beggars loved the road—they couldn't leave it. And
there is no hint of farewell in his cantata.

But the beggars, tho' Robin is unlikely to have known it,
went further back than the King. With an ancestry in art longer
even than Burns' own (and his, as Professor Elton estimates,
goes back straight in Scots literature for at least 400 years). But
the beggars go back further than that—thro' dim centuries of
English literature (Henley and Henderson's 'Jovial Mumper'),
far into the French, and then into the gay Latin of the wandering
scholars, when Christianity was still a new thing in Europe. The
roots of 'The Jolly Beggars',—deeper than any other of Burns'
works—run into no less than four great literatures—Scots and
English, French and Mediaeval Latin. It was a theme that had
already attracted artists high and low, over half Europe. And a
public there also. It was time then that, as a vital and picturesque
part of the country's life, it should now attract a public in Presbyterian Scotland also. For beggars, as experienced as those
Burns saw, have a way of broadening the public mind and divert-
ing it, as there was then much need, from undue concentration on
The Shorter Catechism. Here again Burns was a liberating agent for
Scotland's soul. . . . His cantata follows the plan of such cantatas—
a recitativo, bringing on the first character, who has a song—
then, time about, recitativo and song, for the rest,—until a final
chorus, in which all join. But with variety. Burns varied the
pattern. In fact, variety is the keynote of his 'Jolly Beggars'—
variety in structure, in metre, in subject of the songs (their merit,
their number), in language, in temper,—in everything! The first
recitativo, for example, is a double verse bringing on two, the
sodger and his drab—but the others only one each time. Then his
metres—a sample of nearly everything he had in his pack—the

familiar 'Troubadour's' metre, the octosyllabics of 'The Twa Dogs', 'The Holy Fair' metre with—and without—the bob, the splendid metre of Montgomerie's 'Cherrie and the Slae'—. Variety in the subjects of the songs (the sodger tells you his life-story, but the fiddler does not. And the final chorus is different again). Variety in their number (the fiddler alone gets two)—and in their merit. (The fool's is so poor it has been thought Burns couldn't have written it, and it is actually not in the Edinburgh University MS.—but the fiddler's good enough for anything.) Variety too in the language (the fiddler speaks braid Scots, but the drab formal English—the 'caird' a mixture of both). Variety then in temper (some are drunk like the Merry Andrew and the drab—or wailing like the carlin—dead sober like the 'caird').—It is this impression of overall variety and disorder—reflecting the vast disorder of the vagabonds—that is the most striking thing about the poem—the very air in which it moves and breathes—creating the authentic atmosphere in which the vagabonds can be seen, as the supper and family worship do that other for 'The Cottar'. . . . Nor is the construction as loose as it appears. The fiddler—who alone speaks braid Scots—thus localis-ing the cantata—is the unifying link. He is brought forward (tho' nobody listens to him!) to encore the first song—in the middle he sings his own—at the end he is called on by the others to speak for them (having already spoken for himself in his second song 'I am a Bard of no regard') and expound the philosophy of the road in the final chorus. . . . And as to Carlyle's point about the subject being 'the lowest in nature', Burns, as the *Kilmarnock* shows, had always a liking for 'low' subjects—The Louse—The Mountain Daisy—The Mouse—only this time he'd gone to human life for them. Here he anticipated—as he did also in his diction—the theories of the Lakeside poets, that all subjects are fit for poetic treatment. But he went much further than did they, for 'The Louse' and 'The Jolly Beggars' are 'lower' than anything Wordsworth or his school touched. With one curious, yet im-portant, reservation. For Burns' 'low' subjects are always 'low in nature'. There is nothing pathological in his choice. If his eye is as unembarrassed as any surgeon's, it is also as healthy. Robin sees no 'Idiot Boys'. . . . And his beggars too, are beggars in the full round—seen by themselves, without any onlookers. And drawn 'au naturel', as Shakespeare drew them, with no expurgations on moral grounds. But with no innuendo either. So that the result is art, and not—as it so easily might have been—indecency. Burns' artistic integrity is here complete. . . .

To the opening recitativo then, in Montgomerie's exciting 'Cherrie and the Slae' metre. The intoxication of its carefree diablerie will set anybody's pulses leaping and send the Beggars off to a glorious start. It is Burns' own favourite scene—the bitter winter's night without, the warmth within, with the final four lines giving you the roar and riot of Poosie Nansie's

> 'Wi' quaffing and laughing
> 'They ranted and they sang
> 'Wi jumping an' thumping
> 'The vera girdle rang.'

(Note the 'an's and 'um's carrying on the noise, and the 'r's sharpening it.) Don't you hear the heel-taps? With the recurrent 'r's in the last line echoing them. And, as the girdle doesn't reappear and has no point in a drinking-bout anyway, it is surely introduced just for that ring. Through the hullabaloo you catch sight of the couple 'niest the fire', but in action, just as 'The Cottar' is always in motion. 'She blinket on her sodger.' 'An' ay he gies . . . the kiss', 'While she held up her . . . gab'; 'Ilk smack still' . . . every line at a different stage of the picture, until the last 'He roar'd this ditty up', where 'roar' is the operative word. . . . The soldier's song that follows, is the most remarkable in the whole cantata. Not only is it excessively noisy, the 'sound of the drum' (the concluding words of each stanza) pounding and thundering through the poem, as it does also, twice in particular, in every line—

> 'I am a son of Márs, who have been in many wárs
> 'And show my cuts and scárs, wherever I come.'

It is also extraordinarily fast, the racing and rattling anapaests galloping the words along, with an effect almost as daemonic as that of Catullus' *Attis* (the fastest thing in literature). Metrically, that is, the song is unique in Burns, finished artist in metre tho' he was. And the story it tells, with carefully chosen incident, puts the soldier across triumphantly in just five verses. And the language

—for the soldier has been in England's wars—is English, of the conventional kind, thus bringing in, at a stroke, the soldier's background,—'What tho' with hoary locks, I must stand the winter's shocks'—to the fuming ingle of Ayrshire Poosie Nansie's. But, English or no, the audience like it. And in the next recitativo the applause raises the roof.

> 'He ended and the kebars sheuk (rafters shook)
>   'Aboon the chorus *roar*
> 'While frightened rattons backward leuk
>   'An' seek the benmost bore.
> 'A fairy fiddler frae the neuk (fiddler's first appearance)
>   'He skirled out En*core*
> 'But up arose the martial chuck
>   'An' laid the *loud uproar*.'

(Note the 'ore' throughout the stanza, the 'r's continuing the sound.) You couldn't get more noise than that, into eight short lines, whoever you were. . . . The drab's song, now 'I once was a maid, tho' I cannot tell when', still in the unsteady anapaests but slower and quieter. Autobiographical too, but alas! with moralising—

> 'Full soon I grew sick of my sanctified sot'—

(Note the hisses.) This is surely the indignant voice of the poet of The Holy Fair, and by no possibility, of a drunken drab. Her language too, is unconvincing—

> 'Transported I was with my sodger laddie.'
> 'From the gilded spontoon to the fife I was ready.'

How did a tongue loosened with drink, get round these words? . . . And now it's the turn of the Merry Andrew, in the neuk with his Grizzie. Like the drab, he too makes the Kirk the butt of his worst mockery (suspiciously like Burns' own voice).

> 'Observ'd ye yon reverend lad
>   'Mak' faces to tickle the mob?
> 'He rails at our mountebank squad,
>   'It's rivalship just i' the job.'

But could any drunk sing that last line?—let alone any poet

think it worth writing! No wonder the critics are agreed this
fool's song couldn't originally have been in 'The Jolly Beggars'.
But how did it ever get in? 'Rivalship—just i' the job'! Burns in
a hurry, perhaps? Or Burns not caring? Or Burns on purpose, as
he was writing for a fool? . . . The 'raucle carlin' (sturdy beldam)
gets one good line

  'But weary fa' the waefu' woodie' (gallows)

in the recitativo that now introduces her. She is the weeper of the
party (there is always somebody 'weeping drunk' in a bar), and
in 'sighs and sobs' began 'To wail her braw John Highlandman'—
a different kind of noise from the soldier's ecstatic roar and the
Merry Andrew's song to the pipes ('syne tuned his pipes wi'
grave grimace')—but all contributing to the general brawl. Her
song is different too—the first in the cantata that is not autobiographical. But her diction is just as odd 'The ladies' hearts he
did trepan'—('Trepan' in a song, is wild, even for Burns, tho'
Allan Ramsay uses it once.) and 'Adown my cheeks the pearls
ran'. 'Pearls' indeed! . . . It is the carlin's song that brings on now,
in the very centre of the poem, the little fiddler again, and the
recitativo for him, like his song, is at last in the braid Scots. A
good song this time, with a fine, if borrowed, title 'Whistle owre
the Lave o't' (a further sound, added to the soldier's roar, the
fool's pipes, the carlin's wail—now the whistle). And, in contrast
to her wail, this is a merry song.

  'I am a fiddler to my trade
  'An' a' the tunes that e'er I played
  'The sweetest still to wife or maid
   'Was Whistle owre the Lave o't'.

. . . And now comes the quarrel. Every group of drunks, as Burns
well knew, sooner or later falls to quarrelling, when people get
'fighting drunk', and the 'sturdy caird',—a big, entirely humour-
less fellow—now intervenes. But, after the fiddler's gay song, his
is a slow, dull one.

  'My bonie lass, I work in brass
   'A tinkler is my *station*
  'I've travelled round all Christian ground,
   'In this my occup*ation*.

'I've ta'en the gold an' been enrolled
'In many a noble squadron,
'But vain they searched, when off I marched
'To go an' clout the cauldron.'

You can't help noticing the heavy, double ending—station, occupation, squadron, cauldron—at every second line acting like a brake, slowing up the verse and making the whole poem drag. The 'caird' is a dull fellow. . . . And it's on him the trick is played. By the little fiddler, quick and sly. With the drunk 'carlin' between them. And with the vernacular putting the whole lurid scene across, as naturally as all the rest. And on that, the dramatic part of the cantata ends, for Burns now stands back to admire the fiddler's character 'He was a care-defying blade', at once breaking the emotional tension. And throwing the limelight on the fiddler, who now gets a second song.

'I am a bard of no regard
'Wi' gentlefolks an' a' that'.

But is this the fiddler, or Robin himself? . . .

'I never drank the Muses' stank
'Castalia's burn an' a' that'—

that old cry over the want of learning—and this bold statement of principle

'But lordly will, I hold it still
'A mortal sin to thraw that'.

Robin at twenty-five! As it might be Rabelais (a good deal older) writing his 'Fais Ce Que Vouldrai' over that Abbey of Thelema, where by doing what one wants a man was to find ideal happiness. . . . This song, anyhow, or maybe this doctrine in it, goes to the beggars' heads and makes them, as well it might, drunker than ever, so that—recurring to that breath-taking metre of 'The Cherrie and the Slae', which had so dashingly opened the cantata—they call for another 'A ballad o' the best' which now introduces the final chorus—the only song that Burns, writing to Thomson in 1793, remembered that he liked. And here, in defiant trochees, is the Apologia of the Beggars, carrying Rabelais' doctrine à outrance—

'What is title, what is treasure
'What is reputation's care?
'If we lead a life of pleasure
  'Tis no matter how, or where!'

(Note the testy t's of irritation. For this use of 't' compare Sophocles, *O.T.*, line 370-1

σοὶ δὲ τοῦτ᾽ οὐκ ἔστ᾽ ἐπεὶ
τυφλὸς τα τ᾽ ὦτα τόν τε νοῦν τά τ᾽ ὄμματ᾽ εἶ[1]

But the life of pleasure, as instanced in the next verse, carries nowadays but little conviction—

'With the ready trick[2] and fable
'Round we wander all the day
'And at night in barn or stable
'Hug our doxies on the hay.'

—tho' to an artificial eighteenth century, newly fascinated by Rousseau's doctrines of the simple life, so fantastically remote from their own, it might well have spelt Elysium. Much as gipsy life ('Where my caravan has rested') or hikers' life ('Bed in the bush with stars to see'. R.L.S.) if equally unreal, have fascinated later generations. . . . And now, breaking the thread of this Epicurean dalliance with a thought totally foreign to the singers, there is interposed the usual unhappy Burns' comment. Just as in 'The Cottar' too, Burns stands aside to admire his hero.

'Does the sober bed of marriage
'Witness brighter scenes of love?'

But what was marriage to the beggars? It is Burns himself who thinks of it, with that keen sense of respectability which is always in the background of his mind. And so, to the concluding verse,

---

[1] Teiresias to Oedipus:
      'Tis you that see not clear, 'tis you.
      To ear, to mind, to eye, you tak' no tent
      Whate'er they tell.

[2] As shown by the fiddler a moment ago.

which is the one Robin remembered in 1793 well enough to
quote—

    'A fig for those by law protected
    'Liberty's a glorious feast!
    'Courts for cowards were erected,
    'Churches built to please the priest!'

the cantata ending thus, characteristically, with a final kick at the
Kirk. But 1793 was a Dumfriesshire year, when Robin was up
against the State, as well as the Kirk, and the champagne of the
French Revolution was bubbling over, and this last verse, good
enough to remember, said appropriately much of what he was
then thinking about all that. He remembered it for that.

And as you put 'The Jolly Beggars' down, the reckless abandon
of its spirit, its whirlwind pace and mercurial change of mood, its
marvellous perspective-grouping, even to showing the mutes in
the shadows—the skilful choice of incident—the character-drawing so swift and sure—above all, the creation of the riotous, roaring atmosphere of the shabby, country inn—all these sweep you
off your feet. So that you forget, for the moment, the unrealistic
quality of much of the vagabonds' language. Blind-drunk roy-
sterers in Ayrshire Poosie Nansie's singing forsooth in a starched
and formal English that wouldn't have discredited the stiffest of
eighteenth-century drawing-rooms! Yet Shakespeare, that other
and greater poet of the road, never gives Doll Tearsheet and her
lads words they couldn't have known. Tho' there is this to be said
in Burns' defence. A cantata, like an opera, may not require the
absolute realism of drama. So long as the songs project the
personality of the singer—which the songs of 'The Jolly Beggars'
undoubtedly do—they may have done all that is required of them.
At the same time the abrupt change from the living Scots of the
recitativo to the colourless formalism of the English of the songs,
does jar—and the very fact that it distracts attention from the
people, to the peculiar language the author is now using, stamps it
as inartistic. Still, by and large, a wonderful cantata,—in verve, in
zest, in swing, alone and unrivalled in Scots literature. For it
breathes the very soul of Bohemianism, like Mürger dying in his
Paris garret with the poignant cry of 'Plus de bruit! Plus de
musique! Plus de Bohême!' on his reluctant lips. To Burns'

beggars, as to Mürger, life is but that—noise and song and
Bohemia. Deliriously happy while the bumpers flow but with
no to-morrow at all, even as the volatile Para Handy, their
spiritual descendant, has it too in Neil Munro's gay stories of
Clydeside. . . . But as the severer East Coast surveyed them, and
classic Edinburgh, the beggars took on a different look. Without
one thought of the morrow, true enough—yet here was Scott's
Edie Ochiltree saying 'They'll find as muckle quilted in this auld
blue gown as will bury me like a Christian and give the lads and
lasses a blythe lykewake too . . . sae there's the gaberlunzie's
burial provided for and I need nae mair' (*The Antiquary*, p. 150).
So there were beggars and beggars, it appeared, even on the
road. Then who but Edie had the wits to save the Antiquary from
a salt sea-death? The wits and the will. Whereas this West Coast
riff-raff—the rankest individualists—are incapable every one of
them of a thought or feeling outside self, of an interest even. For,
hark to their songs! Each one expatiating about himself. And with
the rafters ringing all about them for an encore, see that Merry
Andrew and his tinkler-hizzie in their neuk. 'They mindit na
wha the chorus teuk.' Individualists still. Nothing—neither drink
nor lust—can unite this pack. While Edie Ochiltree's life is inter-
woven with everybody else's in *The Antiquary*. And yet he is as
much of the road as any of Burns' beggars, 'I could never bide the
staying still in ae place' (The Antiquary)—as thirled to it as the
sodger and his drab. Is the difference, then, that between the West
Coast and the East? For it was easy Glasgow, that apotheosis of
the West, that first published 'The Jolly Beggars'—taking to it,
it would seem, naturally. While the cantata, it must be owned,
has always been a mouthful for cultured Edinburgh. . . . And
indeed Scotland herself has taken a long time to like it,—if she
really likes it yet? The critics perhaps. For the crabbed Carlyle
did indeed go on to say that, subject or no, 'The Jolly Beggars'
was 'the most poetic of all Burns' pieces'. And an indignant Scott
took the wretched Currie to task for omitting it from the Burns'
canon. While even the supercilious Lockhart, tho' preferring
'Tam o' Shanter' (as did Burns himself) gave it his approval. . . .
But even the orators, on those hectic Burns' nights, fight shy of
'The Beggars', turning rather to Tam o' Shanter who, drunk or
sober, is at any rate riding home to his lawful wife—on the right

road at last—whereas those Jolly Beggars! They do nothing but get drunker and drunker—with morals to match—and not one word of repentance from first to last! What was Robin thinking of,—he that wrote 'The Cottar'? And the ethic of 'The Jolly Beggars' goes dead against the Presbyterian grain. Tho' it is just that ethic impeccably undoctored as it is, that makes the artistic veracity of the poem, and in the end, its glory. . . . In the Highlands it is no better. For beggars do not run on Highland roads. They never have. John o' Lorn down in the South, perhaps. But in the North? Never. What would Lovat say to a Fraser begging, or Lord Reay to a Mackay? It would be a slur on the whole clan. In the Highlands the Beggars have no ancestry. There's hardly a word in the language to express them. And with the Kirk agin them too, the poem in the Highlands is a dead letter. . . . But, furth of Scotland, the cantata fared well. In England, scholars like the eminently proper Matthew Arnold referred to it as 'this puissant and splendid production', and Henley and Henderson (the latter a Scot), Burns' *Centenary* editors, have no doubt about its place, 'this irresistible presentation of humanity caught in the act, and summarised for ever in terms of art'. And the Continent of course, that never has any qualms over the unconventional, rose to it at once. In the view of Angellier, Burns' leading critic abroad, it is Burns' masterpiece. . . . But Robin forgot it. Partly it must have been those songs—good enough, no doubt, for the ribald *Merry Muses of Caledonia* into which he copied most of them—but otherwise? For by 1793 he knew well enough that one doesn't use words like 'rivalship' or phrases like, 'Let inclination law that' in a good song. In a good song, indeed, he would allow by then hardly anything but a monosyllable, certainly never an abstract word. And the 'Jolly Beggars' songs just bristle with abstract words. . . . But it wasn't only the songs. He'd grown out of character-drawing too. Tam o' Shanter in 1790? But Tam was a flash in the pan. Folk like Holy Willie or the sodger and his drab no longer interested him. In his mind's eye he didn't see them now. 'I have forgot the Cantata you allude to.' It is of a piece with the vast disorder of the road.

CHAPTER V

'TAM O' SHANTER.'
'Fou an' unco happy'

THERE IS something about a ride—the quick motion, the thrill, the exhilaration of it—that lends itself to poetry. Even the bookish poet Pope felt it. 'What if you amused yourself in turning an ode?' pleaded a friend. 'Perhaps I may,' said Pope, 'if we ride on. The motion is an aid to my fancy: A round trot very much awakens my spirits.'[1] Scott set a midnight elopement to a ride, in his romantic 'Lochinvar' ('They'll have fleet steeds that follow, quo' young Lochinvar'.) And Browning, the most dramatic of his romances in 'The Last Ride Together'. Burns was no romanticist, but he was well used to riding—on the smugglers' track, after the whisky—up and down the wet Dumfriesshire moors and mosses. (It is significant that 'Tam o' Shanter' belongs to this period, and not to the earlier farming years, when horses were just for ploughing.) Two hundred hard miles a week, he reckoned it would be about, and in wild weather as often as not. And making poetry as you rode. 'As I galloped home at night', he writes from Dumfries in 1792, 'I made a ballad on her' (Lesley Bailey). . . . A ride with whisky in it. The thought must have grown in his mind long before that Captain Grose, the merry fat fellow he met at the Riddells in Friars Carse nearby, asked him for a 'witch story' to put in his *Antiquities of Scotland* alongside the picture of Kirk Alloway. A witch story! And here was Robin on his grey mare 'Jenny Geddes' jogging down Nithsdale, or up by Thornhill, or late of a stormy night galloping home to Ellisland—thinking out his 'witch-story'. Or rather recalling it, for there is nothing invented in 'Tam o' Shanter', as Burns himself wrote in answer to Captain Grose, telling all the tales he'd heard of Kirk Alloway, Tam o' Shanter's among them. . . . A ride with whisky in it, and the witch-story—somehow the two got tangled together. And one day in 1790 down by the Nith—one of those

[1] Pope, August, 1714, letter to Lord Burlington. See Thackeray, *English Humorists*, p. 156.

'trotting burns' that always stimulated his fancy—Burns composed it, 'Tam o' Shanter', the poem of the ride and the story.
He took no more than the day to it, declared Jean, his wife. But
Robin knew better. 'All my poetry is the effect of easy composition, but of laborious correction', and there had been a deal
of correction, after that day, in 'Tam o' Shanter'. Looking back
on April 11, 1791,—nearly six months later, at least—he told Mrs.
Dunlop, his critical Mentor, that 'Tam' now showed 'a finishing
polish' he felt he could never better. 'Tam o' Shanter' was the
best thing he'd written. . . . Edinburgh took to it instantly—
published it in the *Edinburgh Magazine* of March, 1791, before
ever Grose's *Antiquities* came out—Scott found it 'inimitable'—
the fastidious Lockhart gave out that here was Burns' masterpiece
—orators innumerable have quoted from it, or declaimed it (it is
only 224 lines long) and a critic as cool and as recent as the late
Professor Raleigh has called it 'the finest narrative poem since
Chaucer'. But all this (or rather, what he heard of it) failed to
convince the dour Carlyle. For him 'Tam o' Shanter' was 'dead
at the core, like the ivy round the rock. Not so much a poem',
he growled, 'as a piece of sparkling rhetoric.' One moment you
were snug in the Ayr public-house, and the next—hey presto!
—'at the gate of Tophet'. Now how could you make a jump like
that? But Burns shows you how—preparing the ground for it as
cunningly as Scott himself for every step of 'Wandering Willie's
Tale'. (The tale that in some ways is remarkably like Tam o'
Shanter with its midnight ride, its whisky, and its haunted kirk.)
For here, as early as line 30 in the poem, is Tam's wife prophesying
he would some day be

> 'Catch'd wi' warlocks i' the mirk
> 'By Alloway's auld, haunted kirk'.

And, a little later (line 78) as he takes the road in the storm

> 'That night, a child might understand
> 'The De'il had business on his hand',

thus bringing on the principal character, Satan. And close on that,
comes Tam himself, 'crooning o'er some auld Scots sonnet'
(song), and 'glow'ring round . . . lest bogles catch him unawares'.
For—

> 'Kirk Alloway was drawing nigh
> 'Where ghaists and howlets nightly cry'.
>
> (Lines 87-8)

And if you cannot jump to what is to come, from all these clues, you had best leave 'Tam o' Shanter' alone, for the fault is not Robin's. . . . The cavil of Angellier, Burns' best critic, is more acute. 'Tam o' Shanter', argues the Frenchman, stops too soon. We should have been given that fine, dramatic scene—good 'theatre' it would have been—when the returning reveller meets his irate Kate. What does Tam say to his wife? But then Burns never had been interested in what a man said to his wife. Even the Cottar, that model of Scots family life, hasn't a word to say to her, as she sits 'mending the cla'es'. And in 'The Holy Fair' the guidwife deals out the kebbuck, in complete family silence, her guidman speaking only for the grace. For the truth is (as a foreigner wouldn't know) that the Scots husband, drunk or sober, just doesn't talk to his own wife. What would there be to say to her? And Tam would have been no exception. Tam wouldn't have said anything either. Burns knew just the right point where to stop. . . . But what Edinburgh liked in the poem—or what must certainly have caught Scott's ear—was surely its odd resemblance to the Border ballads, then on everyone's lips. The glorious pace of the hard riding in it! Nothing outside 'Kinmont Willie' riding the 'wan water' down into Cumberland, goes quite so fast. And if you don't hear the raiders' bridles jingling—as you do in 'Kinmont Willie'—you hear something else that is just as alluring— the tap-tap of the witches' feet in the delirious reels and strath-speys to the mad music of the bagpipes skirling. And Edinburgh, then dancing the gay night through in the candle-lit cellars of her High Street (where Burns himself had, time and again, heard it) knew that sound too. The riding and the dancing, the bumpers like those you tossed off in the warm taverns of the Old Town— this was a poem after Edinburgh's own heart. . . . After Burns' own heart too. For 'Tam o' Shanter', more than anything else he wrote, comprehends within its short limits all the things— infinitely varied, even contradictory—that he himself liked best, so that he moves in it from first to last with a freedom and ease he shows nowhere else. In 'The Cottar', by contrast, he is on his best behaviour, with a careful eye always on his audience. There isn't a single laugh in 'The Cottar'. It is full dress all the time. In 'The Jolly Beggars' is he, perhaps, on his worst behaviour? Anyhow with a defiant eye cocked as clearly at a probably outraged audience as ever it is for approbation in 'The Cottar'. But you can read 'Tam o' Shanter' through and just feel it is something he is telling you with sheer delight, under no constraint at all—something he enjoys from first to last. . . . There is the wild winter night, and how snug it is in the warm inn parlour with a crony like Souter Johnny (Robin thoroughly understood friendship. It is the very core of 'Auld Lang Syne')—then 'the reaming swats that drank divinely' (And didn't he just know the fascination of that? 'Gae Bring to me a Pint o' Wine')—out in the storm after that (something in Burns, as in Shakespeare, always lifted to a storm) with the thunder and lightning rolling about you and your pulses racing to them both—then that mad ride on the grey mare Maggie (as it might be 'Jenny Geddes')—the dance, 'hornpipes, jigs, strathspeys and reels' in glorious 'abandon', one faster than another, with that most potent and universal of human lures, Auld Nick himself, making music in your ear (and who lit up Burns' imagination like Auld Nick?)—women, 'witches and beldams' here, of course, but—supposing they were girls? Girls! And a close-up of them, with nobody to look at them but yourself! And here *was* one! One of them really was a girl 'Ae winsome wench and wawlie' (choice)! . . . All that on the Epicurean side—and then on the other, the Calvinist, side, 'Tam o' Shanter' is a true tale. None of your meretricious romances that Burns himself loathed, and that the Kirk looked so black on, but 'a tale o' truth'. And furthermore, with a moral purpose. Burns was always, at rock-bottom, your God-fearing Calvinist, and so—those ravishing girls, the Venusberg music, the intoxicating dance, the hilarious fun, even that Arch-Ensnarer Auld Nick himself—what were they but the baseless fabric of a dream—and you weren't to blame for any one of them! You were really riding home to your own wife, as the Kirk enjoined you should,—and her, where Burns always liked her best to be, well out of the picture. So that you had all the credit of the good intention, without any of its boredom. 'Tam o' Shanter' combined every single element that Burns liked best. It gave you the best of both worlds—the World, the Flesh and the Devil, and all the unalloyed ecstasy these supreme enchantments could bring a man (and who knew better than Robin the kick and pull of all that?)—together with the moral approval and commendation of the Kirk, for wasn't 'honest Tam' riding away from it all? Away from the 'reaming swats'—past those girls and the dancing feet—past even the Devil himself—and away home to his lawful wife—and her (thank God!) off-stage! The best of both worlds and no mistake. No wonder Robin liked 'Tam o' Shanter'. It satisfied, up to the hilt, both sides of his nature. . . . And that 'finishing polish' too was plain to see. For had it not every detail just right? Like 'The Cottar', it begins in the evening, the day's darg done. Now is the golden moment—for ease and joy. But, unlike 'The Cottar', this time it's to be a night in town. Over the foaming glasses. And by line 6 we are on to the blissful heights, 'getting fou and unco happy'—that rapturous keynote to which the whole poem thereafter is set. And as happiness for Robin lies always in the present—no dreams of a distant Xanadu for him!—so here his cup of delight is filled full, by a gratifying silhouette of what is still far-off—of 'the lang Scots miles between us and our hame'

'Whare *sits* our *s*ulky, *s*ullen dame'

(Note the hisses)—a startling contrast to the same prospect, as it had appeared to the virtuous Cottar. . . . Into a world of such values comes cantering Tam, and lest you get him wrong (as against such a background you well might) he is, at first meeting, 'honest Tam'. This brilliantly chosen introductory adjective, repeated—as it were, casually—three lines later

'Auld Ayr, wham ne'er a town surpasses
'For honest men an' bonnie lasses'

gives a line on what is to follow, putting the whole adventure into the right perspective. The poem isn't about drunken black-guards. It's about 'honest men and bonnie lasses'. And, with Tam's honesty thus pressed home, Burns can now safely show the other side of him. 'A blethering, blustering, drunken bellum'! But that's what his wife says, isn't it? And what is a wife but that 'sulky sullen dame' we've left sitting at home? Whereas Tam is here with us—here and now—'honest Tam'. Who cares what a wife says? Not her husband anyway. This is a night-out. Burns has got his hero over. And he can give, now without fear, a realistic flash-back on 'honest Tam's' past.

> 'Ae market-night

> . . . . . .

> 'Fast by an ingle, bleezing finely
> 'Wi' reaming swats that drank divinely
> 'And at his elbow Souter Johnnie
> > (Line 41)

> . . . . . .

> 'They had been fou for weeks together',

with even the Puritans savouring those luscious 'reaming swats'. . . . And now the pace has quickened, and the ale-house doors have opened, with the light turned full on to the scene within. But not for long. Soon we are without,—in the dark— while the poet, in the cool, nay, frigid, English of a low-toned obligato comments upon pleasure, with just the one vivid drunken couplet (that triple ending),

> 'Kings may be blest, but Tam was glōrioū̄s
> 'O'er a' the ills o' life victōrioū̄s
> > (Line 58)

shattering the dark. And the low-toned obligato continues, like the accompaniment to a song, of similes all repetitive (Pleasures are like poppies spread—or like the snow falls in the river—or like the Borealis—or like the rainbow) all driving home the one theme, 'happiness and how brief it is!' Even as does the poem it-self, that apotheosis of human happiness. Until, with the solemn and slow spondaic

> 'Nae man can tether time or tide
> 'The hour approaches Tam̄ maū̄n rīde
> > (Line 68)

the verse wakes up to life again. But, as the tense monosyllables show, to an ominous life, for we are out on the road now, in a storm.

'Loud, deep and lang the thunder bellow'd
'That night a child might understand
'The De'il had business on his hand'
(Line 78)

And before us glooms Kirk Alloway, 'whare ghaists and howlets nightly cry' (line 88). The landmarks now are sinister, every one of them, 'whare drunken Charlie brak's neck-bane'—'whare hunters fand the murder'd bairn', with the storm increasing in violence in every line and the verse, with extraordinary skill, imitating it,

'The līghtnings flāsh from pōle to pōle
'Nēar and mōre nēar the thunders rōll
(Line 100)

(hark to the whole gamut of the vowels with the final o's prolonging the sound.) and here, in a glimmer through the trees, 'Kirk Alloway seemed in a bleeze' where language and imagery and versification, all now working together, create a mounting atmosphere of hair-raising terror, so that the concluding couplet of this paragraph breaks on the mind with the most dramatic anti-climax,—that Peripeteia (or Sudden Transformation) that Aristotle loved. Here comes the startling change when the clouds lift and the terror is resolved—

'Thrō' ilka bōre the beāms were glāncing
'And loūd resoūnded-mīrth ånd dancing!'
(Line 104)

The sudden relief of those short, light vowels 'mirth ånd', with the gay trochaic ending (glāncing, dāncing) after the fearsome and sombre ō's and ē's of the preceding couplets (pōle to pōle, the thunders rōll—the grōaning trēes—sēemed in a blēeze, rising to their crescendo of terror) show a mastery of metre and of dramatic power as admirable as it is rare. Tho' the happy issue has been fore-shadowed in the opening lines 'fou and unco happy'. We might have known the terror would be resolved and our breath come freely once again, on that 'Loud resounded-mirth and dancing!' . . . Once more the temperature falls, deliberately lowered now to contrast with the excitement coming, in that

hectic dance (line 115) which is the striking central scene of the
poem, 'Hornpipes, jigs, strathspeys and reels' (line 117) in wild
and whirling confusion—all those dances Burns had seen of a
merry night in the echoing Edinburgh cellars. With the Devil
himself, that soul-ensnaring Auld Nick, piping the Venusberg
music for them, every note aflame with temptation—

> 'He screw'd the pipes and gart them skirl
> 'Till roof and rafters a' did dirl'
>
> (Lines 122-3)

while the candle-lights gleam—as they'd gleamed so often from
their sconces in 'the Coffin', that innermost recess (Burns' favourite haunt) in Johnnie Dowie's dark tavern in Edinburgh—but
from real coffins this time, those (like his father's) that were buried
deep in Kirk Alloway itself, but were now raised up by this mad
demoniac music. And by their light you saw—as you'd seen from
the gallows stark in Libberton's Wynd, not a yard from Dowie's
door—the murderer's bones dangling in their irons, or the thief
dangling from his rope, or—what the Kirk said went to Hell
with both these—'the wee unchristen'd bairns' (the thought of
which always, as in 'Holy Willie's Prayer' made Burns see red)
and then—the knife that had killed a father—the final horror.
But Burns' own father lay buried here, and on that father's deathbed, it was anxiety for his errant son Robin, gone so far astray,
that had darkened his last moments. May some uneasy memory of
that, have crossed the poet's fancy here, to bring in 'the knife that
had killed a father'? But the horrors—true to the poem's primary
intention—again fade out and happiness returns.

> 'The mirth and fun grew fast and furious
> 'The piper loud and louder blew
> 'The dancers quick and quicker flew
> 'They reel'd, they set, they crossed, they cleekit
> 'Till ilka carlin swat and reekit'
>
> (Lines 144-8)

when the verse, now packed with verbs of excited motion, races
and gallops in exuberant and voluptuous frenzy to match the
sense. . . . Till, with the solemn spondees, 'Nōw Tām, Ō Tām'
—the crowning felicity, the ultimate 'joy of joys', sweeps in, with

the delirious thought—'If only these beldams had been girls—
young girls—in their 'teens!'. And here actually—yes—here was
one! 'Ae winsome wench and wawlie' (choice) (line 164). At
that, 'Tam stood like ane bewitched' (line 183)—as Robin must
oft have done—'and thought his very een enriched'. And it
wasn't only Tam who looked. Other eyes too looked hot on
Youth and Beauty—

> 'Even Satan glowr'd and fidg'd fu' fain
> 'And hotch'd and blew wi' might and main'
> (Lines 185-6)

—every verb in the couplet a verb of violent action. But happiness could go no further—

> 'Tam tint his reason a' thegither
> 'And roars out 'Weel done, Cutty-Sark'
> 'And, in an instant, all was dark'
> (Lines 187-90)

Happiness never lasts. And, to mark the bitter change, the poem
is suddenly full of hisses—

> 'Out the hellish legion sallied
> 'As bees bizz out wi' angry fyke
> 'When plundering herds assail their byke
> 'As open pussie's mortal foes
> 'When pop! she starts before their nose
> 'As eager runs the market-crowd
> 'When 'Catch the thief' resounds aloud
> 'So Maggie runs, the witches follōw
> 'Wi mony an eldritch skreich an' hollō.'
> (Lines 192-200)

the hisses dying down in the mournful and calamitous ō (fōes,
nōse, sō, follōw, hollō) of woe. The similes are introduced here
solely, it would appear, for their sound-value, for they con-
tribute little, if anything, to the meaning—only serving to lower
the temperature after the high tension-point of Satan himself, that
arch-enticer, glowering at the girl. . . . But Robin, alas! knew
well enough the fate foretold for those who, like Tam, couldn't
take their eyes off girls. 'In hell they'll roast thee like a herrin'

(line 202). (Note the rough breathing 'h' and the sizzling 'r's'.) . . .
So you must ride for it, if you were to escape, as on many a
tempestuous night, Burns rode back to Ellisland,—to his own
wife. So the verse gallops again, riotously and drunkenly, as they
galloped in Kinmont Willie—

> 'But, ere the keystane she could make
> 'The fient a tail she had to shake'
>
> (Lines 209-10)

Would the girls get Tam then, after all?—Or would he just make
home? Only just—he makes it. ('But faith, he'll turn a corner,
jinkin', an' cheat you yet', as Robin had said in his 'Address to the
De'il'). . . . In the brief conclusion (lines 219-24) this 'tale o' truth'
Burns calls his poem. Psychologically it is so, being based on real
experiences and real beliefs. And literally also,—for, as Burns
wrote to Grose—it hangs on a legend he had heard (and not
invented) and on local tales then current, of drunken farmers. . . .
As for its scenery—the 'ghaists and bogles' and the like—,
eighteenth-century Scotland, with the famous *Satan's Invisible
World Discovered* before her, or devouring the minister of
Aberfoyle's *Secret Commonwealth of Elves, Fauns and Fairies*, or
even rapt in Burns' own 'Hallowe'en', believed as firmly in their
material presence as in that of the buildings they haunted. When
Auld Nick himself might be lurking behind the next fence—as
the Kirk kept telling you—you might well see ghosts and
warlocks, his minions, of a sudden turn in a dark road. 'Tam
o' Shanter' is of a realism as substantial as anything Burns ever
wrote. . . . And he goes on, as he loved to do, to point the moral.
The truly Calvinist moral. If your mind runs to drink and the
girls 'Think! you may buy the joys owre dear' (line 223). . . .
And yet, Calvinism or no, joys they are. He holds to it. But the
final line pulls the other way. 'Remember.' . . . 'Tam o' Shanter'
ends on the moral note, and at precisely the right point, for Tam's
wife, unlike the sober Cottar's, doesn't come in, on the 'Happiness' motif. . . . And Happiness? What a Belshazzar's banquet of
happiness is spread before us in this poem! The warm alehouse-
ingle and your crony Souter Johnnie beside you—those 'reaming
swats' (divine!)—the demoniac music, the whirlwind dance, that
sympathetic Devil who always understood humanity to the core

and would give you all you could ever want—and then, the peak and crown of it all—those girls!—with no other eye to gaze on them but your own—what a veritable Belshazzar's banquet of bliss, Life could provide for a man! And yet—and yet—Robin was not his father's son for nothing. 'Think! Remember!' ring out in sonorous warning in the concluding lines of the poem. 'Damnanda est voluptas', Calvin had written. 'Think! Remember!' And Calvinism for Burns still has the last word.

CHAPTER VI

'BRAW SOBER LESSONS'—
some other poems

BESIDES THE POEMS already mentioned, Burns wrote a vast number of occasional pieces of all sorts—satirical, theatrical, political—epigrams and so on—most of which have no merit whatsoever. It was an ill service to his memory to collect them. But out of this quagmire emerge some few, worthy of attention for themselves, or of interest for the light they cast on his personality. It was a personality that, as his works show, did not develop. True—he discarded the Kirk as a subject, in favour of Scots songs, but the things that interested him in the springtime of the *Kilmarnock*—such as the contrast between rich and poor as in 'The Twa Dogs', Independence, the Devil, and particularly, those girls—are still the things that interested him as he lay dying in Dumfries. Only more ardently now. He never grew out of them. . . .

As a last echo of the Kirk-period, there is one poem, the 'Address to the Unco Guid', published as early as the *Edinburgh Edition* of 1787, and the only reflective poem that Burns ever wrote—that has acquired a well-deserved fame. It is sometimes the only 'Burns' poem that Burns' enthusiasts know. It opens in the emotional Lallans

> 'O Ye wha are sae guid yoursel'
> 'sae pious and sae holy'

thus presaging its stormy character, but, as the poet takes up his role of counsel for poor mortals

> 'That frequent pass douce Wisdom's door
> 'For glaikit (giddy) Folly's portals'

the emotional Lallans, characteristically changes into sober English, the language of thought. Burns puts his case well. He knew, better than most, what he was talking of, here—the temptation for the man

'What ragings must his veins convulse
'That still eternal gallop'—

and for the girl

'A dear-lov'd lad, convenience snug
'A treacherous inclination'—

But the consequent Fall,—shocks him! Instead of delighting in
it, like the real zealots for the Flesh, as the cynical Mallarmé
('*La chair est faible et j'ai lu tous les livres*') or as Swinburne ('The
roses and raptures of vice') would have done, all Burns' Calvinist
blood rises in revolt, and abandoning the defence, he writes
(v. 5)

'See Social Life and Glee sit down,
'All joyous and unthinking
'Till, quite transmogrify'd, they've grown
'Debauchery and Drinking
'O would they stay to calculate
'Th'eternal consequences—

(Note the groaning Ō.) This last idea, it is safe to say, would never
have occurred to the impenitent author of *Dolores*, still less to
Mallarmé. But the Flesh and the Spirit were always at war, in
Burns. It is the last two verses, with that famous beginning

'Then gently scan your brother man
'Still gentler sister woman'

that are most associated with Burns' philosophy. And indeed they
struck a new note altogether in Scots life, unused, as it was, to
viewing either man or woman with gentleness. Was not the Kirk
still hot from burning witches and fresh from chastising folk
like Gavin Hamilton for the heinous sin of lifting potatoes on a
Sunday? And the State was no better, with Lord Braxfield from
the Bench baiting poor prisoners, or sentencing to transporta-
tion for life those like Palmer and Margarot for venturing on new
political thought. For gentleness has never been a Scots virtue.
'Gentle', indeed in this sense does not occur in Scots literature
before Burns but always in its older sense of 'gently born' as in
Ramsay's 'Gentle Shepherd'. Tho' England (*vide* the *Oxford
Dictionary*) as early as the sixteenth century had developed the

secondary meaning gentle=non-violent. Anyone gentle (i.e. gently-born) will act in a 'gentle' way (i.e. non-violent). But, alas in the uproar of the sixteenth and seventeenth centuries, that was a complete *non sequitur* in Scotland. No such meaning could be developed. And it is only in the comparative calm of the closing eighteenth century that it shines out here. But gentleness (i.e. non-violence) is not really a Scottish thought. Nor is the word to-day in the current vocabulary of the people. It was the English who coined the word 'gentleman', and the ideal too— from as early as Chaucer's 'verray parfit gentil knight'. Just as that other word 'cheerful', common in England, is almost unknown on Scottish lips. Why do we never use it, queries that eminent philologist Professor A. W. Craigie, in his study of language?[1] But neither 'gentle' nor 'cheerful' are ideas that would easily dawn on Calvinists. They were not in Calvin's own make-up. From this novel beginning, then, Burns goes on to reflect on the Origin of Evil, and throwing aside the conventional teaching of Calvinism, thinks for himself.

> 'One point must still be greatly dark
> 'The moving why they do it.'—

The clear-cut words, without a single theological cliché, show this to be a subject he has turned over for himself. As does the sequel,

> 'And just as lamely can ye mark
> 'How far, perhaps, they rue it.'

Sunday after Sunday, offenders were made to say they rued it. But whether they really did? Whether anybody really does? Into such mysterious regions of the mind Burns alone, at this time, ventured. His conclusion,

> 'What's done we partly may compute
> 'We know not what's resisted,'

opens out new territory too. The problem of Evil had not been put from this angle to Scotland before, but Scotland, in the new freedom of thought Burns gave her, seized on the morality of the

[1] 'Older Scottish and English—A Study in Contrasts', by Professor Sir William Craigie, M.A., LL.D., D.Litt., read to the Philological Society in Cambridge on Saturday, October 20, 1934.

'Unco Guid' with fervour. Gentleness—humility of thought—making allowances—these were entirely new slogans and if they bore fruit, as they did in the long run, a large part of the credit must go to Burns. . . . Tho' there are some curious black spots in the poem too. Burns' conception of goodness, for instance, is wholly negative—the absence of opportunity or taste for evil. What, for him, distinguishes the 'Unco Guid'? Only their 'better art o' hidin'—the 'scant occasion' they have for a fall—their level pulses. Therein to Burns lies the whole difference between saint and sinner. The idea of someone, full-blooded as himself, but mastering temptation, lay outwith his vision. He had clearly speculated more on the origin of Evil—or to more purpose—than on the nature of goodness. . . .

And then there are some more of those racy Epistles that show Burns at his best, and always at his most natural. Here is one to John Goldie (August 1785) then at loggerheads with the Kirk. Much of this Epistle is undistinguished, but the thought of the Kirk, as ever, lights up Burns' wit. Here is the verse on that—

> 'But, gin the Lord's ain folk gat leave
> 'A toom tar barrel,
> 'And twa red peats wad bring relief
> 'And end the quarrel'.—

That 'toom tar barrel', and the 'twa red peats' (note the 't's of contempt), and what they imply (Scotland's commonest street scene of the witch-fires in all their horror) and their mocking conjunction with 'the Lord's ain folk', make this verse flare out with scarifying power. From this cameo of the Kirk at work, the poem quietens to a talk on himself 'And skill in prose I've nane ava', as the stilted English of most of his Letters bears out, where that tendency to use pompous and grandiose words—a tendency which mars his inferior verse—runs riot. Then, as in the *Kilmarnock* Epistles, there's a line or two on what he likes—

> 'There's naethin' like the honest nappy (liquor)
> 'Whare ye'll e'er see men sae happy
> 'Or women sonsy, saft and sappy
> ' 'Tween morn and morn
> 'As them wha like to taste the drappie
> 'In glass or horn'—

For it is to the taste of the eighteenth century—one of the great 'drinking' centuries—that so much of Burns' poetry turns on drink and the sublimation of it e.g. 'The Jolly Beggars' (par excellence) 'Tam o' Shanter,' 'The Holy Fair,' the drinking songs, etc. . . . But fashions change in literature, and the Victorian nineteenth century had nothing to say to drink. Not a word of it in Tennyson, or Browning—and uncommonly little even in the novelists, except a thought now and then in Thackeray, who broke most Victorian conventions. But with the twentieth century of the cocktails and the sherry, Burns is again in complete harmony, tho' oddly enough neither cocktails (despite their poetic names) nor the more classic sherry have so far found a twentieth-century poet to sing of them. . . . Here, in the Epistle to Goldie, Burns turns from the general to the particular.

'Just ae half-mutchkin (half-pint) does me prime'

with the result

'Then back I rattle on the rhyme
'As gleg's a whittle' (keen as a knife)

Byron would only have his soda-water: Scott liked his tumbler of whisky: Burns' modest 'ae half-mutchkin' must be a surprise to those who fondly picture him as a drunkard. The incontrovertible proof that he was not, must always lie in the superb technical accomplishment of his work. No brain befuddled with drink could ever have achieved 'Holy Willie's Prayer' or, in his later years, mastered the immense difficulties of things like 'The Red Red Rose'. It took the clearest head in Scotland to do both. But drink (the unending toast-lists at any eighteenth-century banquet will rise to mind) was the talk of the day, and in the 'Third Epistle to Lapraik' he recurs to it:

'We'll cry nae jauds frae heathen hills
'Tae help or roose (inspire) us
'But browster wives and whisky stills,
'They are the Muses.'

. . . It is for its bizarre literary interest one remembers his 'Epistle to the Rev. John McMath'. Burns is sending the Rev. John a copy of 'Holy Willie's Prayer' and explaining (a ticklish business to one of the Rev. John's cloth!) how he came to write it—

    'I own 'twas rash an' rather hardy
    'That I, a simple country Bardie
    'Should meddle wi' a pack sae sturdy
        'Wha, if they ken
    'Can easy, wi' a single wordie
        'Louse Hell upon me'

(The last couplet refers to the sentence of the Greater Excommunication which might be, and often was, pronounced by the Kirk.) There is no mockery here. Clearly enough, Burns, for all his daring thought, believed in the power of the Kirk to send him to Hell by its pronouncement. Not Samuel Rutherfurd himself speaks of this with greater conviction. Nevertheless, 'Holy Willie's Prayer' had to be written, for

    'I gae mad at their grima*ces*
    'Their *s*ighin', cantin' gra*ce*-proud fa*ces*
    'Their three-mile prayer*s* an' hauf-mile gra*ces*
      'Their raxin con*s*cien*ces* (elastic)
    'Wha*se* greed, revenge, an' pride di*s*gra*ces*
    'Waur nor their non*s*en*se*.'

(Note the storm of hisses throughout.) If this is meant, as seems likely, for a kind of apology for the Prayer, what did the Rev. John, a minister himself, think of it? It is all very well to be accused of 'greed, revenge an' pride'—the usual counters in controversy—but, nonsense? What did the Rev. John think?

    With Davie Sillar, that Tarbolton teacher who went with Burns to the 'Bachelors' Club, he is more at his ease. Davie wrote verses too, so the talk is of poetry. Here is where Burns would place himself

'For me, I'm on Parnassus' brink (not, be it noted, any higher up)
'Rivin' the words to gar them clink
'Whyles daez't wi' love, whyles daez't wi' drink

    .   .   .   .

      'An' whyles, but ay owre late, I think
        'Braw sober lessons.'

    'To the Guidwife of Wauchope House' has a special interest

as being the only Epistle (as distinct from fugitive verses) that
Burns ever wrote to a woman. He did not write it unsolicited.
It was, in fact, in answer to one of hers. And this time he is far
from at his ease. For Mrs. Scott of Wauchope was a lady 'no bred
to barn or byre'. Worse still, she wrote books, like the impressive
Alonso and Cora, thought to be her masterpiece. He had met her on
his Border tour when 'she had all that . . . intrepidity of face and
bold, critical decision that usually distinguish female authors'.
Robin clearly had not taken to her. But now she had sent him a
plaid. So what could he write to her about? In the defiant metre of
'The Cherrie and the Slae' (only used once before for an Epistle),
and in the broadest Lallans he can find—of books! And, as usual,
of himself.

> 'When I was beardless, young and blate

. . . . .

> 'Wi' clavers and havers
> 'Wearin' the day awa'—

Even then it was his wish

> 'That I, for poor auld Scotland's sake
> 'Some usefu' plan or book could make
> 'Or sing a sang at least'—

When you thought of *Alonso and Cora* you had to put in that
'plan or book' first. Nothing else sounded grand enough. For
what would the distinguished 'female author' think of a mere
'sang'? By the third verse, however, it is only the song remains
in Robin's head. The song, and how you came to write it—

> 'I see her yet, the sonsie quean
> 'That lighted up my jingle
> 'Her witching smile, her pawky een'—

and what it did to you,

> 'I fired, inspired
> 'At every kindling keek'.

It was always like that—the next time as bewitching as the last

—for, when all was said and done, there was nothing like the girls.

> 'The gust o' joy, the balm o' woe
> 'The saul o' life, the heav'n below
> 'Is rapture-giving woman.'

And to think that it was a 'female author' of the 'intrepid face'— and no Jean or Mary of them all!—elicited that from Robin! . . .

To Dr. Blacklock, the blind littérateur to whose original interest Burns owed his Edinburgh visit, he knew exactly what to write. It is from Ellisland now in 1789. 'I'm turned a gauger.' So what of poetry? For that would be the Doctor's first question. But

> 'Ye ken—ye ken
> 'That strang necessity supreme is (note the hisses)
>
> .   .   .   .   .
>
> 'Mang sons o' men.
> 'I hae a wife and twa wee laddies
> 'They maun hae brose and brats o' duddies'—

And yet—the Doctor would persist—the poetry? But the clouds were closing round Burns now.

> 'Lord help me thro' this warld o' care'—

—and upon that, comes the flaming thought, as of old,

> 'But why should ae man better fare
> 'And a' men brithers?'

But it was no use getting angry. The fury of Edinburgh days was long since past. He grits his teeth—

> 'Wha does the utmost that he can
> 'Will whyles do mair'.

That was the sort of spirit in which to write to Dr. Blacklock. . . .

And then, as Robin lay dying in 1796 comes the 'Epistle to Colonel De Peyster', of the Dumfries Volunteers—a bitter retrospect on Life.

'Ah now, sma' heart hae I to speel
'The steep Parnassus'—

How steep it was when you looked at it now! You could see the angle of it better from a deathbed. Parnassus that had haunted him all his days. How steep! . . . And what a fine world it would be, if Life played fair—

'And Fortune favour worth and merit
'As they deserve
'And aye a rowth—roast-beef an' claret
'Syne wha wad starve?'

But instead, 'like baudrons by a ratton', there stood the Enemy, 'Auld Satan'—

'Our sinfu' saul to get a claut on (clutch)
'Wi felon ire'—

Clearer than ever he had seen it, Robin saw that now. That, indeed, was all there was to Life—the steep Parnassus—the roast beef and claret (if you could get it)—and, for the rest, the Devil. All the hours and every hour playing with you 'like baudrons by a ratton', to get you in the end. Even as the sensitive Thomas Boston had known it, and the learned Samuel Rutherfurd had feared it. The Devil, indeed, overweights the poem. Five of its eight verses are on him alone, real enough now. And it is on that same, grim thought the Epistle ends—its final line, almost the last Burns ever penned—

'The Lord preserve us frae the Devil!
'Amen! Amen!'

A long road, surely, from the gay *Kilmarnock* mockery of the 'Address to the De'il'. . . . But deathbed thoughts can be out of focus, too. And the airy epigram he wrote, years before, by Wade's road at Dalnacardoch, may more truly represent him—

'When Death's dark stream I ferry o'er
'A time that surely shall come
'In Heaven itself I'll ask no more
'But just a Highland welcome'.

For while it is true that, historically, the thought of the Devil never left him—oppressing him ever the more grimly, the older he became—it is, nevertheless, his lighter moments that held more of the quality that 'made' Burns. And this Highland epigram gives just that verve and colour, that waft of diablerie that must have come into any company when the opening door brought in—Burns!

CHAPTER I

BURNS' LYRICAL ART— ITS BASIS.
SCOTS FOLK-SONG, HIGHLAND TUNES,
THOMSON'S *SCOTISH AIRS*

SCOTTISH LITERATURE, in legend, begins with a song—
Thomas the Rhymer (thirteenth century) singing it, Thomas
who still lies in an enchanted sleep, but throughout the centuries
never dead, beneath the Eildon Hills;—with a song, that is, in the
Border country, where song lies always latent. And indeed
Scotland is particularly rich in old songs—or rather, now in the
fragments of them, recovered chiefly through the zeal of Herd,
that poor Edinburgh clerk Burns knew and who made it his life-
work to collect every line or patch of any old Scots song he could
come across. There had been earlier collections, of course. George
Bannatyne, the poetically-minded Edinburgh merchant fleeing
from the city in 1568 because of the plague, occupied his en-
forced leisure in copying out (in 800 folio pages, now the precious
Bannatyne MSS.) most of the fifteenth- and sixteenth-century
poetry—a collection largely drawn upon by Ramsay for his
Evergreen. And a little later, old Sir Richard Maitland (father of
Mary Queen of Scots' subtle Minister, Maitland of Lethington)
made his collection, now the Maitland MSS. of 1586, with some
old songs in it, like 'The Wooing of Jok and Jenny', with a
resounding smack at the end of each line for a kiss, or 'The
Wyf of Auchtermuchty' on the 'John Grumlie' theme, giving
you a good laugh at the foolish husband. . . . But Scotland
must have been a singing country from the earliest times.
'Cockelbie's Sow', the old poem of the fifteenth century, lists
any number of popular songs and tunes—all of them lost now.
The learned were interested in them too. Here is Gavin Douglas,

that Provost of St. Giles who made the first translation of Virgil into any European vernacular, looking up from his *Aeneid* round about 1500, to note the song they were singing out there in the High Street, 'The Joly Day Now Dawes'. Dunbar, the Court poet at Holyrood, heard it in the fashionable Canongate some years later. And the *Complaynt of Scotland* of 1549 is full of the names of more songs and tunes—tantalisingly enough, when you reflect that these too are all lost now. For, with the Reformation, like a thunder-clap, the singing stops. By 1570, all you would hear—openly, anyhow—were those 'Gude and Godlie Ballates' of the brothers Wedderburn of Dundee, who made sanctimonious parodies of the old, lively songs. It was hard enough, as the brothers found, to parody some of them, like

'John cum, kiss me now
'John cum kiss me now
'John cum kiss me by and bye
'And make no more adow.'

What could you make of a thing like that? How could anybody turn it into religion? Yet the brothers tried—with a result that has almost a blasphemous air, for you can't turn earthly love into Divine simply by changing a name, which was about all the brothers had skill for. . . . But the Kirk grew stronger. And the singing, perforce, lower. And in the dismal seventeenth century, with the gallows gaunt in the Grassmarket and the torturers aye at it, you could hardly hear it. And never at all in the houses that mattered, like that of My Lord Warriston, the Scots judge, groaning over his prayers, or of the scholarly Samuel Rutherfurd, penning his revolutionary *Lex Rex*. The songs were in the kitchen now, or the stable, or in a dark and drunken corner of a Close. . . . So that, when they emerged into the free air of the eighteenth century, they came with the stains and tatters of their evil sojourn on them. But with their vigour, their salt, their piquancy still unimpaired. Rather like those Mediaeval Greek folk-songs—the *Klepht* or bandit-songs—full of the same gay spirit because of the danger thro' which they had lived, and like many of them, with only a line or two left. It may be that, had the songs survived in full, they would have been duller. For, like enough, it's the wittiest, the freshest, the most alluring lines that have survived—

the lines the people couldn't forget, because of some graphic touch, some vignette they draw, some dramatic phrase. 'De'il tak' the wars' now—could you put that any better? For vigour, directness and good humour it is unsurpassable. But, like enough, the lines that followed it, were not. But only 'De'il tak the wars' survives. Then the famous 'Over the hills and far away' that Gay, in *The Beggar's Opera*, tried to find a second line for, but couldn't find one good enough. Or 'We're a' kissed sleepin' '—what was the story behind that? Burns knew all these as titles. They were names of tunes in that Oswald's *Caledonian Pocket Companion* (600 tunes, almost, in it!) that was never out of his hand, and that he passed on, with his own notes, to the famous fiddler, Nathaniel Gow, son of the immortal Neil, who knew all the tunes that were.... How these stray lines catch the imagination, lighting up glittering vistas, even as a drop of attar of roses distils the essence of a thousand flowers,—'Laddie, lie near me', 'I kissed her while she blush't', 'I wish my love were in the mire'.... Sometimes there's a casual line or two, as

> 'Sweet, let me lie beyond thee
> 'Until it be break o' day'—

that Sappho herself might have written, or a challenge like this

> 'Lass, an' I come near thee
> 'Lass, an' I come near thee
> 'I'll gar a' your ribbons reel
> 'Lass, an' I come near thee.'

Snatches of wild wine-songs too, that once rang out to the pewter mutchkins dunting on the board, and echoed and re-echoed on the sleepy midnight causey of some auld Scots town, like that roaring favourite, 'Andro and his Cutty Gun'—careering along—

> 'When we had three times toom'd our stoup
> 'And the neist chappin new begun,
> 'In started, to heeze up our hope
> 'Young Andro, wi' his cutty gun'.

Allan Ramsay, the jolly wigmaker, printed that one in 1740. Or the slower 'Guidwife, count the lawin' ', that Burns took up—

'The cock's at the crawing
'The day's at the dawing
'The cock's at the crawing
    'We're owre lang here'—

There were bits of Jacobite songs too (not as ladylike as those to come) like that outspoken 'The Muckin' o' Geordie's Byre'—

'It was ne'er my faither's will
'Nor yet my mither's desire
'That e'er I should fyle my fingers
'Wi muckin' o' Geordie's byre'—

Sometimes Herd would light on the treasure-trove of nearly a whole song. 'Eppie Macnab' was one like that. You couldn't get the whole picture without both verses—which is probably why both have survived.

'O saw ye Eppie Macnab the day?
'O saw ye Eppie Macnab the day?
    'She's doun in the yaird
    'She's kissing the Laird
'She winna come hame the day, the day!

'O see to Eppie Macnab as she goes
'O see to Eppie Macnab as she goes
    'With her corked heel shoon
    'And her cockets aboon,
'O see to Eppie Macnab as she goes.'

Who would have thought they'd be singing that still in Edinburgh, when the roar of all John Knox's sermons had passed into oblivion? For even in sober Scotland, a song outlives a sermon. . . . Other singers besides Burns delved into the gold-mine of the old songs. Lady Nairne took her 'Cockpen' from this,

'When she cam ben, she bobbit
'And when she cam ben, she bobbit
'And when she cam ben, she kissed Cockpen
'And then denied that she did it.

'And wasna Cockpen richt saucy?
'And wasna Cockpen richt saucy?

'He len'd his lady to gentlemen
'And he kissed the collier lassie.'

And it would be hard to say that she improved on it, for there's an originality about these fragments burnished at street-corners that is absent from the more laboured drawing-room songs of a later day. Sometimes Herd would happen on a poignant song, like 'There's Nane Shall Ken', with its

'I'll gang nae mair to yon toun
'O never a' my life again,
'I'll ne'er gae back to yon toun,
'To seek anither wife again'—

—a verse so steeped in emotion and drama that it's hard to think of it as Scotch at all. For later Scotland habitually watered its emotion into sentimentality. . . . But indeed the old, lost songs cover the whole range of feeling—touching now one string, now another—and all with a sureness of touch that nothing can excel, and that belongs only to folk-art at its very best. Broad, sometimes, from their stay in the stable, and coarse, they offended that eighteenth century that re-discovered them and that was all for politeness. Nowadays, however,—with politeness of the eighteenth-century kind, out of fashion—we read most of the old songs without a blush. But Burns was deeply exercised by them. Not that he minded coarseness himself. The 'Merry Muses' that he wrote for the Crochallans is witness to that. But the wide audience he sought, was dead against coarseness. So at first he set out to re-write the loose old songs, in correct eighteenth-century dress —Needless to say, such tinkering with the peerless 'Eppie Macnab' and 'When she cam ben, she bobbit' was riding for a fall. Any copy, set against originals of that rank, will crash. As do Burns' attempts. For, what the folk-song had to teach—and it was the whole art of song—was not to be learned that way, but by hard and intelligent study of its technique. It was only when Burns had mastered that—and it took him some considerable time as well as labour ('Those who think composing a Scotch song is a trifling business—let them try': R.B. to James Hoy, Chamberlain to the Duke of Gordon)—it was not till then, that he was able in the end to write a good song. For, until his Edinburgh visit of

1786, his primary interest was not in song. The Kirk and its impact for evil on the community, was what filled the foreground of his mind. A song, no doubt, now and then. But his *Commonplace Book*, begun at Mossgiel when he was a young man of twenty-four, shows how the interest grew. His start, for instance, at song-making. 'I never had the least thought or inclination of turning Poet, till I once got heartily in love, and then Rhyme and Song were, as it were, the spontaneous language of my heart. 'O once I lov'd a bonie lass' my earliest (written at the age of seventeen). . . .' But if a love-affair set you off (and there is no more talk of that),—what gripped you, was the technique of song-making. 'There is a certain irregularity in the old Scotch songs, a redundancy of syllables with respect to that exactness of accent and measure that the English poetry requires, but which glides in most melodiously for the respective tunes to which they are set.' And as those tunes were, in general, strathspeys, the irregularity is natural—for the strathspey is itself irregular—consisting of two measures of four bars each, with an essential eccentricity, an uneven-ness of beat (in contrast to the even beat of the reel) within these bars. The extra syllables of the song follow this uneven-ness of the tune. . . . And here it may be in place to consider those tunes, the second and more powerful of the two formative influences that went to the making of Burns as a song-writer. Stemming from Speyside, as their name indicates (tho' that name is not found in print till late in the eighteenth century) they traversed the whole breadth of the realm—crossing the Highland line without let or hindrance when nothing else could. To their wide dispersal Sir Walter Scott is himself a witness, with his Wandering Willie 'the best fiddler that ever kittled thairm with horse-hair' in *Redgauntlet* (Waverley Edition, p. 139) —Darsie Latimer speaking, 'I asked him if he was of this country' (*sc.* county). "This country," replied the blind man (Wandering Willie). "I am of every country in broad Scotland and a wee bit of England to the boot. (Scott making this very point of the wide dispersal.) . . . Will I give your honour a touch of the auld breadwinner?' . . . I expressed my surprise and pleasure (*sc.* at the tune). "A rant, man—an auld rant," said Willie. . . . "Here's another—it's no' a Scots tune, but it passes for ane—Oswald made it himsell, I reckon," ' where the reference is to Burns' own textbook, Oswald's *Caledonian Pocket Companion* that Scott also knew. And over from this Solway dykeside to Poosie Nansie's lighted windows in Ayrshire, with the Jolly Beggars' fiddler scraping out one of the 'auldest rants' of them all, 'Whistle Owre the Lave o't', from Bremner's *Collection of Reels and Strathspeys* (the first ever made), published at Edinburgh round about 1749. And to all the Penny Weddings, like those Wilkie was to paint later in Fife, and to every harvest home went the ubiquitous fiddle. The tunes were, in fact, the ancient traditional music of all Scotland. . . . Tho' Highland in origin and spirit. And it was the fiddle, by good luck, interpreted this Highland spirit—with its gaiety, its insouciance, its devil-may-care charm. The fiddle and not the bagpipes. For, had it been the grander pipes, the music would of necessity have struck a fiercer note. Pipe-music reflects a different and a more rousing spirit—pibrochs of war and battle, laments to wring your soul—the spirit, that is, of the Western Isles and in particular, of Skye, the home and training-school of those great hereditary pipers, the MacCrimmons. But the rants the fiddler played—of an antiquity even with the old Scotch songs and of an authorship as unknown—had a lighter, headier quality, an intoxicating magic like the whisky of their own Speyside. And, in fact, it's from a radius round the Spey that the rants all derive—from East of it, as far as Buchan, from the South as far as Atholl—but none from the frigid North and never a one from the serious Isles. The rants, like the whisky, cling to the Spey. . . . Strathspeys and reels, the eighteenth century called them—dividing them according to pace. The strathspey was slower and more complicated—full of dotted notes and semi-quavers—and it had to have a kick or 'snap' in it. Twenty to twenty-five seconds you allowed to play its full eight bars, whereupon you started again da capo—and again—and again—till (if ever!) you got tired of it. After that, you plunged full tilt, head on, into the reel—the same number of bars, but an even beat here, and faster than ever. Fifteen seconds was all the fiddlers ever took to the reel. Stirring rants, both of them,— and didn't they just, between them, make the songs go? There was more to the strathspey, of course, with that kick,—and to the strathspey most of the old songs, with the irregularity Burns noticed, were set. But some also to the reel. And as both reel and strathspey repeated themselves thus with no definite end, so likewise did the songs. There is no real reason why a Gaelic song, set to such a tune, should ever stop (and some don't!), for, with this repetition, one line will make a verse, the second line another and so on,—like this, the first verse (probably the oldest version) of Tullochgorum, a reel.

> 'Theid mi null, gu Taoth Loch Gorm
> 'Theid mi null, gu'n teid mi null
> 'O Theid mi null, gu Taoth Loch Gorm
>   ' 's thig mi null a maireach.'[1]

The Scotch songs, like 'John cum kiss me now', being set to the same tunes, do very much the same thing—the repetition arising not only from the character of the rants, but also from the nature of folk-song itself which, unlike the written word, lives by monotony. Make a catch-phrase simple enough ('Tea for two and two for tea'—'John cum kiss me now') and say it often enough, and you will set the whole world singing it. The monotony has the arresting power of the drummer's beat, or of the African tom-tom, monotonous both as can be. And the needed variety is provided by the tune (in this case, the strathspey)— vivacious, exciting, intricate—throwing the plain words into relief, so that plain words and coloured tune, like two of Spey-side's complementary whiskies, blend into one potent and glorious whole. . . . It is interesting to note Burns's reaction to all this. While in his early work like 'Mary Morison' he thinks out new and elaborate words for every line—thus making a poem, but not a song—by the time his hand is really in and he is on to work like 'Auld Lang Syne', it's on the figured tune he relies to carry the words. And the words themselves are repetitive and the simplest he can find—following the folk-song's model. . . . He was fortunate also in coming to the rants when they were in their heyday. He heard them at their golden moment. For here (to anticipate) at Gordon Castle by the Spey, was William Marshall, composer of the loveliest strathspeys ever made (some of them

---

[1] 'I'll go away there, to the side of Loch Gorm
'I'll go away there—I'll go away there
'I'll go away there to the side of Loch Gorm
'And I'll come back to-morrow.'

used by Robin for his best work) and down in Atholl was Neil Gow (whom he heard) the finest fiddler Scotland ever saw. The best rants and the finest fiddling—both to his hand. Destiny presiding with such care over every step of Burns' career, was never more alert to his needs than when she brought him just to that part of the Highlands—and just then. For, if ever the strangle-hold of the Kirk on his imagination was to be broken, now was the moment. If ever he was to lift his eyes from the Mountain Daisy and the Louse and the humdrum Ayrshire earth, now was the moment, when—the brilliant Edinburgh episode fading out, he was going back to the old life he knew. Back to the Kirk again? It well might have been that. And no longer with the old gay mockery of youth, but with the sour and bitter disillusion-ment of a disappointed middle age, harping on twice-told grievances. What then should raise his eyes and set him free? Edinburgh, for all her intellectual eminence—the Borders, for all their ballads and their romances—had not inspired him. When all else had failed, the Highland tunes and they alone proved strong enough to stir him, lift him, change the whole current of his thought and being—release him alike from the thraldom of the Kirk and the banality of poor Mailie—and stimulate him to a gaiety and passion, a wild diablerie that opened a dazzling new world to him. For they and they alone appealed to that Dionysiac element in him that nothing so far had awakened and set a match to it. With the riotous breath of their own Speyside hot upon them, they swept him—for good and all—completely off his feet. Henceforth the nightmare of the Kirk was over. Ministers there must have been in populous Dumfries, as there had been in holy Ayrshire, but never the name of one of them passes through the alembic of his mind. Gone too are the mountain daisies and all the rusticity they stood for. His whole being is now keyed up to something wild and strange, something that, like the Pied Piper's music, was to hold him and enthrall him to his dying day. The Highland visit was the turning-point in Burns' life. Let us return now to his *Commonplace Book* and see how it all came about. . . . He was talking of the irregularity in the old Scotch songs. 'This', he goes on, 'has made me sometimes imagine it might be possible for a Scotch poet to set compositions to many of our most favourite airs . . . independent of rhyme altogether.' With just, perhaps, that rhythm and assonance on which the Gaelic songs are built (like 'Tullochgorum' quoted above)? For Gaelic, tho' there is no evidence Burns knew the language, was spoken habitually in Carrick (Ayrshire) as late as 1800, so there must have been some local knowledge of Gaelic songs too. More probably, however, he has here in mind that other Highland singer, Macpherson's Ossian, under whose spell he then was, and who uses no rhyme either. But while Burns in practice does not abandon rhyme, he commonly, like Byron, prefers it inexact. This inexactness, no doubt, is sometimes more apparent than real, the dialect pronunciation giving often a good spoken, tho' not written, rhyme—but some of it too, is intentional. The old songs themselves, in this respect, were inexact. As the ballads, by contrast—are not. For with their Border provenance, nearer that England which, as Burns had noted, likes exact rhyme—the ballads like it too. Maybe Scotch folk-song, harking as it does, largely from the North and making use of the Gaelic tunes, derived this inexactness too from its association with the Gaelic. It is interesting to see Burns' mind here, anyway, like the old songs, moving away from rhyme. . . . And—moving to the tunes. 'These old Scottish airs are so nobly sentimental that, when one would compose to them, to sooth (hum) the tune, as our Scotch phrase is, over and over, is the readiest way to catch the inspiration and raise the Bard into that glorious enthusiasm so strongly characteristic of our old Scotch poetry.' The tune, that is, is the heart of the song. Its heart and soul. Giving you that all-important atmosphere which will suggest the words. And the tune—and the atmosphere—are both alike Highland. For Burns' debt to Highland music and the Highland spirit can hardly be over-estimated. In his songs he is as much a debtor to the Highlands as he is, in his satires, to the Kirk. . . . You 'soothed' the tune until you got under its skin. But sometimes you couldn't. A tune now, like 'Over the Hills and Far Away' (Gay's favourite for his *Beggar's Opera*)—but what could you make of that, when, unlike most Scots, you had never wanted to see as much as the road to London? Whereas a tune like 'Oh Whistle and I'll come to you, my lad'—ah! that was a different story. You were on to that, at once. Into the 'glorious enthusiasm' straight away. For every girl you ever loved (or, for that matter, ever could love) had answered to that whistle on the dot. You knew where you were here. And a first-class song you made of it. The 'glorious enthusiasm' was as necessary to Burns as the tune. The tune and the atmosphere—the one as necessary as the other. For his best work, Robin had to have both. Unlike the other great song-writers of the world—Shakespeare, Heine and the rest—who composed, as it were, in vacuo, with just the words in mind. Not so, Burns. His songs, by contrast with theirs, have no objective reality of their own. They are projected by the tune. Fused into one with the music, they are like fire, struck from the tinder of the tune. . . . That tune! How it haunted him! 'I set about composing an air in the old Scotch style', is almost the last entry in the *Commonplace Book* in 1785. But 'composing an air' proved even harder than writing a song. And Robin gave it up. Gave up songs too—for a time. For the *Kilmarnock* was on the way—and Edinburgh on the horizon. And in Edinburgh—on the first visit—he wrote no songs at all.

But there were tunes. Staggering home from the New Town he heard them—from every oyster-cellar in the High Street—strathspeys and reels—the Devil's own music, as he always thought them, alike in 'Tam o' Shanter' and in 'The De'il's Awa' wi' Th' Exciseman'—the tunes and the tap-tap of heel and toe. They were the undertone to all the parties and the high talk with the Judges and the savants and the fine ladies. It was to the tunes dirling in his head he fell asleep on his pallet in the Lawnmarket. . . . But he wrote no songs. . . . And, in the late summer of 1787, set out with Willie Nicol on his eventful Highland tour. Eventful, for now he was going into the very home-country of the strathspeys, where he would meet fiddlers of the authentic and immemorial tradition. Into the Atholl country, with the great Neil Gow himself playing to him? Robin dancing reels 'Bob at the Bowster', 'Tullochgorum', 'Loch Errochside' till three of a June morning at Arrochar, with 'the ladies singing Scotch songs, like angels'—then up to Inverness, the heart of the Highlands—where—for the first time, apparently—he heard Gaelic songs. 'The air is admirable—true old Highland', he is writing later to Peggy Chalmers, one of his more intelligent correspondents. 'The tune of a Gaelic song an Inverness lady sang me when I was there—and I was so charmed with it I begged her to write me a set of it from her singing—for it had never been set before' (*Burns*, ed. Scott Douglas, Vol. IV, p. 307). And so on to Castle Gordon where, had he but known, he could have met William Marshall himself, then in the Duke of Gordon's service and the greatest of all strathspey-composers. Two of Marshall's best strathspeys, indeed, 'Miss Admiral Gordon's Strathspey' and 'Mrs. Hamilton of Wishaw' he was, in fact, to use later, the first for 'O' A' the Airts', and the second for 'My Love is like a Red Red Rose'. But, as like as not, on that September night (just the night for a dance) when Burns sat down to dinner in bonnie Castle Gordon with the Duke and Duchess, strathspeys were never even mentioned for—Willie Nicol thinking himself offended—the poet had to hurry off with his boorish friend. And missed the finest tunes in all the Highlands. . . . Back in Edinburgh in October, 1787, he stayed, not now in the old Lawnmarket lodging of his first visit, but with Nicol's friend, Cruickshank who—had a young daughter, who—could play the harpsichord! And, stirred by the Highland visit,—it was tunes now, day in—day out. 'There is a certain something in the old Scotch songs' he is writing, October, 25, 1787, to Rev. J. Skinner ('the author of the best Scotch song ever Scotland saw, 'Tullochgorum's my delight'), 'a wild happiness of thought and expression which peculiarly marks them.' This is the first time that (possibly with the rants in his head) he has noticed the Dionysiac quality in the songs too, as distinct from the tunes, and he returns to it. Then comes the momentous entry: 'An engraver (Johnson) in this town has set about collecting and publishing all the Scotch songs, with the music, that can be found. . . . The music must all be Scotch. . . . I have been absolutely crazed about it, collecting old stanzas and every information. . . .' And with that, the thread of the old Scotch songs was joined to that of the tunes. The meeting with Johnson and possibly with Herd, brought the two strands together. What the Highlands had begun, Edinburgh—the old town—now perfected. So Burns at long last was launched on his life-work—the patching of old songs and making them like new—for Johnson's *Musical Museum*, five of whose six volumes are mostly his own work, and to which he contributed in all 184 songs. The old songs came from Herd's MSS.—from 'The Lark' —from Ramsay—: the tunes from Highland collection after collection, as his letters show, like this one to Peggy Chalmers, 'One of them—is already set. The tune is Neil Gow's Lamentation for Abercarney—the other is to be set to an old Highland air in Daniel Dow's *Collection of Ancient Scotch Music*—the name is "Ha a Chaillich air mo Dheidh" ', (1787, *Burns*, ed. Scott Douglas, Vol. IV, p. 305) or this one from Dumfries to Mrs. Dunlop, 'Looking over with a musical friend McDonald's *Collection of Highland Airs*, I was struck with one—an Isle of Skye tune entitled Oran an Aoig, or The Song of Death—to the measures of which I have adapted my stanzas' (1791, *Burns*, ed. Scott Douglas, Vol. VI, p. 8)—or this, from Ellisland to Mr. Cunningham (W. S., Writer in Edinburgh), 'I have this evening sketched out a song—my song is intended to sing to a strathspey or reel, of which I am very fond, called in Cumming's *Collection of Strathspeys* 'Ballindalloch's Reel', and in other collections that I have met with, it is known by the name of Candelmore' (1791, *Burns*, ed. Scott Douglas, Vol. V, p. 358). Burns was as thirled to the Highland tunes, as he was to the 'auld Scots sonnets' (songs): 'You know I am an enthusiast in old Scotch songs', he is writing from Ellisland to Mrs. Dunlop. . . . It was good going now, with Johnson's *Museum* open to him,—and the old Scotch songs before him—and the Highland tunes in his ear. Good going, if one had the inspiration. What of the 'falling in love' that had originally started Robin song-writing at all, when he was a callow youth of seventeen? But much water had flowed under the bridges since Burns was an unsophisticated seventeen. 'I believe that my heart has been so oft on fire', he writes from Edinburgh to Peggy Chalmers, 'that it is absolutely vitrified. I look on the sex with something like the admiration with which I regard the starry sky in a frosty December night' (1787, *Burns*, ed. Scott Douglas, Vol. IV, p. 298). And on a frosty December night, as everyone knows, a million stars and more glitter in that sky—one, alas! as bright as the other! From the point of view of art, however, this change is all to the good. Unsophisticated seventeen had produced nothing better than 'Once I lo'ed a bonie lass'—a dead plain statement and in the past at that— damned on both counts. For no work of art can be a transcript from life and still less can a love-song deal with the past. But, with his starry sky and its million stars, Robin had at least advanced one step. He had now got away from personal emotion. He was to go one stage further before he could write the good love-song. . . . And with his move to Dumfries in September, 1792, and his meeting with George Thomson, publisher of *Scotish Airs*, that stage was well on the way. For Thomson—not just a simple enthusiast like the amiable Johnson—but a pretentious amateur, was the final agent in the creation of Burns the great song-writer. It was the carping Thomson put Burns on his mettle and made him think out what points in a song could be conceded, and what could not. For while it was certainly unfortunate that Thomson held—and held with mulish obstinacy—the completely tasteless views he did of the qualities of a good Scotch song, in another way it was a Heaven-sent boon. For only this astringent tonic could have taken the froth off Burns' 'enthusiasm' and that 'craze' for Scotch song, of which he so often wrote—and made him settle down soberly to an analysis of what song required. Here Thomson's opposition (for Thomson was as critical as a Government Department, to which indeed, he belonged) helped him far more than had Johnson's easy acquiescence. And it is not too much to say that, had it not been for Thomson's constant pin-pricking, Burns' supreme achievement in song might never have been attained. As the famous Thomson-Burns correspondence (from 1792 to Burns' death in 1796)—the most fascinating in Scottish literature—makes clear. In its pages, as almost nowhere else, we see a great artist in the making. And to this period belong all Burns' best songs—the only songs worth remembering—tho' they were not by any means all sent to Thomson. (He sent Thomson about 120, of which only six were published in his lifetime.) But it was the cold shower-bath of Thomson's disapproval that brought them to perfection. . . . For Thomson,—as befitted a principal clerk to the Board of Trustees and unlike the humble engraver Johnson—moved in those Edinburgh circles where the 'high English' alone was heard. It is true he was collecting *Scotish Airs*, but with an eye to improving—re-modelling—in fact, de-Scoticising them. Burns is alarmed. 'If you are for English verses', he writes from Dumfries as early as September, 1792, 'there is, on my part, an end of the matter. Whether in the simplicity of the ballad (i.e. folk-song) or the pathos of the song, I can only hope to please myself, in being

Neil Gow, Scotland's finest fiddler, who played reels to Burns at Dunkeld in August, 1787. Portrait by Raeburn

(By courtesy of the Scottish National Portrait Gallery)

Gordon Castle, Fochabers, as Burns saw it—'a fine palace, worthy of the generous proprietor' (R.B.)—when he dined with the Duke and Duchess of Gordon on his Highland tour, 7th September, 1787

allowed at least a sprinkling of our native tongue.' . . . With these dynamic words 'a sprinkling of our native tongue', Burns has here hit upon the true literary language of Scotland, reflecting the country's dual position not only as a self-contained unit in itself but also (and more important) as an integral part of a larger English-speaking whole (Great Britain). And while from the first aspect comes the native tang, that 'sprinkling' giving the local colour and appeal to the homeland,—from the second—and the consequent use of English—derives the more valuable result,— the cosmopolitan status of Scottish literature, its European membership and appeal to a world-wide audience. . . . And for the 'sprinkling' Burns has historical precedent too behind him, for the old songs like 'Andro and his Cutty Gun', 'Hame Cam oor Gudeman at E'en', etc., do just this,—using English for the main thought and the Scotch for colouring. Even the fifteenth-century poets also,—from Henryson to Dunbar— sensing the poverty of the vernacular, sought to eke it out,— in their case, by the 'aureate' Latin or French. An experiment which failed, the vernacular refusing to assimilate these florid and often uncouth terms. And then with the dominant figure of John Knox and his great *History*, English with a sprinkling of Scotch, became the established literary language (and not less import- ant) the normal speech of educated Scotsmen, a twofold thread which cannot lightly be broken. In this tradition too are the great Scots novelists, Scott—Galt—Stevenson—who, however familiar with the vernacular, never use it in its entirety for their work. And with reason. For great literature cannot be expressed in a vernacular of always limited and sometimes vulgar thought. If a literature is to be great, the first condition is that it must be written in a language that is worthy of it and can convey it, i.e. a language noble and urbane in quality—capable of every shade of thought, high as well as low—equal to every flight of imagination—and sensitive to every nuance of feeling—requirements to all of which English answers absolutely, as Lallans does not, and never has done. Indeed, the use of 'Lallans and nothing else' by the modern Scots Renaissance versifiers carries in itself the certain seeds of failure, for not only is it historically completely at variance with the centuries-old practice of Scottish song (and also, it may be added, of Scottish poetry) but linguistically also it limits itself

I

to a dialect spoken only by a fraction of the populace and these,
the least educated—a dialect that, by its narrow range of expression, the ignoble, if not vulgar, associations of its words, its
severely circumscribed vocabulary and powers, is tied to the
muddy earth. Such a dialect could never speak for a nation. . . .
But Burns made no such mistake. A completely Lallans song—
in the broad Lallans of his 'Hallowe'en', or of his letter (his only
Lallans letter) to Cruickshank from Carlisle—he seems never to
have envisaged. As for completely English ones, he had tried
only too many of these, like that deplorable 'Eliza' of the
Kilmarnock, to be set on any more. But, confronted now with
Thomson's yearnings for the English, he reasons it out. 'A
sprinkling of our native tongue', he must have. It is that and no
more of the Lallans that carries him to success. In support of his
decision, he turns to the tunes. 'In the sentiment and style of our
Scottish airs, there is a pastoral simplicity, a something that one
may call the Doric style and dialect of vocal music, to which a
dash of our native tongue and manners is particularly, nay
peculiarly, apposite (1792, *Burns*, ed. Scott Douglas, Vol. VI,
p. 220). The Doric tune too demands 'a dash of our native tongue'.
But, for all their simplicity, the tunes were difficult. That irregularity he had noted just nine years before, in his *Commonplace
Book*—now he sees what it involves. 'A peculiar rhythmus' in
many of our airs and a necessity of adapting syllables to the
emphasis, or what I would call the feature-notes of the tune, that
cramp the poet and lay him under almost insuperable difficulties'
(1792, *Burns*, ed. Scott Douglas, Vol. VI, p. 222). There was 'the
light-horse gallop of the air' too, that ran away with you in the
reel. The tunes were not easy. . . . In January, '93, he writes of it
again to Thomson, this time in relation to the song itself. 'A
naïveté, a pastoral simplicity', that is what you must have to go
with 'the simple pathos or rustic sprightliness of our native music'
(1793, *Burns*, ed. Scott Douglas, Vol. VI, p. 235). Away from the
ponderous phrases like, 'Let inclination law that', and all that
heavy stuff he had used in 'The Jolly Beggars'. The more he
worked on the old songs, the more increasingly clear it became—
their emphasis on naïveté—with again, that 'slight intermixture
of Scots words and phraseology'. And how thrilled he was with
the old songs! 'In the course of my several peregrinations through

Scotland', he, rather unexpectedly, lets out, 'I made a pilgrimage
to the individual spot from which every song took its rise'. And
what tremendous fun it was, this task of patching them up for the
so-critical Thomson! 'You cannot imagine how much this
business of composing for your publication has added to my en-
joyments' (1793, *Burns*, ed. Scott Douglas, Vol. VI, p. 239). He
had never written in such terms to the mild Johnson. Tho'
Thomson was an exasperation too. 'Give me leave to criticise
your taste. You know I ought to know something of my own
trade. Of pathos, sentiment and point you are a complete judge.
But there is a quality more necessary than either in a song, and
which is the very essence of a ballad (folk-song). I mean simplicity' (1793, *Burns*, ed. Scott Douglas, Vol. VI, p. 245). He had
got it now, at last,—the kernel, the essence, the secret of the finest
song-writing in the world—that supreme quality, simplicity,
that was to make 'A Red, Red Rose' and 'Auld Lang Syne' songs
of an international appeal. . . . By September '93 he is telling
Thomson, in perhaps the most interesting letter of the whole
correspondence, just how he sets about writing a song. It is over
'Laddie, lie near me', which he can't do just yet. 'I do not know
the air, and until I am complete master of a tune, in my own
singing, I can never compose for it. My way is—I consider the
poetic sentiment correspondent to my idea of the musical expression—then choose my theme—begin one stanza—when that
is composed, which is generally the most difficult part of the
business, I walk out—sit down now and then—look out for
objects in nature round me in unison or harmony with my fancy
(this may account for the perpetual presence of singing birds, the
mavis, the blackbird, the lintie and what not—an interminable
series at times—in most of Burns' songs), humming every now
and then, the air. . . . Then I retire to the solitary fireside of my
study, and there commit my effusions to paper—swinging, at
intervals, on the hind-legs of my elbow-chair, by way of calling
forth my own critical strictures as my pen goes on. Seriously
this, at home, is almost invariably my way' (1793, *Burns*, ed.
Scott Douglas, Vol. VI, p. 274). Except that it is more detailed,
this simply corroborates the earlier 'soothing the tune' of the
Commonplace Book, and makes clear that, from first to last, the
tune to Burns is all-important. It is the tune that inspires him

—the tune—when he has it by heart—that suggests the atmosphere of the song. Only after both of these processes, can he find the words. The only new point in this description is the vital final one of self-criticism. And that came to him from his arguments with the stubborn Thomson, even as the sword-play between opponents eventually makes the perfect fencer. . . . And now Thomson, not content with girding at the words, was threatening to interfere with the tunes! That leading Edinburgh expert, the fashionable Mr. Pleyel, would tinker them up. Burns is up in arms. 'Whatever Mr. Pleyel does, let him not alter one iota of the original Scottish airs. . . . They are, I own, frequently wild, but on that very eccentricity, perhaps, depends a great part of their effect' (1793, *Burns*, ed. Scott Douglas, Vol. VI, p. 249). But Thomson, who played in Edinburgh's most high-class St. Cecilia's Hall orchestras (and such classical works as Handel's choruses!) couldn't away with the lowly Highland tunes. Again Burns is emphatic in their defence. 'Many of our strathspeys, ancient and modern, give me most exquisite enjoyment—where you and other judges would probably be showing disgust. . . . In fact, unless I am pleased with the tune, I never can make verses to it' (September, '94) thus reiterating, more clearly than ever, his original standpoint, of complete dependence upon the tune. . . . And finally, for the inspiration—with the 'bonie lassie' of artless seventeen, and the 'vitrified heart' of a blasé Edinburgh alike in the limbo of the past—what now? What, in the drudgery of an exciseman's life in provincial Dumfries, could inspire Robin now? Certainly not his wife. As he had told that old boon companion Davie Sillar, as far back as 1789, when he was newly wed and more might be expected of a bride—a wife wouldn't do at all. 'I know not whether the Nine Gypsies are jealous of my Lucky, but they are a good deal shyer since I could boast the important relation of husband.' And it wasn't any better now, in November, '94. 'Conjugal love', laments Robin, 'is a passion which I deeply feel . . . but somehow it does not make such a figure in poesy, as that other species of the passion.' And with that, he lets fly at Thomson in a sudden rage, 'Do you think that the sober gin-horse routine of existence could inspire a man with life and love and joy,—could fire him with enthusiasm, or melt him with pathos? No! No!' (*Burns*, ed. Scott Douglas, Vol. VI

p. 311). But inspiration a poet must have. And more than most poets, a love-poet. Where then was Burns to get it? It was simple enough really, when you came to think of it—the inevitable third stage in a poet's progress. 'Whenever I want to be more than ordinary in song . . . I put myself on a regimen of admiring a fine woman' (*Burns*, ed. Scott Douglas, Vol. VI, p. 311)—a deliberate induction of the required emotion, with a 'fine woman' as artist's model, and drawn from those peasant classes where artists of all ages—from Raphael onwards—have always found their most congenial material. Thus, with all the experience of the past, distilled by memory—like honey garnered from a thousand blossoms—you thought yourself into the desired mood —more or less that 'emotion recollected in tranquillity' the authors of the *Lyrical Ballads* later declared to be the only means of creation of great poetry. For, with your senses released from the bondage of passion and reacting at will to the chosen object floodlit by memory, with your intellect sorting out—selecting —universalising—you were able, with no interference from the senses and with the full strength of your genius, at length to create in peace. It was the last secret of the poetic art. Master of it now, Burns had no further on the poetic road to travel. It was now that, guided by the old tunes, trained on the old songs, and inspired by years of unbroken personal experience, he wrote the songs that have made his name immortal. But all three had been necessary, to this end—the Highland tunes to give the atmosphere, the Scots folk-songs as a model, the years of personal experience to give the song its identity and its colour. Leaning on these three, as one can read in the *Commonplace Book* and the *Letters*, Burns slowly attained maturity in his art.

CHAPTER II

THE LOVE-SONGS

'You know I am a cool lover.'
BURNS TO CLARINDA,
18 MARCH 1788.

IT IS ON THE love-songs Burns has made his name. He was writing them, it is true, all his life, but, of the multitude he wrote, only about a score or so still linger on everybody's lips. That, however, is a very large number to be at the credit of any individual poet, as songs there is no forgetting. For a love-song, more than any other, takes a deal of writing, and the percentage of successful ones must be the lowest in all art. . . . For the pitfalls here are not a few. First, over the song's length. Your inexperienced poet, like Burns at the beginning, is apt to go on for too long. For love evaporates. And, in a song, nothing goes so quickly off the boil. Burns' earliest love-song, written when he was seventeen, 'O Tibbie, I hae seen the day', runs to no fewer than nine whole verses and a chorus, and all just to show how clever Robin is, in scoring off Tibbie. But, apart from the fact that raillery is not love, posterity is not going to be interested in singing ten long verses, however neat. As a love-song, 'Tibbie' fails. There is altogether too much of her. . . . As there is of most of the world's second-rate love-songs. Sometimes it is the fault of the language, luring you on, like Gaelic, with its hundred words for 'darling'. Why shouldn't a poet use them all? But cataloguing the fair one's beauties, verse by verse—tacked on to a different endearment each time—which is all that the Highland songs ever arrive at—can be just as exasperating as raillery. You never get anywhere with either. And by the time you've come to an end, no woman in the world will believe you. Your phenomenal fluency damns you. And there is no first-rate love-song in Gaelic. . . . Or you spread your net too wide, like those charming

'Carmina Burana', the twelfth-century love-songs that the
Wandering Scholars sang all over Europe. For the Scholars were
steeped in the lusciousness of the Song of Songs,—that gorgeous
'Song of Solomon' (who had, unfortunately, a whole miscellan-
eous harem to please)—and their Carmina, like his, are written for
all sorts of girls. One exotic verse, full of ravishing comparisons,
for some Italian Juliet, then a plain one for Gretchen, then—.
If you didn't get her with the one, you might with the next.
On and on. Charm? Yes. But, of love? No more than 'Tibbie'.
There are too many flowers in the garden here. Your good love-
song concentrates on one, as Goethe, of wide experience in these
matters, counsels.

'Nun begrüss' ich sie sogleich
'Sie, die einzig Eine'—

It is to 'die Einzig Eine' that the world's great love-songs, without
exception, are addressed. . . . Short and hot, then, is the only safe
rule for the good love-song. You cannot have it too hot and
therefore—human passion being what it is—you cannot have it
too short. The great love-songs, indeed, are all short. Like those of
golden Sappho who knew, no one better, how to put it across,
as in her immortal 'To Anactoria' φαίνεταί μοι κῆνος ἴσος
θέοισιν (no lower than a god he seems to me) of four verses
only, with but two brief phrases about the girl to whom it is
written: ἄδυ φωνείσας (her sweet speech) . . . καὶ γελαίσας ἰμέροεν
(her lovely laughter). Praise of the girl doesn't matter. What
does matter, and what that girl is dying to hear—is of the man's
overwhelming ecstasy at the mere sight of her. And it's on that,
the whole song turns. Sappho knew. She gives him, however
only four brief verses to say it. And every phrase in them hand-
picked. Chosen, as the great critic Longinus long ago pointed out
admiringly, with the very subtlest art. Sappho knew. So too
Catullus, in his superb 'Vivamus, mea Lesbia, atque amemus',
the shortest and greatest of all love-songs, uses only thirteen lines.
Or, from modern times, Goethe's lovely 'Haidenröslein' but
fifteen lines, or Burns' own 'Red Red Rose' written when he had
learned his trade, at the end of his life, four verses only. The great
love-song is short. . . . As it is bound to be. For its emotional
content must be at white heat throughout. In this genre, unlike

others, there must be not one moment's cooling off, no let-up anywhere. The poet who introduces scenery, as Burns so often does, does so at his peril. Corn-rigs perhaps, with the girl's face peeping out of them, as in Hornel's pictures,—but 'gay green birks', 'hawthorn trees', and 'the mavis' evening sang', Afton or Ayr purling by—etceteras like these tell a different story altogether. He shouldn't have eyes to notice things like these. Here the high tension must be unrelieved. The song suffers by these distractions. . . . Furthermore, he must sweep her off her feet, if he can, in the first line. If he doesn't do it then, the odds are he'll never do it. 'O' A' the Airts the Win' can blaw', might be the prelude to anything—to sheep in a fold, as like as not. Poets are always thinking of sheep or shepherds as indeed Molière had noticed long before, satirising this tendency in 1670 in his inimitable *Le Bourgeois Gentilhomme*. 'Pourquoi toujours des bergers?' laments the practical hero. 'On ne voit que cela partout.' And in Scotland everywhere too the sheep and the winds. So why should a girl stop to listen? But 'My Love is like a Red Red Rose', or 'Ae Fond Kiss'—with their keynote in the first line— these catch her ear at once. Like the folk-song's forthright 'John cum kiss me *now*'. There's no mistaking that. Horace's rule of plunging 'in medias res' on the first word applies to nothing more certainly than to the love-song, as the masters well know. Hark to one of them—the magnificent poet Donne opening his most famous love-lyric with 'For God's sake hold your tongue and let me love'. Any woman in the world would find her head whirl at that. . . . The short poem, then, at white heat, with the explosive first line and—most vital of all—that air of guileless simplicity which only the most experienced lover can achieve. Innumerable girls went to the making of the seemingly so artless 'Red Red Rose'—as of Goethe's 'Haidenröslein' also—both of which look as if the poet had never loved before. It's on this last rock that most love-songs founder. For flowery words and periphrases nowhere more assuredly than here, damn you at the post. Yet it was Solomon's way of it too—his 'tower of ivory', his 'heap of wheat set about with lilies', his luscious 'I will cause thee to drink of the spiced wine of the juice of my pomegranate'. What glowing imagery it all is! Yes—but imagery and no more. Tho' Flecker indeed, in his Eastern *Hassan* follows this lead:

'How splendid in the morning grows the lily
'With what grace he throws, his supplication to the rose.
'Do roses nod the head, Yasmin?'

But, ever since classical Athens, love-talk like that has cut no ice
in Europe. The Parthenon girl had no use for it. The Parthenon
girl, with the Elgin Marbles behind her, liked it simple. And it's
she who has set the standard for European love-songs ever since.
Like Sappho again in her simple φαίνεταί μοι κῆνος ἴσος θέοισιν
(no lower than the gods he seems to me) where every word is
simple enough to be used in ordinary speech—or Catullus' plain
'Vivamus, mea Lesbia, atque amemus' of which the same is true
—or Shakespeare's 'Mistress mine, where art thou roaming?', or
Burns' 'My Love is like a Red Red Rose'. No precept is more
uniformly observed by all the great masters of this art. It's from
the high tops of Parnassus—and from nowhere else—the examples
come, like Marlowe's 'Come live with me and be my love'.
Even the involved Ben Jonson is here unexpectedly clear, with his
'Drink to me only with thine eyes.' For only simple words can
convey successfully the deep emotions ('Would God I had died for
thee, O Absalom, my son, my son') and only simple words are
equal to those great moments of life, of which the love-song
sings. . . . But in simplicity there lurks a danger only too apparent
in much of Burns' work. Simplicity must not degenerate into
banality, as in his bald 'From thee, Eliza, I must go' (the *Kilmarnock* song) which strikes rock-bottom here. Nor into raw
rusticity, like his 'Ca' the yowes to the knowes', reeking of the
yokels. Nor must it call up infelicitous images, like 'O Wert
Thou in the Cauld Blast', psychologically wrong from the
outset,—that 'cauld' followed by the even worse 'blast' conjuring
up such a realistic picture of Scotland's weather, as to drive all
other thought out of a girl's mind. Who wants love in a tearing
gale? As well write 'O Wert Thou at the North Pole' and expect
the song to generate heat. And indeed none of the three songs
recovers from these initial 'gaffes'. . . . For the weather, or climate,
associated with love, obeys a rigid convention—as the writer of
Ecclesiastes lays it down, 'A time to embrace, and a time to
refrain from embracing' (Eccles. iii.5). And, for the poet, moonlight—which carries Burns' 'Corn-rigs' and many another to an

easy triumph—is by far the safest. But if moonlight you cannot have, then starlight, with the planet Venus showing, as Tennyson uses it in his alluring

> 'Come into the garden, Maud
>
> .   .   .   .   .
>
> 'And the planet of Love is on high
> 'Beginning to faint in the light that he loves,
> 'In a bed of daffodil sky.'

But no love-song could survive a breakfast-table setting. Any such departure from convention at once distracts attention from the main theme and so destroys the unity of the song—while equally, any use of convention aids the poet by putting the reader into the required mood. . . . And the season, no less than the time, runs to rule—the merry Spring, hallowed from Mediaeval times in the joyous 'Pervigilium Veneris',

> 'Cras amet, qui nunquam amavit
> 'Quique amavit, cras amet.
> 'Ver novum, ver jam canorum, ver renatus orbis est
> 'Vere concordant amores, vere nubunt alites.'[1]

But that is the Continental Springtime with its foam of cherry-blossom and pear and its rose-glow of plum and almond—as in 'Alt Heidelberg du feine':

> 'Und kommt aus lindem Süden,
> 'Der Frühling übers Land,
> 'So webt er dir aus Blüten
> 'Ein schimmernd Brautgewand.'[2]

[1] Never Loved? Then love to-morrow.
Lovers all,—ah! love to-morrow
To-morrow when the Spring is new
When the ringing Spring is here,—
Spring when the world is born again
Springtide is the hour for love—spring when the bird on the wing goes mating—

[2] When out of the sweet South he comes,
The Springtide over the land,
From blossoms a-blow he weaves for thee
A shimmering bridal-robe to thy hand.

It takes Shakespeare himself, however, to put across the English Spring—

> 'Springtime is the only pretty ring-time,
> 'Sweet lovers love the Spring.'

Lesser poets, like Marlowe and Herrick do not venture out before 'the Merry Month of May'! But the Scots Spring, like the Scots May (those 'May Gobs') are both very different affairs and the less said about either in a love-song, the better. Lady Nairne, in her songs, wisely avoids the weather altogether, and Burns would have much greater success, if he did the same. For the love-song, in Scotland, pre-eminently requires an indoor setting, as in the second verse (the only happy one) of Burns' 'Mary Morison'.

> 'Yestreen, when to the trembling string
> 'The dance gaed thro' the lighted ha'
> 'To thee my fancy took its wing—
> 'I sat, but neither heard nor saw—'

As to the approach, however, there is no convention. Almost any way will do, if you can bring it off. Sappho in her 'To Anactoria' puts it into the mouth of the man. The folk-song on the contrary, does it the other way round 'John cum kiss me now'—like Burns himself often, as in 'O Whistle and I'll come to you, my lad'. The expert Catullus, gaining thereby a very great initial advantage, starts off with the united 'We' ('Vivamus, mea Lesbia, atque amemus')—that perilous cheek-to-cheek effect which Burns in only one of his love-songs 'Ae Fond Kiss' so much as attempts. For the initial 'We', tho' the most ardent of all, is alight with danger. If the lovers are united at the start, it is difficult to keep the temperature of your song hot enough. The interest flags. And Catullus, half-way through his song, abandons the dangerous 'We' for the passionate second person,

> 'Da mihi basia mille, dein secunda centum
> 'Da mihi—'

Burns solves the problem otherwise, by introducing the idea of parting. 'Ae Fond Kiss' (united enough) 'and then' (immediately) 'we sever', where the prospect of parting is enough to keep the temperature high throughout. . . . But, in his early love-songs

Burns generally speaks—the easiest way—as the man to the girl.
And as, among the Ayrshire girls, he hardly ever knew defeat,
those early songs, like 'Corn-Rigs' of the *Kilmarnock*, brim over
with gaiety.

> 'I'll ne'er forget that happy night
> 'Amang the rigs wi' Annie'

all aglow with personal triumph, which—not being passionate
love—admits of, and indeed demands, a much longer poem to
savour its full delight. And 'Corn-Rigs' has thirty-two lines and
a chorus as well, developing its theme from the first line—

> 'It was upon a Lammas night
> 'When corn-rigs are bonnie'—

the night (the perfect time for love-making), the moon (that
has shone on lovers from Sappho on)—the corn-rigs, only high
enough to frame Annie's face—all adding to, and accentuating
the love-atmosphere, instead of that unseemly 'Cauld Blast' of
Burns' last song, obliterating it. Of this type of song—the world
and the flesh without the devil—Burns is the complete master.
The lightness of touch—the verve—the zest—he has them all.
And gets them all across by merely outlining his picture with
phrases like 'I'll ne'er forget', and 'That happy night' which the
reader, filling in from his own experience, finds the whole
song flash for him into living flame. It moves quickly too—
carrying the imagination with it—'I set her down—I kent her
heart was a' my ain—I lov'd her—I kiss'd her—I lock'd her in my
fond embrace'—with nothing static—all verbs of motion sweeping the thought along. So that the song is full of hidden electric
points that, at a touch, catch fire. . . . Despite the handicap of its
being written in the past tense. When the true time for the
love-song as Burns himself learned later, is the present—'My Love
is like a Red, Red Rose'—'Ye Arena Mary Morison'—.
It was Sappho too set the model for that, with her emphatic
φαίνεταί, and Catullus with his 'Vivamus'. Even the diplomatic
Solomon jumps to it—East meeting West here, on this funda-
mental issue—'Thy lips are like a thread of scarlet', 'Thou art all
fair, my love'—. Not one of the whole harem wanted these in the
past.

It is interesting too, that, for this song, as for most of his others, Burns uses English—the language of thought—with but the merest sprinkling of dialect, to give it local colour. That, indeed, was his favourite medium and despite the remonstrances of Thomson (his editor who wanted 'high English') he kept to it. On the other hand, the broad vernacular of 'Hallowe'en', of a purely local appeal, does not occur in the songs, tho' occasionally a mild Lallans does, as in 'O for ane an' twenty, Tam'. But, in general, Burns uses the language that possesses the wider content of association and speaks to a wider public. Even tho' he himself was not always at home in it. The prosaic 'sever' and awkward 'heart-wrung' of 'Ae Fond Kiss' are instances in point. But even at the cost of such solecisms, he preferred the wider range of English—always with that sprinkling of dialect 'kent', 'amang', 'awa''.

To the same class of light-hearted love-songs belong some other gems, like 'Green grow the rashes O', the very apotheosis of flirtation—

> 'The sweetest hours that e'er I spent
> 'Are spent among the lasses, O'.

And flirtation, as all but the moralists know, is the most heavenly fun. Even the staid Victorians lit up to it, 'How sad and bad and mad it was', sighed the pensive Mr. Browning, 'But Oh! how it was sweet!' And Scotland had been trying to say so too—with but little success—for centuries, for this is a very old song indeed. It had never been anything but muddy when Allan Ramsay lit on it—and left it muddier than he found it—. But the essential truth of it wasn't necessarily muddy at all. And the truth of it was in Burns' blood. Light as champagne is his song—and nearly as heady—all set round that recurrent 'O' running like laughter through the whole. Flirtation *was* fun! And with wit in it too.

> 'The wisest man the warl' ere saw
> 'He dearly lo'ed the lasses O.'

It's that recurrent 'O' of laughter that 'makes' the song—its keynote—keeping it to the gay, light-hearted level and the kind of love where you forget even her name to-morrow. There isn't a name at all in Burns' song. Why should there be? It's the experience that matters. And on the experience there's never been a finer song.

In the same vein, tho' of later date (1790) is 'My Love She's but a Lassie Yet'. Burns has progressed here. 'My Love' is shorter, with only three verses and a chorus, as against the five and chorus of 'Green Grow the Rashes O'. The titles of both songs are old, but while Burns re-writes 'Green Grow the Rashes O' from scratch, he is beginning to patch together bits and pieces of other old songs to form 'My Love'—the treatment he was later to carry to perfection in 'The Red Red Rose'. This early 'My Love', however, shows the patching plain, as the finished 'Red Red Rose' does not.

v. 1   I rue the day I sought her O
       I rue the day I sought her O
      Wha gets her needna say he's woo'd
       But he may say he has bought her O.

v. 2   Come draw a drap o' the best o't yet
       Come draw a drap o' the best o't yet
      Gae seek for pleasure where ye will
       But here I never miss'd it yet.

v. 3   We're a' dry wi' drinkin' o't
       We're a' dry wi' drinkin' o't
      The minister kiss'd the fiddler's wife
       He couldna sleep for thinkin' o't.

That first verse is clearly Burns' own. Its four short lines, characteristically packed with no fewer than twelve verbs, carry his authentic signature. But v. 2 'Come draw a drap o' the best o't yet' strikes off at a tangent. Robin has eyed that line in a chapbook and with no care for relevance, stuck it in here. So that the heartsome couplet following 'gae seek', etc. is ambiguous. Is it meant for the lassie (left high and dry in v. 1)? Or for the nearer (and dearer?) drap? There's no knowing. The patching is loose. While the third verse—a magnificent verse, but again irrelevant—comes straight from Herd. That closing couplet, with its vignette of high romance, is far too romantic ever to have occurred to Burns himself. So the song is a composite affair of one verse on the theme, and the rest a heterogeneous collection of fine

lines. There is no unity in it, and unity is a necessity for any work
of art. Yet the lines Burns has picked, are telling ones and he has
learned the folk-song's lesson of repetition, each verse repeating
its own first line. And 'My Love' albeit an affair of shreds and
patches, is singable, because each patch is singable. But its technique is clumsy, not to say elementary. And the interest of the
song lies just in this—that it shows what a long road Burns had to
travel, before he was able to darn his patches, so that the seams
do not show.

'The Silver Tassie' of the same date, experiments in a different
way.

> v. 1. Gae fetch to me a pint o' wine
>   An' fill it in a silver tassie,
>   That I may drink, before I go
>   A service to my bonnie lassie.
>
> v. 2. The boat rocks at the pier o' Leith,
>   Fu' loud the wind blaws frae the Ferry,
>   The ship rides by the Berwick-Law,
>   And I maun leave my bonnie Mary.
>
> v. 3. The trumpets sound, the banners fly
>   The glittering spears are ranked ready
>   The shouts o' war are heard afar,
>   The battle closes thick and bloody—
>
> v. 4. But it's not the roar o' sea or shore
>   Wad make me langer wish to tarry
>   Nor shouts o' war, that's heard afar,
>   It's leaving thee, my bonny Mary.

The stirring first verse is taken over entire from an old song. And
the second (Burns' own) this time follows its lead, ending with
'An' I maun leave my bonnie Mary'. So far, the song has unity,
but the third verse strikes a new note altogether, with its abrupt
and inartistic change of scene. The third verse comes from no old
song, with those ugly 'shouts o' war', and that prosaic fourth
line, 'The battle closes deep and bloody'. Burns had never seen
war and as always with anything outside his own experience, his
imagination gives out. This wholly conventional third verse, with

not an ounce of real feeling in it, cuts across the original theme and destroys it. But in parting (the original theme) Burns was always interested, so that the fourth (and last) verse rings sincere again. 'The Silver Tassie' is an unequal song, spoilt by the affectation of the third verse. Burns had yet to learn that when he took over a fine verse (like his first here) from an old song, he must keep to its leading idea and import no new ones, if his song was not to jar. One song, one theme. By 'Auld Lang Syne'—also taken from an old song—he has learned his lesson. The unity of thought is there complete. No discordant or variant idea is admitted. 'The Silver Tassie' by contrast, is immature. Burns was still unsure of his technique.

As he still is, in 'Mary Morison', also an early work and the only serenade that Burns ever tried. But serenades, as a form of art, do not ring true in a Scots climate, and an atmosphere of unreality swathes 'Mary Morison' from the start.

> 'O Mary at thy window be
> 'It is the wish'd, the trysted hour'—

But what is the poor girl to do shivering there, with a wooer (presumably) out in the open, amidst the gusts of a Scots October? —for the setting is autumnal. Nor does the exaggerated language help.

> 'How blithely wad I bide the stour
> 'A weary slave frae sun to sun'—

Robin a 'weary slave' to any girl? Who is going to believe that? This first verse is a failure. But the second verse pulls the song up.

> 'Yestreen, when to the trembling string
> 'The dance gaed thro' the lighted ha'—

Here, on the contrary, is a picture drawn from life with that sensitive choice of detail, of which Burns in the 'Jolly Beggars' had already shown himself a master. And now that we are indoors, the feeling at once grows more natural—

> 'To thee my fancy took its wing
> 'I sat, but neither heard nor saw'—

That is the language of truth—the packed verbs, the directness,

Burns' letter to Clarinda with the MS. of 'Ae Fond Kiss'. Note how the MS. of this song, unlike that of others, contains no corrections. Burns' mind was made up

(By courtesy of the National Library of Scotland)

Old Inverness as Burns saw it on his Highland tour in 1787. He may have crossed this old bridge. From Carr's 'Caledonian Sketches' (London, 1809)

the simplicity—. And the thought moves on naturally too—

> 'I sighed and said amang them a'
> 'Ye arena Mary Morison'—

v. 2 is high art. But the last verse falls off again, with its clichés ('wreck his peace') and recurrent hyperboles ('Wha for thy sake wad gladly dee'). For the serenade, a foreign form of art, really demands the syringa-scented background of a moonlit Verona, against which all exaggerations take on the light of truth, and all violence seems in place. Whereas in icy Scotland, the whole setting cuts against probability—that fatal mistake, as Aristotle points out in the *Poetics*, for any work of art,—the thing which no work of art can afford to do.

To this early period too belong the 'Highland Mary' songs, more famous than they deserve. The first one (1790) 'Thou lingering star with less'ning ray' has almost every fault a song can have. Choked with artificialities, 'departed shade', 'blissful rest', 'transports past', etc. stiff with exaggeration 'Eternity cannot efface, Those records dear' (with Jean just round the corner, not to speak of Clarinda!)—rough with ugly forms 'usher'st', 'th'impression'—it seems, at first, without one shred of real feeling. Feeling, however, it has—tho' not for Mary. (Could any man who had truly loved a girl, call her 'dear departed shade'?) The feeling is for Ayr—'winding Ayr', the first 'real' adjective Burns lights on. He has looked at the Ayr. It stays in his mind too, so that he returns to it in v. 3—the only natural verse in the song—

> 'Ayr, gurgling, kiss'd his pebbled shore
> 'O'erhung with wild woods thickening green
> 'The fragrant birch and hawthorn hoar—'

Not a first-class picture, perhaps, but not a conventional one either. The river and the wild woods are drawn from life, and how much more interesting to the poet than the now defunct Mary, who elicits only clichés! For Burns was not a realist for nothing. Only the girl on the doorstep was real to him. And it is to the Ayr he returns in v. 4 (the last). 'Still o'er these scenes my mem'ry wakes'—But the scenes are the 'winding Ayr' with its birch and hawthorn (his favourite tree)—and not the girl. The very thought of her indeed in the final four lines, drives him back

K

on the same old clichés—'departed shade', and 'blissful rest'—
even 'the groans that rend his breast'. Not one single original
idea can he rake up. . . . The second song, two years later (1792)
shows the grief, if grief there was, considerably assuaged. No
funeral panoply here. And the second song

> 'Ye banks and braes and streams around
> 'The Castle o' Montgomery'

gets off to a dancing start, for this earthy background puts a
realist poet much more at his ease than any star, lingering or
otherwise. So it is 'woods' now and 'flowers' and 'waters' till
finally, at the end of the verse, he does bethink himself

> 'There I took the last farewell
> 'O' my sweet Highland Mary'.

But it's the woods he's really thinking of, for v. 2 begins

> 'How sweetly bloom'd the gay, green birk
> 'How rich the hawthorn's blossom—'

And there are 'golden hours', and 'lock'd embraces'—almost
as happy as the memory of 'Corn Rigs'. But—she's dead! And
—realist to the end—it's the vision of her physical death ('O pale,
pale now those rosy lips—'And mouldering now in silent dust')
that haunts him, rather than any feeling of his own loss. Dead
indeed—

> 'But still within my bosom's core
> 'Shall live my Highland Mary.'

That gratifying thought should console her, dead or not,—on
which cheerful note the song ends. . . . As love-songs, of course,
both are failures—where is the love? But as testimony to the
contemporary view of death, they are of high interest. The stiff,
set phrases of the first,—formal as the crape, the weepers, the tall
hats, all de rigueur at an eighteenth-century funeral, its highest of
'high English', as far removed as possible from the homely vernacular—reveal Death as the show-piece the eighteenth century
made of him. The second song, with its insistence on physical
decay, recalls the skull and cross-bones of the eighteenth-century
tomb. It is, no doubt, partly owing to our changed attitudes to

both that the 'Highland Mary' songs to-day seem made of fustian.

In the songs of a later date, Burns sometimes speaks as the girl. By then he had great experience of girls, at any rate of the particular girl he had chosen as his type. She, like the Beggars and Holy Willie, is a character not confined to Ayrshire or the eighteenth century, but likely to be found anywhere, at any time—'universal', in fact, and as such, the proper subject for immortal song. And Burns got to know her like the back of his hand. Why, it is sometimes asked in this connection, did he not fall in love with a brilliant woman like Maria Riddell or a delightful bourgeoise like Peggy Chalmers? Neither the one nor the other would have served his purpose (which was merely animal)—even had they been willing to look at him, which they were not,—whereas the girl he really did bother about, is the girl of like animal nature to himself, who would sing 'An' O for ane-an-twenty, Tam', or 'O Whistle an' I'll come to you, my Lad', or who would tell you all about it in 'Tam Glen', or lament aloud, when things went wrong, as in 'Bonnie Doon'. Not an elevated type perhaps, but a constant one, and the only one that appealed to Burns. Every century knows her, and every country. She is the girl who doesn't date. And it's the same girl in all of them. 'Tam Glen' a genre-song of 1789 shows her first—fresh, lively, with Youth's usual point of view,

> 'What care I in riches to wallow
> 'If I maunna marry Tam Glen'—

She keeps on at it too—as they do—dinning the name at you in verse after verse, with Youth's true sense of values for his rival,

> 'He brags and he blaws o' his siller
> 'But when will he dance like Tam Glen?'

And the Scots touch comes in with the Kirk and Predestination in the last resort,

> 'But if it's *ordain'd* I maun tak' him
> 'O wha will I *get* but Tam Glen?'

Of its kind, a very good song—putting the girl across as clearly as the beggars in Poosie Nansie's. . . . But by 1792 Burns had learned a great deal more. Eight verses for 'Tam Glen'? This new

one 'An' O for Ane-an-Twenty, Tam' has but three and the
chorus, and gets its text across in the very first line, as swiftly as
the old folk-songs had, and in language as divertingly simple—

> 'An' O for Ane-an-Twenty, Tam
> 'And hey, sweet ane-an-Twenty, tam
> 'I'll learn my kin a rattlin' sang
> 'An' I saw ane-an-twenty, Tam'—

This is the first sign of that masterly economy of diction that
Burns was to show to such perfection in 'Auld Lang Syne'.
(Here he gets the last ounce of meaning out of his 'Ane an'
twenty', and drives it home with repetition.) Every word too
could be used in ordinary speech, and yet this ordinary speech,
as in Catullus' 'Vivamus, mea Lesbia, atque amemus', by some
subtle alchemy is here transmuted into poetry. (Listen to the
vowel-music!) And as Burns, with true dramatic instinct, gives
her only Lallans, there are no solecisms this time (like 'sever' in
'Ae Fond Kiss'). Every word here carries the right associations.
And then look at the monosyllables—125 out of the song's total
of 141 words. But monosyllables—the most concentrated form of
expression—do not come by chance. Their simplicity depends on
hours of hard thinking—and a touch of genius after that. And yet
the air of natural ease—as if the words just flowed of themselves—
that pervades the whole of this song! In its light-hearted grace
'An' O' for Ane-an-Twenty, Tam' cannot be bettered. All the
lessons of the folk-song have been learned here—its simplicity,
its ease—its repetition of a catchword first line—its brevity—its
music—. All the lessons— Together with its projection of
dramatic personality, as striking as the folk-song's own 'Eppie
Macnab'. It is true the mood suited Burns—the mood and the
girl—he was always at home with a rebel. . . . But in 'Bonnie
Doon', 'Ye Banks and Braes o' bonnie Doon' (a reminiscence of
Highland Mary?) the mood did not suit him so well. This was
sorrow, and he did not really understand sorrow. That was left
for his great successor, Lady Nairne. And so, not being at his ease,
he slips into the English clichés, like 'warbling bird'. Sorrow was
a solemn thing. You didn't talk of it in the Lallans. You just kept
a grim silence. If you were to make a song of sorrow—then use
the remoter English—'the warbling bird, that wantons thro' the

flowering thorn' and that sort of thing. But this is not the authentic language of grief—rather of the versifier with an eye to poetic diction. . . . Nor did the Gaelic tunes help Burns here. Badenoch and Buchan, so rich in the strathspeys and reels, had produced no laments, which indeed, like the great 'MacCrimmon's Lament', belong to the pipe-music of the Western Isles. But even had Burns heard the *cumha*, it is doubtful whether he would have felt any affinity for it. For there was no chord in his being that it could touch. To the wild gaiety of the strathspey and the reel he responded with all that was in him. To the deeper notes of sorrow he was tone-deaf. . . . The last two verses, however, of 'Bonnie Doon' (there are only four in all) improve, for Burns has here thought of the rose, and the Lallans comes back, and the metaphor (a very rare figure of speech in Burns) of the rose and thorn carries him through, with the sorrow just hinted at, in the final couplet,

> 'And my fause lover staw the rose
> 'But ah! he left the thorn wi' me'.

The artistry of this song, despite its laboured beginning, marks a distinct advance on work like 'The Silver Tassie'. Here the personality of the singer is preserved throughout. There are no abrupt changes of thought,—no disconnected lines. The unity of the song is complete. . . . But the high-light of all this group is undoubtedly the alluring 'O Whistle and I'll Come to You, My Lad', of 1793. It was a song he'd been working on for years, for the fragment (all that was left) in Herd, had attracted him,

> 'O Whistle and I'll Come to You, My Lad,
> 'O whistle and I'll come to you, my lad,
> 'Tho' faither and mither an' a' should gae mad,
> 'O whistle and I'll come to you, my lad.'

Surely he could make something of that? He had known so many girls, from Jean Armour on, whose signature tune it was. But the version he sent to Johnson in 1788—with Jean, it is thought, in mind,—is poor stuff. In it he even tinkered with the Herd original—a thing that, at the height of his powers, he never did—slowing down that galloping third line to the stiff 'Tho' father and mither should baith gae mad'. But the song haunted

him. He could do better than that—with the right girl. And when,
down in Dumfries, he met the 'Lassie wi' the Lint-White Locks',
who'd eloped at seventeen to Gretna Green with a rake of an
Englishman who'd left her plump at the blacksmith's anvil, he'd
got what he wanted. She would do. And, with that wild lass to
inspire him, the version he sent to Thomson in 1793 has all the
kick you could desire. For his first verse (and chorus) he goes back
to the Herd fragment—now word for word—and for the next
three (all there are) he writes a genre-song,—and all so perfectly
blended with the Herd fragment you could never tell (did Herd's
MSS. not survive) they were not all written by the same hand.
A genre-song in Lallans gave Burns' narrative powers, seen already in 'Death and Dr. Hornbook', full scope. The monosyllables, the crowded verbs, the quick motion with the action
advancing in every phrase, the rich humour—all these are the
sign-manual of Burns at his best.

> v. 1. But warily tent when ye come to court me
>
>   .   .   .   .   .   .
>
>   And come as ye were na comin to me.
>
> v. 2. At kirk or at market, whene'er ye meet me
>   Gang by me as tho' that ye car'd na a flie.
>
>   .   .   .   .   .   .
>
> v. 3. But court na anither tho' jokin' ye be
>   For fear that she wyle your fancy frae me.

Note the monosyllables pouring out naturally and with the
appearance of the most unstudied ease. Not since 'Holy Willie'
had Burns achieved such perfection of diction, and as in the satire,
here too he has etched with consummate skill, in just three verses,
the character behind it. It was that congenial character, plus the
hint in the Herd fragment, plus his own now very great experience
of song-writing,—all three factors combining—that produced in
1793 this marvellous song. Hark to it racing along—gay, provo-
cative, challenging—with the bravado of Montmartre and the
outspokenness of Scottish peasant life!

The songs Burns wrote as from a husband to a wife reveal him
in a different light. 'O' A' the Airts' (1790) the honeymoon song to

Jean, does not as has been said, get off to a good start. And for a
honeymoon song, you well may think, it is remarkably cool. If
you like a honeymoon song to be that way, you will never get a
cooler one than this. The 'wild woods' and 'the dewy flowers',
the 'bonie birds', the 'flowers' again—he's looking at them all
with considerable interest, and tangled among them all somewhere
is—Jean. The whole thing is too geographical. Robin had a roving eye. A little passion in 'O' A' the Airts' would give it some
depth. As it is, one feels that the wild woods, the birds, the bonie
flowers with which the song is packed, provide an equal attraction
with Jean.... But he does better with 'My Wife's a Winsome Wee
Thing' of 1792. Only two verses in this, the briefest of all his love-
songs, a 'random clink' as he called it, but this time he brought it
off. Not, perhaps, because he was thinking of Jean, who doesn't
occur, but because he'd come across an old air. An intriguing old
air—its title 'My wife's a wanton wee thing'. And with that, he'd
sat him down and written this song, as he told Thomson, 'ex-
tempore'.

> Chorus: 'She is a winsome wee thing
> 'She is a handsome wee thing
> 'She is a lo'esome wee thing
> 'This sweet wee wife o' mine
>
> v. 1. 'I never saw a fairer
> 'I never lo'ed a dearer—'

That word 'wanton'—how it did fire you! And the song has
a breathless 'go' in it. Whisky this time he made of it—not
lemonade!

And then there are the songs—the two or three—when his
powers and his skill were now at their height. Of these 'John
Anderson my jo, John' stands out as easily the first—'John
Anderson' so far out of his usual beat that it sets you wondering,
until you remember 'The Cottar'. For the Cottar and his wife
were drawn, at the outset of Burns' career, from the same model
as here. Our 'John Anderson' is not, of course, a first attempt.
Far from it. Burns had tried his hand at mending it—for it is a
very old licentious song—already several times. A version for a
chapbook (1787)—another, not so clean, for 'The Merry Muses'

—still it would not do. And then he must have remembered the fireside and the old couple by it, for the new 'John Anderson my jo, John' he sent to Johnson in 1790 keeps nothing of the old song but its title. The setting is entirely new and Burns's own. And while it has all the hallmarks of his best work, it has certain other qualities too, only found in his masterpieces. A severe restraint, for example, alike in subject-matter and in treatment, characterises this new style. The subject indeed—the contrast between Youth and Age—is one in which pathos is implicit. But it is never allowed to become explicit. Nothing like the wallowing emotion of the 'Highland Mary' songs occurs here. And yet every line of its short four verses is fed from hidden springs that well up afresh at each new reading. The pathos is as intrinsic to this song as it is to Simonides' great epitaph, 'Stranger, tell the Lacedaemonians that we lie here, obedient to their orders'. And it is of the same order. . . . The treatment is severe too. Not an otiose word here. No irrelevant birds or whatnot go careering through this song. Here every word tells. Every thought bears on the theme. The full flood of the limelight falls on the old couple and on them alone. Nor is the theme laboured. The detail carries it. 'Your bonnie brow was brent, But now your brow is beld, John'—with everything else left to the imagination, so that the reader has to meet the poet halfway—the co-operation that quickens the artistic delight. Even as a line of Rembrandt carries the suggestion of the whole picture for the reader to visualise. The theme too is not a momentary thing, resting on a passing phase of life, like the girl's gay brilliance in 'O Whistle and I'll Come to You, My Lad'. It wells up from something deep in human nature—the tried and seasoned love of husband and wife. 'John Anderson my jo, John' has an appeal for all time, for all sorts, in all places—fulfilling thus all the conditions of the Mediaeval critic Adam de St. Victor's definition of a masterpiece . . . '*quod semper, quod ubique, quod ab omnibus*' (an appeal for all time, in all places, to all sorts.) . . . Of this class also is 'My Love is like a Red, Red Rose'. For, while it is true enough, as all the commentators point out, that there are innumerable precedents for this song—chap after chap—blackletter after blackletter—a fragment in Herd— another song by Burns himself 'O were my Love Yon Lilac Fair' (using in its second verse, Herd's fragment, viz.

'O Gin my Love were yon Red Rose
'That grows upon the Castle wa'
'And I mysel' a drap o' dew
'Into her bonie breast to fa'—)

it is incontestable too that not one of the precedents here reaches anything like the level of Burns' great song. Not even Herd's fragment—usually the outstanding jewel in a Burns' song. Here —for once—Burns has far outstripped all his models. The precedents, by comparison, are awkward and ungainly in diction, like

'Now fare thee well, my Dearest Dear
'Now fare thee well awhile
'Altho' I go, I'll come again
'If I go ten thousand mile'—

of an old black-letter. How much simpler is Burns' version!

'And fare thee weel, my only luve
'And fare thee weel awhile,
'And I will come again, my luve
'Tho' it were ten thousand mile'.

The thought in Burns' last couplet flows velvet-smooth— without a jar—instead of the jerky repetition of the black-letter. And so it is throughout. . . . Each of Burns' four verses leads on to the next, with the love, like a thread of gold, linking them all together. Love is the recurrent motif. Burns has at last realised you cannot have too much of it in a love-song. Or bring it in too soon. Or pitch it too high. By the second verse it is good going

'And I will luve thee still, my dear
'Till a' the seas gang dry'.

But how, with the emotion at this peak, to find an end that shall not let you down? For an end there must be, almost at once. And cooling off will never do. Catullus, in his Lesbia song, facing this difficulty too, found the same solution to it as Burns. Do it with vast numbers, fading into infinity—kisses without number. Leave that as the final thought, with no real end—kisses more and more. Burns'

'And I will come again, my luve,
'Tho' it were ten thousand mile'

follows the same plan. His 'come again', is the last thought, and
the song fades out, rather than stops, to a sense of infinite distance.
This indefinite ending, like Catullus' indefinite number of kisses,
leaves you thinking that the love goes on—and on. . . . The
diction is simplicity itself—every word (except only seven out of
a total of 109) monosyllabic and such as could be used in ordinary
speech—but not arranged as ordinary speech would do it—with
just that subtle difference that Aristotle prescribes in the Poetics,
That explosive opening line, for instance 'O my Luve is like a
red, red rose', shows a brilliant repetition of the adjective (Burns'
own effect, and not present in the 'Herd' original 'O gin my luve
were yon red rose') here making all the difference between poetry
and prose. Then the vowel-music charms the ear, so that the
whole song sings itself, even as you read it. And, a further point,
its anonymity—for there are no 'Mary's or 'Jean's here—makes
it of universal appeal. This is any man to any girl. So that the 'Red
Red Rose' would seem to be Burns' most perfect love-song for
young lovers—a masterpiece of technique, however, rather than
of passion. For it is by the superb blending of the varied units
into one harmonious whole that the song achieves its beauty—
carrying the passion over, if it does carry it, from the originals
from which Burns patched it. 'Ae Fond Kiss' the third of the trio
of masterpieces, is the song Burns wrote for Clarinda in 1791.
A song of parting, it derives much of its effect from that emotional 'Ae' at the start, repeated in the next line and again in the
final verse, which is the same as the first. Burns had studied the
effect of that 'Ae' in Herd's fragment—

'O let me in this ae night
'This ae, ae, ae night,
'O let me in this ae night
'And rise and let me in'—

where the wail of the 'Ae' carries the whole song,—as it does in
'Ae Fond Kiss', setting the keynote from the start. For the diction
here is more than questionable. 'Heart-wrung tears', 'warring
sighs and groans', 'dark despair' etc. come perilously near Burns'

besetting weakness, clichés. But the slow motion of the song, which is written almost entirely in spondaes—a thing unprecedented in Burns but extremely effective for its subject—somehow carries the diction too. And unlike Burns' custom also, this song has very few monosyllables, except in the famous couplet of the middle verse (by far the best verse of the three) where Burns is really thinking—not feeling—

v. 1. Ae fond kiss and then we sever
Ae fareweel and then for ever,
Deep in heart-wrung tears I'll pledge thee
Warring sighs and groans I'll wage thee.
Who shall say that Fortune grieves him,
While the star of hope she leaves him,
Me, nae cheerfu' twinkle lights me
Dark despair around benights me.

v. 2. I'll ne'er blame my partial fancy,
Naething could resist my Nancy.
But to see her was to love her
Love but her and love for ever
Had we never lov'd sae kindly
Had we never lov'd sae blindly,
Never met—or never parted—
We had ne'er been broken-hearted.

v. 3. Fare thee weel, thou first and fairest!
Fare thee weel, thou best and dearest!
Thine be ilka joy and treasure,
Peace, Enjoyment, Love and Pleasure!
Ae fond kiss, and then we sever!
Ae fareweel, alas! for ever!
Deep in heart-wrung tears I'll pledge thee,
Warring sighs and groans I'll wage thee.

'But to see her was to love her,
'Love but her and love for ever—'

monosyllables for thought. It is a longer song too (six verses instead of the usual four) than Burns habitually wrote in his best moments, but that, too, is appropriate here—for the length, as

well as the slow motion, emphasises the length and quality of the
farewell kiss. . . . The vowel-music, too, is here played very subtly.
For in the first line, as in the second, the only accented long vowel
is the 'Ae'—the opening word—suggesting each time that the kiss
is carried on right through the line. It is not till line 3 that the
varied music begins. 'Dēēp in heārt-wrung tēars I'll pledge
thēē'. . . . But 'Ae Fond Kiss' is an unequal song. Without the
middle verse concluding with the much-quoted

> 'Had we never loved sae kindly
> 'Had we never loved sae blindly
> 'Never met, or never parted,
> 'We had ne'er been broken-hearted'

it is unlikely that much would have been heard of it, for the
language of the other two, is the sort of language that dates. And
yet—those sensational spondaes, catching the ear at once—the
explosive first line with that piercing 'Ae' ('Ae Fond Kiss and
then we Sever')—the heavy undercurrent of passion surging
slowly through the whole—unmistakably this is a song for the
World, the Flesh, *and* the Devil—a foretaste of Swinburne. As
such, it is the most unusual—in one sense, the most original of
Burns' songs. For he slows down the gay Highland dance-tune
('Rory Dall's Port') which inspired him, to this tense music, and
with the help of the Herd fragment, makes the awkward English
words convey just the atmosphere he wants. In this song, as in
'The Red Red Rose', it is the matchless technical mastery of his
art, that stands out. For in quality of emotion, he is much more
uncertain. It is sometimes there, sometimes not. But at the end of
his life he had mastered—as no other poet in Scotland has ever
done—the whole art of song-making. . . . It had been a long
road to travel, since he was seventeen and wrote ten cheeky verses
to 'Tibbie' ('O Tibbie I hae seen the day') and it had taken him
all his life and sent him after 'lights o' love' innumerable, learning
his trade, but it had been worth the trouble, for the end was high
art. . . . On the whole, it is the gay songs he manages best. The
Highland tunes suggested gaiety. The lilt of a reel or a strathspey
had you on your feet in an instant, all your being keyed up to its
dancing music. A bar or two—and you could tell the very words
it wanted to say—. It was the gay songs he managed best—the

songs that, in this genre, were in line with 'The Jolly Beggars' and 'Tam o' Shanter'. It was this kind of atmosphere that stirred his pulse, like the corn-rigs in the clear moonlight, or the low whistle in the night air. . . . For life was graver indoors—where you saw John Anderson and his wife quiet by the fireside—or there was a tearful Clarinda waiting for that kiss on your way out —or there were books and books—Herd and black-letters and old chaps, all about a red rose and love, so that you had to sit down and patch them together, tho' it took all you had to do it —but out-of-doors now—Ah! that was the place!—with the gay green birk and the scented hawthorn and the Ayr—and oh yes! wasn't that where you'd left Mary?—and the wind that always made you think of Jean—and back again to the ripe corn-fields or the rye on a golden September night—who knows but there'd be a girl—down there among them? . . . And you'd get a song out of that—a song,—that was the thing—a song . . .

CHAPTER III

OTHER SONGS, DRINKING, POLITICAL, SOCIAL

OF WINE-SONGS, strictly so-called,—apart from the extravaganza of Tam o' Shanter—Burns wrote only two, possibly three, to challenge comparison with the great wine-songs that have come roystering down the ages, like that glorious 'Mihi est propositum, in taberna mori' of that graceless twelfth-century Archdeacon of Oxford—the song that raised the roof from Paris to Bologna and sent the flagons clattering even in the duller Leyden and Utrecht. Earlier wine-songs, of course, there had been, like Horace's famous Ode 3.2 Ad Amphoram ('O nata mecum consule Manlio') or even before that, in the Greek fragments of Alcaeus. But it was the irrepressible Archdeacon who first struck the note of gay 'abandon', with its undertone of mockery, that captured the imagination of Europe. Not that it is likely Burns had ever heard of him, or of his song. But many a Scots student—for in the Middle Ages they travelled far—must have done both. And brought back the witching words dancing in his head along with the staider maxims of Justinian or Aquinas to lighten a Mediaeval Scots manse or a lawyer's desk in Edinburgh. And from the outspoken 'Mihi est propositum' stemmed —in spirit, anyhow—the anonymous seventeenth-century 'Todlen Hame' that Burns thought the best Scots drinking-song ever written.

> 'Todlen hame, todlen hame
> 'Round as a neep, come todlen hame'.

How strange to think they were singing that in seventeenth-century Scotland, Killing Time and all! . . . But when Burns came to write his own wine-songs, he took a different line. In his earlier one, at least, 'Guidwife count the lawin', it is Horace's reflective mood ('Tu spem reducis mentibus anxiis') that he follows—

> 'My coggie is a haly pool
> 'That heals the wounds o' care and dool'.

And it is not a little extraordinary that, realist everywhere else—in his wine-songs he goes out of his way to avoid realism. The language of v. 1. of 'Guidwife, count the lawin' is highly imaginative—the mirk night, ale and brandy and blude-red wine, stars and moon and the risin' sun. (How easily the old wines slip into poetry! And with what difficulty their teetotal counterparts, gingerbeer and lemonade could enter any form of art, at all!) v. 1, then, lifts you clean away from harsh reality, into the realm of stars and moon and risin' sun. By v. 2 the singer is feeling political and aggrieved (the usual second effect).

> 'There's wealth and ease for gentlemen
> 'And semple folk maun fecht and fen!'

While v. 3 (the final one) brings unalloyed delight

> 'My coggie is a haly pool
> 'That heals the wounds o' care and dool,
> 'And Pleasure is a wanton trout
> 'An' ye drink it a', ye'll find him out.'

Not one hint of the coarser side of drinking, as emphasised in 'Todlen Hame'! Everything here is exalted and peculiar—the 'haly pool', 'the wounds o' care and dool', the very curious 'Pleasure is a wanton trout'. (More metaphors here than in anything else Burns wrote.) If the sense of the whole scene is drunken, the language is not only imaginative—it is noble. The Chorus of deep satisfaction that begins and ends the song

> 'Then, guidwife, count the lawin'
> 'The lawin', the lawin'
> 'Then, guidwife, count the lawin'
> 'And bring a coggie mair'—

is taken from an old song, and leaves you with the idea of the drinking going on—and on—, that indefinite and highly artistic ending, of which Burns is fond. The song is but an interlude in the drinking. This is the song of the philosophic drunk, who has settled down—as the slow, deliberate movement of the words shows—to a night's complete enjoyment. . . . The second and better-known one 'Willie Brew'd a Peck o' Maut' is the song of the hilarious drunk. But it is just as imaginative and written with even more care. How simply it begins—

> 'O Willie brewed a peck o' maut
> 'And Rob and Allan cam to see'—

but the next couplet is highly complicated, introducing the element of strangeness, remoteness from the humdrum that good wine soon brings. Here it is—

> 'Three blyther hearts that lee-lang night
> 'Ye wadna found in Christentie'—

'Lee-lang' and 'Christentie' swing you out into Fairyland. The second verse rings with merriment ('merry' three times over) but the third takes you right out to the cool night air and a lovely moonlight scene—

> 'It is the moon, I ken her *horn*
> 'That's blinkin' in the *lift* sae hie
> 'She shines sae bright to *wyle* us hame
> 'But, by my *sooth*, she'll wait a wee'.

All monosyllables but one, and the diction, the unpretentious Lallans, has an unusual word in every line (horn, lift, wyle, sooth) to give it distinction. While the final verse, with its one realist line 'Wha first beside his chair shall fa', has in the next line the very unusual image 'He is the King amang us three' to take your mind off all that. The chorus, beginning and ending this song too —and this time Burns's own—is the most carefully written, of all.

> 'We are na fou, we're nae that fou
> 'But just a drappie in our e'e!
> 'The cock may craw, the day may daw,
> 'And ay we'll taste the barley-bree'.

Not only the monosyllables (twenty-eight out of thirty words), not just the vowel-music (playing on all the vowels), but the humour, the care with which the realism ('We are na fou', etc.) is balanced by the imaginative 'The cock may craw, the day may daw', and the skill with which the last thought, apparently with

complete naturalness, should be 'the barley-bree'—all these show
Burns writing at his very best.—Why both these great songs,
unlike the realistic 'Todlen Hame', should dwell on the mental,
rather than the physical effects of drunkenness, and why both—
in a writer as earthy as Burns,—should be packed with images of
beauty, raises an interesting question. But most of the great wine-
songs of the world do the same. The old Archdeacon himself set
the fashion. His opening 'Mihi est propositum' is dignified enough
for a royal decree. And if he does propose to die in a tavern, that's
all of the tavern there is in it. By the third line he is in the celestial
spheres, with choirs of angels fluttering round. So that this strange
paradox seems to be true. You can't sing of wine, as it should be
sung, without bringing in beauty and laughter and imagination.
If you leave out any of those, you won't do better than 'Todlen
Hame'. For the essence of wine is the lifting power of imagination
it brings with it—as Burns saw also in 'Tam o' Shanter'. . . . As a
pendant to these two, may well be taken that rattling song of 1792
'The De'il's Awa wi' th' Exciseman'. The very thought of the
De'il stimulates Burns, as it always did in his prime, to his most
uproarious mood. Here the De'il is dancing, the De'il is fiddling
(like the fiddling and dancing in 'Tam o' Shanter')—both of
them practices, as the Kirk taught, entirely given over to the
Devil. Furthermore, the dances are particularised.

> 'There's threesome reels, there's foursome reels,
> 'There's hornpipes and strathspeys, man'—

those Highland dances he'd seen in Edinburgh and that Burns
always associates with the Devil's own music. It is a short song
—only three verses and full of verbs—and its success depends on
the dancing metre, intoxicating as wine itself, and the presence of
the De'il in each verse, with its necessary corollary (as Burns saw
it) outrageous fun. This is the humour the outside world had
noticed—with a shock, in the *Kilmarnock*. Now the De'il imports
it into a song.

THE POLITICAL SONGS

More famous than the wine-songs are the two political songs
'Scots wha Hae' and 'A Man's A Man for a' that', which Burns

wrote later still (1794-5) within a year or so of his death. Unlike the wine-songs, where you use the familiar Lallans, the political songs appealing to a wider public, are in English—the sort you'd shout from the hustings. For here Burns was deliberately setting out to inflame an audience, to put a match to their emotions. And for anyone who wants to do that, there is only one language, as John Knox also had found, when he too set out, with a similar intention, for his *History*. If you want to set your audience on fire, then use the English—a language that has all the keywords ready and soaked in paraffin already from centuries of inflammable tradition—a metropolitan language that appeals and on the instant to all sorts. No mere dialect like Lallans has the resources you require. So, by a strange irony, both 'Scots Wha Hae', and Knox's *History of the Reformation*—those twin pillars of Scots nationalism—are written in English. . . . Not that 'Scots Wha Hae' hasn't one or two dialect forms, like the two in the title, or that unheard-of 'Wham' in the next line. But none of these is likely to set anybody on fire. The great names, Wallace and Bruce (significantly enough for Burns, Ayrshire men both, as well as national heroes) do that first, and then the clear-cut alternative, shot at you of 'gory bed' or 'victorie'. Blood, even camouflaged as 'gory' will always do it. And then the time, 'Now's the day and now's the hour', v. 2. (Give them not a moment to think) so that 'see approach proud Edward's power' can be put across as the venomous 'Chains and Slavery'—loaded words, both of them, with their age-long train of political associations. (What, as a matter of interest, are the Lallans equivalents of either?) v. 3 follows up with more, like 'traitor', 'coward', 'slave'—the stock-in-trade appellations of political opponents (on the hustings anyhow) so that by v. 4 you can turn to yourself. For you it is 'Freedom's sword', and 'Freeman stand or freeman fa' '—with, in mounting climax for the other side, 'oppression, chains, usurpers, tyrants'—words of deeper and deeper dye, until you get the red flag itself, of 'Liberty' for the last line, and on that, the blood now up, 'Let us do or die'. . . . But the recipe is too conventional—the make-up too obvious—to be great art. Cunningly contrived the song is, but of pre-fabricated units, the regular (and monotonous) vocabulary of every war-song. And the real criticism of 'Scots Wha Hae' is that it has always

been a platform song, and no other—its appeal blatantly emotional. But Scotsmen, emotional as they undoubtedly are, have
also an underlying layer of intellect, which emotion never touches.
In the light of that, 'Scots Wha Hae' has always remained—just
a platform song. Whereas a great song appeals also to the intellect. Not relying on catchwords ('chains and slavery', 'tyrants',
'traitors', etc.) it fashions ordinary words to give new effects,
as does Burns himself in 'The Red Red Rose'. But a war-song,
of course, does not allow of this treatment. It must use old words,
such as wake a long train of heated reminiscence in the hearer—
in all sorts of hearers—and at once. There is no substitute for a
word like 'traitor'. It cannot be rethought. To get the effect, the
word itself must be used. So that, relying thus on loaded words
for its emotional appeal and appealing to the emotion only, the
war-song can never attain the same rank as a song which re-
moulds its material and appeals to the intellect as well. . . . And
indeed, over the Channel in Revolutionary France at about the
same date (1792) they were using much the same material as
'Scots Wha Hae', for the Marseillaise. A little more of it, perhaps
—five double verses as against Burns' short six single—but the
material is the same. 'Enfants de la patrie' stabs you awake, like
Burns' staccato 'Scots'. And there's 'tyrannie' and 'l'étendard
sanglant' (gory bed?) and 'traîtres' and 'esclaves', and 'ces fers,
des longtemps préparés' (chains and slavery?) with 'Liberté
chérie' to sum up, like Burns, in the last verse. With a great deal,
too, about blood. After every verse 'qu'un sang impur abreuve
nos sillons', to which Burns, high in his inflammatory crescendo
'We will drain our dearest veins'. For blood in a war-song there
must be. The vocabulary of the two, in fine, with one interesting
exception, is identical. But where the French song harps on glory,

> 'Allons, enfants de la patrie
> 'Le jour de gloire est arrivé'—

and ends with it too,

> 'Que tes ennemis expirants
> 'Voient ton triomphe et notre gloire'—

Burns, well aware that glory as a war-cry cuts no ice in Scotland,
writes

'Wha for Scotland's King and Law
'Freedom's sword will strongly draw'—

that highly improbable 'Law' (for what Scotsman in his senses ever fought for Law? And certainly not the rebel Burns!) being introduced as a desperate rhyme for 'draw'. . . . And how then does Shakespeare do it, rousing the English before Agincourt (*King Henry V*, Act III, Scene 1)? Not with 'glory', you may be sure—far less with that fantastic 'Law'—and there's never a mention of 'Liberty'. 'Be copy now' urges Shakespeare, with penetrating insight into the English national character, 'to men of grosser blood, and teach them how to war', and, as an after-thought 'The game's afoot' (as it might be, cricket) 'Follow your spirit'. It is only in the last line and a half he lets himself go.

'Upon this charge
'Cry God for Harry, England and St. George.'

No catchwords here—only the one infallible motif 'God' for bringing England in. The Englishman always fights for a righteous cause. . . .

More original than 'Scots Wha Hae' is the stirring 'A Man's A Man for A' That'. 'This piece is not really poetry', avowed Burns candidly (and truthfully) sending it to Thomson in 1795. But pretty good politics, perhaps? The thought of it had been simmering in his mind ever since 'The Twa Dogs', the opening poem of the *Kilmarnock*, where 'They're nae sae wretched's ane wad think' declared Luath, the poor man's dog, of the poor. And the idea grew. Then, what with the bitterness of his Edin-burgh experiences and the excitement of the French Revolution blowing hot over all Europe, by 1795 it had got to boiling point. 'The honest man, tho' e'er sae poor', he flings out now—'is king o' men for a' that'. As the bloodstained guillotine in the Place de la Concorde had been proclaiming him loud and large. Yet poverty and honesty—far from being synonymous—are sometimes incompatible and Burns' classification is here too crude. Indeed the emphasis on honesty and independence throughout the song ('the honest man', 'the man of independent mind') rings strange to-day in a Welfare State where both words have fallen out of current speech. Independence, indeed, whether of mind or

of State, is not a twentieth-century ideal. But ideal it is, nevertheless, and one that will always be associated with Burns and that
still makes much of his appeal to the Scottish people. And tho'
by denying the 'pith o' sense' and 'pride o' worth' to 'yon birkie
ca'd a lord' ('But a cuif for a' that') he—ironically enough—falls
into the identical mistake (in reverse) of the class he censures, there
is a rightness and novelty in his commendation of that same 'pith
o' sense' and 'pride o' worth' which greatly needed saying. Like
some other startling truths, in the song, that were entirely new to
the eighteenth century, and that haven't ceased reverberating
yet, as

> 'For a' that an a' that
>   'Our toils obscure an a' that
> 'The rank is but the guinea stamp
>   'The man's the gowd for a' that.'

The emphasis, too, on 'hamely fare' and 'hoddin' grey' was
just, with its undoubted corollary 'A Man's a Man for a' that'.
You have only to read the novels of Miss Ferrier, a leader of
Edinburgh society about 1820, or those of Miss Catherine Sinclair in Edinburgh a generation later, to see how completely unheard-of—even then—were such sentiments. But the fatal flaw
in the poem—which has turned it into a 'class' song—lies in
Burns's ascription of these virtues solely to the poor, of whom
they have never been the prerogative—let alone the monopoly.
Indeed, even in Edinburgh days—had Burns only stopped to
think—there had been Lord Glencairn

> 'And I'll remember thee, Glencairn
> 'An' a' that thou hast done for me'—

who'd had enough 'pith o' sense' to introduce a raw Ayrshire
poet to the best Edinburgh society. . . . But the great final stanzas
of 'A Man's A Man' rise above class feeling.

> 'Then let us pray that come it may
>   'As come it will for a' that
> 'That Sense and Worth o'er a' the Earth
>   'Shall bear the gree an' a' that!

'For a' that an' a' that
'It's comin' yet for a' that
'That man to man the world o'er
'Shall brithers be for a' that.'

(All monosyllables but two.) These, embodying the highest
hopes of humanity in language as clear and telling as in Holy
Willie long ago, rise to a height of imagination and a nobility of
thought that surely here, at least, carry them into the sphere of
poetry. . . . 'A Man's a Man' is written in English but with more
dialect words than 'Scots Wha Hae', for here Burns was calling
for no Red Revolution. Rather was he talking, as it might be, to
Gavin Hamilton, or the crowd that gathered round him in a
Tarbolton Club. Not poetry perhaps. But a dangerous kind of a
song. There's dynamite in it still.

THE SOCIAL SONGS

It is not uncommon for a great painter, like Rembrandt,
to leave us his own portrait. But few poets have done so, which
makes Burns', 'There was a Lad was Born in Kyle' of more than
usual interest. The old song, 'Rantin', rovin' Robin', on which
it is based, had a title that fitted him exactly, so that it was in the
same key he went on,—the blast o' Januar' wind (the best-known
wind in the world to-day), the 'misfortunes', and the 'hert'—
and then, in a tone as assured as Horace's own 'Non omnis
moriar',—the prophetic

'He'll be a credit till us a'
'We'll a' be prood o' Robin'—

which should introduce the most famous of all his songs 'For
Auld Lang Syne'. What exactly is the secret of this song that has
carried it into every company beneath all sorts of skies? It has, of
course, like most of Burns' songs, many predecessors, 'Old Long
Syne's without number, 'Auld Lang Syne's in Watson, in
Ramsay, in collection after collection. But there's only one that
the world knows,—the simplest of all—Burns' own. It's the
shortest too—five verses and a chorus—full of repetition, monosyllables and a veneer of Lallans. Only a veneer, for there are but

four dialect words in the song. But there are no clichés. And no
false notes in English. The diction is perfect. There's vowel-
music too, if you look for it. But it's neither the diction nor the
music nor the Lallans that has carried it over the world. Rather
a quality of spirit that Burns has managed to infuse into it, by
throwing a glamour over the past. For this song, as its fame
testifies, is more subtly constructed than almost any other Burns
wrote. . . . v. 1 shows the past in the vague distance, where
everything looks beautiful,—with only 'acquaintance' to pin it
down.—

> 'Should auld acquaintance be forgot
> 'An' never brocht tae mind?
> 'Should auld acquaintance be forgot,
> 'An' the days o' Auld Lang Syne?'

This idea of the past—the one idea in the verse—is driven home in
line after line, in different words, by a kind of hypnotic suggestion. v. 2 brings in you and me—and a drink, which always
heightens the atmosphere, but still with a look to the past.

> 'We'll tak' a cup o' kindness yet,
> 'For Auld Lang Syne'.

v. 3 and v. 4—the centre and heart of the song—both say exactly
the same thing. You and I have become the close-knit 'we twa'
—the opening words of both verses—on whom the limelight
now falls full, with the past a mere breath of a dream, 'gowans',
'braes', 'wander'd monie a weary fit'. Imagination, as in the early
'Corn Rigs' leaps to fill in that picture. v. 5 returns to the thought
of v. 2—you and I not so close—and the drink before us,

> 'We'll tak' a richt gude willie waught
> 'For Auld Lang Syne'—

and the past we share. v. 6 the chorus, returns to the thought of
v. 1—the theme thus coming full circle—with the spotlight,
three times over, now flooding the past.

> 'For Auld Lang Syne, my dear,
> 'For Auld Lang Syne
> 'We'll tak' a cup o' kindness yet,
> 'For Auld Lang Syne'.

—but with the 'acquaintance' delicately changed into the warmer 'My dear',—and the drink still before us! . . . No song in the world, it may safely be said, rests on fewer ideas (and certainly none simpler!). But there's a miraculous skill in the play of them —the past—we twa—and the drink. The timing is perfect, and so is the perspective—'the past' suggested, but never stated—you and I who, in the light of that past, become 'we twa'—and then, back to the past again, with the new tenderness of 'My dear'. And the undercurrent of the 'willie-waught' keeping the excitement up throughout. The magic of the song thus lies more in what is left unsaid and what the imagination reads into it,—like the artistry of Franz Hals conjuring up his masterpieces from just four colours. A glance at the earlier 'Old Long Syne's' makes this clear. Earlier poets had strewn flowers all along the wayside of the past. Burns strews none. Their 'You and I'—several, it might be—roved at random through the earlier songs. It is only Burns who, at the very heart of his, links us precisely into 'we twa'. He will have no crowds. And it's on that magical 'we twa' the power of his song depends. It's round 'we twa' and what we share, that the emotion of the song surges. There surely lies the wizardry that keeps it always alive. . . . It took all Burns' genius, at the height of his powers, to write 'Auld Lang Syne', but, as no work of genius is unheralded, the early traces of it go back as far as the 'Corn Rigs' of the *Kilmarnock*.

> 'I'll ne'er forget that happy night
> 'Amang the rigs wi' Annie'.

The hand that left 'that happy night' unparticularised, was the same hand that later wrote the simple 'Auld Lang Syne',—and left it at just that.

CHAPTER I

THE BACKGROUND OF BURNS' THOUGHT
—BURNS' QUALITIES—BURNS AND
ROUSSEAU—BURNS AND HOMER—WOMEN
IN SCOTS LITERATURE AND HISTORY—
BURNS AS A POET

'He'll be a credit to us a''
'We'll a' be prood o' Robin.'

WITH THE SATIRES and the songs to his credit, Burns stands
out above any of the other poets in Scots literature. It is true that
in the faculty of imagination, Dunbar is his superior, for there is
nothing in the Burns' canon to equal the brilliant picture of
Renaissance Edinburgh in the 'Twa Mariit Wemen and the
Wedo', or that Villon-like 'Lament for the Makars' with its
haunting refrain 'Timor Mortis Conturbat me'. In learning, again,
Henryson, Gavin Douglas and many others easily outclass him.
But in sheer intellectual power and brilliance—to lay his finger
unerringly on the weak points in an apparently impregnable wall
of dogma and expose them, as in the satires—or to pick out the
right pieces from a mosaic of old songs and to mould them into a
completely new and fascinating whole, as in his songs—no one
in Scots literature comes anywhere near Burns. And in English
literature, in this particular quality, only perhaps Shakespeare
himself. An intellect, then, of deadly power and of almost infallible sureness of touch. And, if this be a true assessment of
Burns' genius, it falls into line with Maria Riddell's famous verdict
on him, just after his death, that 'poetry was not really his forte'.
For, in the aesthetic qualities that usually go to make up poetry, he
was undoubtedly deficient. . . . In achievement too, if not in

range, Burns stands supreme. No one else wrote satire as unforgettable as his—no one else wrote satire that does not date.
And in song, tho' his rivals here stand closer—Lady Nairne in
her matchless 'Cockpen' and in some others, Lady Anne Lindsay
in 'Auld Robin Gray' are almost at his side—yet, in mastery of
technique as in universality of appeal, Burns here too takes the
lead. All the world can sing his 'Auld Lang Syne' or his 'Ae
Fond Kiss', for both transcend the barriers of nationality, in a
way the purely Scots songs of his rivals do not. . . .

The quality in his best work (and nothing else is under con-
sideration here) that marks him most notably is—deriving from
his intellectual power—a well-packed brevity. It was an eighteenth-century cult. Pope, from whom Burns perhaps learned it,
was its great devotee—but no Scots poet before Burns possesses
it, and almost none after. And it is this quality, unspectacular as
it may seem, that, whenever he scores a triumph, carries him to
the crest of the wave. This quality and no other. In a manner, it
was forced upon him—partly by his lack of learning, which
prevented him from filling out his work with the usual stuff of
poetry,—as mythology, romance or history. The only 'stuffing'
Robin knew or used, and never in his best moments, is an interminable and generally inappropriate list of birds. But conciseness was also imposed on him by the very circumstances of his
life. With no long spells of leisure, he had to work in repeated
odd moments of high concentration—intense concentration
made possible by the alternation of manual work, relieving and
resting the creative mind. Had Burns had the leisure of a Lord
Byron, his satires, roving at random, would have been no better
than his Lordship's—perhaps not so good. But, with the dull
hours at the plough nursing and fanning the heated intellect, the
thought grew white-hot. It had boiled down to its irreducible
minimum and to its transparent clarity by the time Burns got to
his attic desk. . . . And so too, for the songs. Riding all day long,
you thought them out, with the tune running in your head. But
who could remember a lengthy twenty verses or so, that came like
a flowing tide to the wigmaker Ramsay at his ease at home?
In the saddle you thought of, maybe, four or five, trimmed and
cut them—trimmed and cut. Brevity and concentration were
thus, alike by his mental and physical environment, forced upon

Robin. His manual labour, and later, his excise-duties—far from being a handicap—proved an actual advantage to his creative work. They made him think long hours before ever he wrote a word. Through them he had to prune his words and pack his thought. It is thus from his limitations—as is the way with genius—that arose the master-qualities of his art. . . . But he was fortunate too in the form that art took. Song and satire, in which he achieved his triumph, are both built for brevity and concentration. But it is not so with the other forms he tried. Here, brevity and concentration limit his vision. For it is still true that you can't see the whole of life in an evening out. Yet 'The Cottar's Saturday Night', 'The Jolly Beggars', 'Tam o' Shanter',—all Burns' longer works, in fact—show nothing else. Something here escapes him. In 'The Cottar' the whole household gather under the family roof-tree of a Saturday night—when no one, oddly enough, wants to be anywhere else! In 'The Jolly Beggars', from first to last, there is never a thought of quitting the road. The revelling Tam o' Shanter—revels or no—is going home. Burns' world, that is, is an enclosed one—without ambition and without windows. Nobody ever sees out. . . . For there is something in Ruskin's contention that for Robin the moon must always rise over Cumnock hills. Yet, for millions of Scotsmen ever since Robert the Bruce (a wanderer himself, as also an Ayrshire man) and like enough before him, it has risen—tantalisingly enough—'beyond the last blue mountain barred with snow'. Soldiering with Gustavus (didn't Dugald Dalgetty know?) or with the old Scots Guard in France as in Sir James Melville's (sixteenth century) *Memoirs*, trailing after the White Rose like Neil Munro's exiled John o' Lorn—studying in the twelfth century with Duns Scotus in a Paris garret, or in Utrecht in the eighteenth with Boswell—translating the Psalms like George Buchanan in a Portuguese prison—pioneering with Mackenzie in Canada or with Livingstone in Africa—down in the engine-room with Kipling's Macandrew wherever a ship sails, o'er all the Seven Seas—the moon rises for most Scotsmen, Highland or Lowland,—to their torment—beyond that 'last blue mountain, barred with snow'. And all that, escaped Burns. Ambition and Wanderlust alike—two of the mainsprings of Scottish character —lie both outside his cognisance. In his world you stayed put—

and liked it! So that Scots had better go to the familiar Second Paraphrase 'O God of Bethel', almost Scotland's national anthem

'Through each perplexing path of life
'Our wandering footsteps guide—'

when the Spring fever takes them, for on this point Robert Burns has not a word to say to them. But a writer who is blind to such a vast tract of national character and experience, suffers under grave disabilities when it is claimed for him that he speaks for his country. Brevity, then, and concentration—his major qualities—while they make him a classic, also blind him. . . . But it is on brevity and conciseness that the songs too are built. For, while songs like Lady Grisell Baillie's bright 'There was Ance a May' or John Ewen's 'The Boatie Rows' go rambling on, to the exhaustion of their material, Burns' best songs do not. Indeed, the longer he lived, the shorter he made his song. And, like the Impressionist in painting, the less he said in it. Till, with the masterpieces like 'Auld Lang Syne', and 'The Red Red Rose' he fills only the outlines in. By leaving all the rest to the reader's imagination, he keeps that reader's mind always at the stretch. There is no chance of your getting bored. And, it is to this pleasurable sense of co-operation between poet and reader that most of Burns' world-wide appeal is due, for a work of art into which you can read your own interpretation, is a work of art with ever-living springs of attraction. The leading ideas too (one idea, one song) are all simple, of a simplicity cut to the very bone, and so clear you need never think twice about them—rammed home too by the figure of repetition, imported from the folk-song, but also from the strathspey or reel, to all of which repetition is intrinsic. On brevity then, and conciseness, aided by repetition, the Burns' song is built. But here too, as in his other work, these qualities carry him only so far. For it is on the choice of the idea, as is easily seen, that the success of the song, under these conditions, depends. Let the idea be pretentious, like

'Thickest night, surround my dwelling,
'Howling tempests, o'er me rave'
(Strathallan's Lament.)

or parochial

'What will I do gin my hoggie die?'

or suggestive

'The tailor fell thro' the bed',

and the song crashes on the first line. No amount of conciseness can save it. But to Burns, a poet, as has been said, without aesthetic taste, one idea is as good as another. He writes as readily, trash like 'What will I do gin my hoggie die?' as the beauty of 'The Red Red Rose'. He has no aesthetic criterion. So that a large proportion of his songs are for the waste-paper basket only. . . . And then brevity and conciseness, at best, do not touch on the scope of a song. A great song should be an epitome of life. But life to Burns comprehends only what is actual, what is real for the moment. Any deeper meaning he does not sense. His songs, therefore, with rare exceptions, mean only what they say. In this, like Ayrshire itself, of a physical clearness of atmosphere unparalleled elsewhere. But the greatest poetry, it may well be argued, must see something more than the actual. Life is never really as clear as Ayrshire would have you believe. And a poet who does not paint the shadows, leaves something out. It isn't only that Burns could never go on for long (the other way of looking at his most excellent quality of brevity!). Nobody could, with his subject-matter, for the actual soon gives out. . . . And amidst the misty Highland Bens there's an uneasy feeling that life isn't all common sense. In the Highlands you write long poetry —sometimes boring enough—but it does give you a chance to get more into it,—as imagination now. In flashes, Burns has it. 'Auld Lang Syne', and 'The Red Red Rose' will always keep his place for him, but that place would have been higher if he could have shown imagination oftener. Even the paucity of ideas that makes his songs masterpieces, argues at the same time against the poet himself. Such thoughts as Drayton's 'Since there's no help, come let us kiss and part' with the conciseness shot through with passion, or as Catullus' meteor-like imagination in

'Nobis cum semel occidit brevis lux
'Nox est perpetua una dormienda'—[1]

[1] But we—once our brief light is out
It's night for us—one long unbroken night for sleep—

or Shakespeare's noble 'So are you to my thoughts as food to life' (Sonnet No. 75) are completely and altogether outside his range. Beyond a kiss and an embrace, as has been said, he has no conception of passionate love. For him the standpoint

> 'That, gin the lassie winna do't
> 'Ye'll fin' anither will, jo'.
> ('O Steer her up an' haud her gaun',)
> *Burns Centenary Edition*, Vol. III.

is the highest he ever attains. And the unknown Borderers who wrote the tragic 'Lowlands of Holland' knew more of passionate love than ever Robin did. . . . And it is this lack of response to something profound in human nature that keeps him from the highest place of all. Reflection—the one quality denied him— would seem to be a sine quâ non for the great poet. Humour? He has it. There is 'Holy Willie' or 'Tam o' Shanter'. Pathos, that Jeffrey called his supreme quality? And 'John Anderson' will rise before you. Gaiety? 'Oh Whistle an' I'll come to you, my lad'—Dignity? The Cottar round his ingle—Tenderness? 'The Red Red Rose'—all the qualities that appeal to his countrymen, not very great readers of poetry at any time. But when it comes to his international status and he is placed alongside other poets, this lack of reflection tells against him. It is that, that keeps him, and will always keep him, from the summit of Parnassus. . . . But, on the brink of it, where he would place himself

> 'For me, I'm on Parnassus' brink'.
> ('Epistle to Davie Sillar.')

there is much in him to delight. A certain earthiness, for example, like the good smell of a ploughed field, with a relish for homely fare, Ayrshire cheeses and buttered farls, 'reaming swats' to soak them down—in the hodden grey and the auld mended cla'es, with a flash of scarlet (as in 'The Holy Fair') for the girls,—in dogs about—a kiss or two—in a little field-mouse—in an earthy world, in short, that was on the whole new to Scots literature. It is true that Sempill of Beltrees' 'Blythesome Bridal', printed in Watson's *Collection of Scottish Poems* (1706) side by side with that 'Christ's Kirk on the Green' that Burns had studied, may well

have given him the original idea of using country fare, for
Sempill's bridal supper has the richest and most breath-taking
native menu in Scots literature, related with a verve and gusto
that sweeps all before it.

'And there will be . . .

.   .   .   .   .

'And there will be fadges and brachan
  'Wi' fouth o' guid gabbocks o' skate,
'Powsowdie, and drammock, and crowdie,
  'And caller nowt-feet on a plate . . .

'And there'll be . . .

.   .   .   .   .

'And there'll be lapper-milk kebbucks
  'And sowens, and farles, and baps,
'Wi' swats and weel-scrapit painches,
  'And brandy in stoups and in caups—

'And there'll be . . .

.   .   .   .   .

  'And a mill o' guid sneeshin' to prie
'When weary wi' eatin' and drinkin'
  'We'll rise up and dance till we dee'.

Burns' eye couldn't have missed the Gargantuan revelry here,
on the same page as 'Christ's Kirk on the Green'. And then
Fergusson in his 'Farmer's Ingle' set you down to it too—buttered
bannocks, kale, 'nappy liquor owre a bleezin' fire'. But Burns,
toning Sempill down and rounding Fergusson out, strikes a
middle course,—by the same method as he used later on in blending old songs. And so makes his picture convincing. For Ramsay's
'Gentle Shepherd' is mere theatrical stucco, as unreal as Watteau's.
And the alehouse and buffoonery of early Scots poetry, as in the
well-liked 'Christ's Kirk on the Green', present only the holiday
side of life. But Burns' earthy world is an everyday one and an
integrated whole—the food, the drink, the hodden grey, the
auld mare, the kiss or two, the warm ingle at night with worship
—the sort of static rural background that Scotland has always

known. Every facet of Scots country life is there. Nothing is overdrawn and everything smells of the good earth. Its appeal to the home of good farming—of the Ayrshire dairy cow—of the stolid shorthorn—of the fat Aberdeen-Angus—is therefore instant and peculiar. You don't want Xanadu and Kubla Khan in a country like that, or even Kisimul's galley that they sing of in the remote island of Barra. You want crude facts. Burns' picture is full of such and he gets it across to such an audience as inevitably to-day as on the morning he first created it. It is to his contact, like Antaeus, with the good earth, that he owes his strength. . . . It gives him too his contemporary air, for the details of his picture —as is soon seen—are all timeless. Unlike the rustic Scotland of Sir David Lyndesay's *Three Estates*, for example—based on topical and passing conditions, or Allan Ramsay's, based on eighteenth-century fantasies,—and both, therefore, bearing the stamp of their age—Burns' picture bears none. Resting on detail as ultimate as the earth itself, it remains as fresh. . . . For all that, cunningly put together as it undoubtedly is, it shows a wholly unreal world. As unreal, indeed, as Jane Austen's and in much the same way—i.e. with all the unpleasantnesses shut out. It would seem that Burns created it thus deliberately.

> 'Sworn foe to sorrow, care and prose
> 'I rhyme away'.
> ('Epistle to J. Smith', v. 25.)

No one in the Cottar's circle (a farming one!) has any troubles over money or loss or death. The Jolly Beggars, on the brink of starvation, haven't a care. There's nobody left sick or sorry at home in 'The Holy Fair'. But a world like that can be real only in the material sense. The poet loses in artistic breadth by his arbitrary exclusions. And yet—what a delightful world for the homesick exile to recall when, like Burns, he wishes to forget all about Scotland's problems! This is the way the folks live at home —the farls—the 'reaming swats'—the cosy ingle. You remember every one of them. And there's nothing in the picture you'd rather not remember. So this is the Scotland they always see under the Southern Cross—an idealised Scotland. And, paradoxically enough, it is not the romantic Scott, whose characters have the cares and worries of ordinary folk,—who does the glamourising.

Here it is the realist Burns. . . . Yet, whatever the gain, no artist can leave out the whole spiritual sphere and not suffer a corresponding loss. And Burns, undeniably, is the poet of the moment. It is for the moment he is read. You do not take him up in a library, as you would Shakespeare or Milton, to dig for hidden treasure. Here there is none. All the reactions are obvious and on the surface. Study him never so long, you will get nothing more. . . . It makes him too the poet of the middle distance. A close-up destroys the illusion of reality. If you want to believe in him, you must read him apart from his national background. For in an eighteenth-century when you could find a well-thumbed Boston's *Fourfold State*, not to speak of a *Shorter Catechism* in every but and ben in Scotland, it is hard to believe in a milieu of gaiety like 'Tam o' Shanter', 'The Holy Fair', 'The Jolly Beggars' —even with 'The Cottar'—as in any way representative. You keep thinking of folk like Scott's eighteenth-century Covenanter, Davie Deans, in *The Heart of Midlothian* arguing on points of law, or of his Andrew Fairservice, the gardener in *Rob Roy* so hot over 'the sad and sorrowfu' Union'. But in Burns' world, the high-water mark of thought is the Cottar's (Burns' most serious character)

> 'Their masters' and their mistresses' command
> 'The younkers a' are warned to obey—'
>   ('The Cottar's Saturday Night.')

You are to stay put in your mind, it seems, as well as in your lot. The Jolly Beggars, it is true,—but only when blind drunk— (and is it the Beggars then, or only Burns?) fling out in final chorus—

> 'Courts for cowards were erected
> 'Churches built to please the priest'—

But, generally speaking, no one in Burns' world thinks at all. . . . So that, for the home-bred, an air of incongruity hangs over the poems. With those hectic 'Burns' Nights' when the emphasis, like their own, falls on food and drink and the absence of all things unpleasant—on the absence, in particular, of any hard thinking—they go well enough. But, in the stern light of the morning after, a page of Burns carries little conviction. . . .With

M

his peasant world, however, he caught the tide. Peasant worlds were now the vogue. Rousseau had started it, with his shattering *Discours sur l'Origine de l'Inégalité* of 1757, picturing a world idyllically simple and in consequence—averred Jean-Jacques— idyllically happy. In a soberer England, Crabbe—Burns' con- temporary—not going quite so far with his *Village* of 1783, yet threw a spotlight on peasant life too. Literary Europe was all eyes now for the peasant. And Burns—without Rousseau's wild exaggeration and without the depression of Crabbe—stole the picture from both. Unlike Crabbe's, his was a happy world. Unlike Rousseau's, it looked natural. So that, while a logical France has long since shot up Rousseau's pastiche, and a 'merrie England' leaves the dismal Crabbe unread on her shelves,— Scotland unfortunately remains still obsessed with kitchen life —till outsiders may well wonder if there is any other room in her literary house now at all. For Burns here has had many des- cendants. Even in painting, the craze caught on. Sir David Wilkie (whose 'Cottar's Saturday Night' still hangs in the Glasgow Art Gallery) with his 'Blind Fiddler', his 'Reading the Will', later his 'Penny Wedding' carries on the genre tradition undeviatingly in this same kitchen background. And in literature, on the sentimental side, the 'Ian Maclaren' school with its Drumtochty, and later Barrie's self-conscious Thrums, both derive from Burns, while on the realist side George Douglas Brown's grim *House of Green Shutters* (Ayrshire too!)—on the sensual, Lewis Grassic Gibbon's revolting *Sunset Song* set in a Nor-East as humdrum as Ayrshire—all, dealing with an earthy 'kitchen' world, stem directly from him. But each and all of these, in some respect or other, exaggerate and overdraw. Burns never overdraws. He balances his facts—how carefully is only realised when you see what these, his successors, make of it, who didn't balance them at all. The Cottar, for example, takes family worship but, for several verses before that, the Cottar has been labouring in a field. The light falls evenly on both aspects—the one side as genuine and to the poet as interesting as the other. . . . Nor will Burns have any extremes. No sob-stuff like Drumsheugh's love-story in Ian Maclaren—no mawkish prodigal as in Barrie's Thrums— and on the other hand, no sordid meanness as in Douglas Brown's Barbie, no foul vulgarity as in Gibbon's *Sunset Song*. With a taste here as severe as Shakespeare's own, Burns keeps implacably to the middle of the road. He alone, of this school of Scots writers, has the wit to do that. His world, in consequence, clean and normal as a potato patch (if nothing more) puts all the others out of focus. Head and shoulders above them all, he alone makes earthiness attractive so that you forget that, metaphorically as well as physically, his windows never open. No ideas circulate. No one sees out.

How then does Burns present his world? Largely, as Aristotle says all drama should be presented, by action. It is action that gives the illusion of life. So—the Cottar putting away his spades —going home—meeting his children—'cracking of horses, pleughs and kye'—the Holy Fair out in the road, at the Fair itself, drinking, going home—the Beggars at their byplay in the inn, and so on. Everything is put over in verbs, the unit of action (almost as many verbs as Molière himself, that consummate master of action on the stage) till his whole world seethes with motion—which is just as well, when there is to be no thought. . . . But if Burns uses more verbs than do most English poets, he uses —significantly enough—far fewer similes, the unit of imagination. And what few there are, prosaic in the extreme. 'A runt was like a sow-tail' is Hallowe'en's first ('Hallowe'en', v. 4). And in the whole poem, Burns' longest (28 double verses) there follows but one other, of the same calibre 'as cantie as a kittlin' (kitten). The 'Cottar' is without a single simile, and with only two metaphors, both clichés, 'the hours swift-wing'd' and 'the conscious flame' (of love). The more lively 'Jolly Beggars' has still but four similes, all of the crudest e.g. 'like daft'. 'The Holy Fair' but one, cruder still—'his gestures—like Cantharidian plasters'. 'Tam o' Shanter', the most imaginative of Burns' works, rises—it is true—to more—but of the most ordinary ever found on poet's lips—a repetitive group of five, all emphasising transience and reading like a catalogue 'As bees flee hame'— Pleasures are—like poppies, or like the snow, or like the Borealis, or like the rainbow'—with three more later, introduced obviously for their sound-value rather than for any imaginative content 'As bees bizz out—as open pussie's mortal foes—as eager runs the market-crowd—so Maggie runs'. And you can read through nearly all the 'Epistles' and 'Addresses' without encountering a simile at all. It is to this poverty of imagination—when one remembers the coloured richness of tapestry and the brilliant intellectual illumination given by the simile to poetry from Homer on—one must put down that thinness of texture so apparent in Burns' poems. Had he been able to see likenesses— which, except in his best songs, he never was—the lack of learning, which he so often deplores, would not have incommoded him. For the simile would have given the required depth. Without it, his poetry remains, to his mortal loss, incurably superficial. . . . The poet, then, of the material—the poet of action—but not, as has been said already, one of the 'reflective' poets.[1] But some reflections there are—mostly in the Epistles—and at first sight, original enough. Scots literature certainly had not heard them before, nor—for that matter—English. But, across the Channel, they were on all men's lips—ever since Rousseau's epoch-making *Émile* and still more inflammable *Contrat Social* of 1762, had set a match to France. Every wind from the Continent blew the new ideas over. On the political side, folk like the patriots Muir, Palmer, Margarot and Skirving picked them up—only to be tried later in 1793 before the Hanging Judge, Lord Braxfield, for the first bold stirrings of democracy. And, on the philosophical side, —long before he ever saw Edinburgh—the ideas had reached Burns. They were just the sort of ideas to appeal to him,— thoughts later crystallised into the French Revolution slogans 'Liberté, Égalité, Fraternité'—and most of them appear in Burns' work as early as the *Kilmarnock*. But, however new they were to Scotland, the man who first gave them currency, was not Burns (at no time an original thinker) but the visionary Rousseau.

And Burns' debt to Rousseau is in every way so remarkable that some notice should here be taken of it. . . . In temperament the two were not unlike, Rousseau avowing in the *Confessions* that he felt before he thought, and further laying it down that 'Nature and immediate feeling are the basis of all determinations of Worth'. To which Burns would assent, singling out, as he does, Mackenzie's maudlin *Man of Feeling* for his highest praise, 'a book I prize next to the Bible' and declaring

[1] 'Burns felt and saw too much to have much time for thinking', Saintsbury, *History of English Literature*, p. 595.

'The hert's aye the pairt aye
'That maks us richt or wrang'.

Here feeling, not thought, is to Burns too, the moral criterion. . . .
Again, it was the sound of running water, in solitude, that
inspired the one, as the other. Burns' verse on this ('Epistle to
Wm. Simpson', v. 15) is well-known—

'The Muse, nae poet ever fand her
'Till by himsel' he learned to wander
'Adown some trottin' burn's meander
'An' no' think lang
'O sweet to stray, an' pensive ponder
'A heart-felt sang'.—

Rousseau's rhapsody on the same theme, as what stimulated his
feeling, in *Les Rêveries* (cinquième promenade) is perhaps not quite
so well-known. 'J'allais volontiers m'asseoir au bord du lac, sur
la grève, dans *quelque asile caché*. Là le bruit des vagues, et
l'*agitation de l'eau*, fixant mes sens et chassant de mon âme toute
autre agitation, la plongaient dans *une rêverie délicieuse* où la nuit
me surprenait souvent sans que je m'en fusse aperçu. *Le flux
et le reflux de cette eau*, son bruit contenu, mais renflé par intervalles,
frappant sans relâche mon oreille et mes yeux, suppléaient aux
mouvements internes que la rêverie éteignait en moi et suffisaient
pour me faire *sentir avec plaisir mon existence, sans prendre la peine
de penser*.' Moreover, when Burns, in that 'Epistle (so full of
advice) to a young Friend' urges

'The great Creator to revere
'Must sure become the creature'
(v. 9.)

he is here voicing no tenet of Calvinism, but, on the contrary, of
sheer Deism—the very same that Rousseau uses for his young
eighteen-year old Émile, who, brought up in ignorance of God,
is suddenly faced with the splendour of the Alps, in the hope he
will discover for himself and worship (as he does) their Creator. . . .
But it is not only a likeness of temperament between the two.
Burns owes Rousseau a real debt. Those French Revolution
slogans 'Liberté, Égalité, Fraternité' (all derived from Rousseau)

run like a vein of fire through Burns' poems. . . . And it is often
—but mistakenly—assumed that Liberty is a theme native to
Scots literature. Such, however, is not the case. Far from it. Neither
in Scots history nor in her literature, does Freedom play any great
part. While Scots independence—not to be confused with freedom—was certainly won at Bannockburn in 1314, that was all.
Of civic liberty—the freedom of the individual—achieved in
England by Magna Carta as early as 1215—there is, in Scotland,
neither then nor for centuries after, any trace. 'There is no
Scottish equivalent to the Habeas Corpus Act' points out the
learned Lord Constable (that distinguished Judge of the Court of
Session, in his *Law in the Making*, p. 8) 'until 1701, c. 6.'[1] This very
belated recognition in Scotland of the individual's rights was due,
firstly no doubt, to the country's intense struggle for independence, but secondly—and over a longer period—to her major
preoccupation with religion. Both these ideas, most unfortunately,
ousted the idea of freedom from the national consciousness. And
indeed John Knox, in his *First Book of Discipline* of 1561 puts it
with a peremptoriness that admits of no doubt. 'For no man may
be *permitted* to live as best pleaseth him, within the Church of
God. But every man must be *constrained* by fraternal admonition
and *correction* to bestow his labours where of the Church they are
required, to the edification of others'. Here is 'direction of labour'
with a vengeance—that tyranny that gives pause even to the
twentieth-century Welfare State in full career. But not one voice
in Scotland was ever raised against it. A submissive country
accepted it, without murmur or question, for centuries, as the
first-fruits of her Reformation. There was no nonsense about civic
liberty in the mind of Scotland's Reformer. But a country that
tolerates the intolerable, cannot claim for herself a place alongside
Harmodius and Aristogeiton in the shining annals of the world's
liberators. . . . Nor is it otherwise in Scots literature apart from
Barbour's solitary outburst after Bannockburn 'Ah! Freedom is a
noble thing' in the fourteenth century. The fifteenth-century

[1] See also Cosmo Innes' 'Lectures on Scotch Legal Antiquities' p. 149. 'In
everything the freedom of the subject was less protected with us, than in
England. We had no habeas corpus, nor anything equivalent to it. The practice
of judicial torture continued with us after it had virtually ceased in England'
etc.

galaxy of poets were more concerned with Life (Dunbar's 'In Prais of London', Henryson's 'Robin and Makyn', Gavin Douglas' *Aeneid*, Lyndesay's *Thrie Estates*). And then in the sixteenth century fell the barbarous Reformation, enslaving all freedom of thought. 'All interpretation (*sc.* of the Scriptures) disagreeing from the principles of our faith . . . is to be rejected' (Knox, *First Book of Discipline*). Plunged in Stygian darkness therefore lies the ensuing seventeenth century, like the first half of the eighteenth. It is only with the clarion call of *Le Contrat Social* in 1762—and its immortal opening words 'L'Homme est né libre' with which Rousseau burst the chains of France—that the voice of Liberty, if only as yet in a whisper, comes over from France to Scotland. Fergusson (1773) may have heard it, tho' it is in a social context—of the caged bird—that he apostrophises it, over and over again, in his 'Ode to the Gowdspink'

> 'Ah! Liberty, thou bonny dame—
> .   .   .   .   .
> 'And reft of thee, fient flee we care
> 'For a' that life ahint can spare
> .   .   .   .   .
> 'For when fair freedom smiles nae mair
> 'Care I for life?' . . .

But with Burns there is no doubt. With him it is liberty in a political context from the start. And by the end of the eighteenth century he rings it out full and clear. But after him—with the re-emergence of the thraldom of the Kirk in the Disruption nineteenth century—Liberty, if not Life itself, fades out again— clean out of Scots literature. It is not till the clipping of the Kirk's wings and the rise of secular interests in the twentieth, that Liberty, in the new Scots Renaissance school, is in these latter days reappearing. But 'L'Homme est né libre' shrilled Rousseau (if mistakenly!) in 1762, and here is Burns, hearing the call, in the *Kilmarnock* (1786)

> 'If I'm designed yon lordling's slave,
> 'By nature's law designed,

'Why was an independent wish
'E'er planted in my mind?'
('Man was Made to Mourn.')

That was new talk in Scotland, and carried further in the two
famous political songs 'Scots Wha Hae'

(Liberty's in every blow
'Let us do or dee')

and 'A Man's A Man for a' that'

(The man of independent mind
He looks and laughs at a' that.)

But some of the lesser-known pieces show even more clearly
the way Burns' mind was moving, like the remarkable 'On
Glenriddell's Fox Breaking his Chain' (1791) beginning 'Thou,
Liberty, thou art my theme' and going on to

'Couldst thou enslave a *free-born* creature,
'A *native denizen* of Nature?'—

where Burns with 'free-born', and 'native denizen' seems to
be actually quoting Rousseau's theories. Or again, in 'On
Commemoration of Rodney's Victory' (1793)

'And here's the great fabric, our free Constitution
'As built on the base of the great Revolution'.

Or in that 'Ode for General Washington's Birthday' ('Tis
Liberty's bold note I swell') on which Burns himself wrote to
Mrs. Dunlop (June 25, 1794) just two years before his death,
'The subject is Liberty. You know, my honoured friend, how
dear the theme is to me.' It was indeed a theme that, more and
more, in that Dumfries-shire period when the Kirk had lost its
interest for him, possessed and enthralled him. But Scotland had
nothing to do with it. The new wine came from France.

To the second of the trio 'Equality', Burns makes also frequent
reference. The injustice of inequality had struck Rousseau (*Discours sur l'Origine de l'Inégalité*, '57) even before he had begun to
think of Liberty, and it probably came earlier with Burns too.
Here it is in the *Kilmarnock*—

'It's hardly in a body's power,
'To keep at times frae being sour,
    'To see how things are shared'—
        ('Epistle to Davie', v. 2.)

or its sequel in the same Epistle—

'I grudge a wee the great folks' gift,
    'That live sae bien and snug,
'I tent less and want less
    'Their roomy fireside—
'But hanker and canker,
    'To see their cursed pride'—

This is the very spirit that inspired those shrieks of the French
mob, 'À la lanterne! À la lanterne' with the Aristos, that were
soon to deafen Paris. Or here again, is Burns viewing it from a
different angle, but still in the *Kilmarnock*.

'The sun that overhangs yon moors
    'Outspreading far and wide
'Where hundreds labour to support
    'A haughty lordling's pride—'
        ('Man was Made to Mourn,' v. 3.)

or, more clearly, in the 'Epistle to J. Smith', v. 17—

'Some, lucky, find a flow'ry spot
'For which they never toiled nor swat,
'They drink the sweet and eat the fat—
    'But care or pain,
'And happy eye the barren hut
    'With high disdain'.

all written, it is to be noted by those who claim that Edinburgh
soured him, before Burns had ever set foot in the Capital. But
this rage against the inequalities of society, so prominent in Burns,
and the demand for equal shares in riches, are both cardinal points
of *Le Contrat Social*.

And then,—Fraternity. 'L'Homme est un être naturellement
bon', proclaimed Rousseau's Émile, in defiant and flagrant
contradiction of the cherished Calvinist doctrine of Original

Sin—that hated doctrine which Burns pilloried in 'Holy Willie's Prayer'. But if Man is naturally good, it follows all men are brothers, and the Revolution cry 'Fraternité' enshrines this. How it lights up the *Kilmarnock*—

> 'But ye who hold your being on the terms
> 'Each aid the others,
> 'Come to my bowl, come to my arms,
> 'My friends—my brothers'.
> (Epistle to Lapraik, v. 21.)

or the familiar 'Then gently scan your brother man' of the 'Address to the Unco Guid', or the exultant cry of 'A Man's A Man for a' that'—

> 'It's comin' yet for a' that
> 'That man to man the warld o'er
> 'Shall brithers be for a' that.'

Liberty, Equality and Fraternity are the keynotes of all Burns' social thought. And while it cannot be claimed that he had read Rousseau—it is almost certain he had not—there were other opportunities. Rousseau himself had lived in England in the 1760's, as guest and friend of the Scots philosopher Hume who, Rousseau's ideas with him, came back to live in Edinburgh. And the inflammatory *Contrat Social*, spreading like wildfire over all Europe, had been out for a good twenty years before Burns sat down to the *Kilmarnock*. Fashions—even fashions in thought—take much less time than that, to cross the Channel.[1] But the whole trend of Burns' mind, it is true, was in line with the new ideas. They found in him a soil ready prepared to receive them. Nevertheless those reflections—so startlingly original as they appeared to Scotland (an additional proof that here they had no ancestry) and however genuine they were as utterances of his own feelings—and they were incontestably both—nevertheless those reflections owed both their origin and their content to another. It was not Robert Burns thought them out first. They sprang full-grown from the master-mind of Rousseau. . . . And indeed the

[1] E.g. Calvin's *Institutes* were published in Basel in 1536. Its ideas had already borne fruit in Scotland by 1546, when George Wishart was burnt there for heresy.

truly reflective poet, as history shows, expresses himself—as did the earlier Scots Montgomerie, author of 'The Cherrie and the Slae', not to speak of the great thinking poets, Shakespeare and Milton—in that special literary form, the sonnet, designed above all others, to show up every nuance of thought. It was a form which Burns thrice attempted and in which he signally and completely failed. He was not, in fine, a reflective poet. . . . Nor is he, you would say, apart from the power to suggest uproar and gaiety in 'The Jolly Beggars', and a witches' dance in 'Tam o' Shanter', a musical poet. There are no long, slow harmonics like Tennyson's 'The splendour falls on Castle walls', or the lovely bell-like tones of *The Lady of Shalott*—nothing that you can turn over on your palate and savour slowly like drops of nectar. No wild thrills in him either, like the Border ballad of Bailie Nicol Jarvie's delight (*Rob Roy*, Waverley Edition, p. 361), 'a' fu' o' venturesome deeds and escapes, sic as folk tell owre at a winter ingle in the daft days'. It wasn't in agricultural Ayrshire you could write a Border ballad! Being then without original reflection, and largely without musical power and without allusiveness (for his poetry, as has been often said, tends to be on the surface) how then comes it that Burns—more readily than poets who have all these gifts—captures and holds his audience? Popularity, of course, must not be confused with fame—still less is it a sign of genius. But yet, popularity apart, there must be something in Burns that accounts for his continuing hold on human nature. His well-packed conciseness for the scholar—his couthie earthiness for the exile—his flamboyant political ideas for the Continent and the Scottish Nationalists—but none of these would necessarily make him a great poet. And yet,—apart from the songs and satires not at present in question—a great poet he sometimes is. . . . Or so you think, reading the much-worked-over 'Tam o' Shanter'. Unlike the satires, whose appeal is only to the intellect, 'Tam o' Shanter' appeals also to the imagination. There is the storm, the Devil and the ride. To the senses too, in its vivid pictures and macabre dance-music. 'Tam o' Shanter' is unquestionably the poem of widest general appeal that Burns ever wrote. Here, par excellence, is the poetry of rapid motion—a much rarer kind in English literature than either the reflective, the musical or the allusive. And of this kind Burns is the complete and absolute master. It is this sort of poetry too that is the most spell-binding of all. The vast audience of all sorts, in every corner of the Mediterranean, that listened to Homer's breath-taking race of Achilles after Hector in the twenty-second book of the *Iliad*, well knew that. As did the Elizabethans thrilled and inspired by the moving speeches of Shakespeare's *King Henry V*. But Burns' theme is, in a sense, more difficult than either of these, for, unlike them, he has no national hero to provide a ready-made magnet for enthusiasm. He does it all in a highly original way, through no more than a country farmer,—with drink, certainly (one of the three great sources of poetry) to help him out, and, as a good second, his own unfailing and illustrious source of inspiration, the Devil—the same that carries him to immortality in the satires. But even with these two well-tried aids, 'Tam o' Shanter' marks a supreme achievement. It has, indeed, something of an epic quality about it. Its pace—not uniform, but with acceleration, so giving variety and interest—; the way it clings, at every step, to something real and material—the drink, the storm, the earthy images, the piper, the beldam's clothes, Maggie's tail, so that you get the illusion of reality throughout—; the presence of the supernatural lifting a drunken ride to the plane of the extraordinary and incalculable—; all these recall the great art of Homer, who uses much the same means to put across the terrific pursuit of Hector at the climax of the *Iliad*. Homer too framed it in a homely domestic setting—in the opening scene the women doing their washing, as in any Southern town, at the sunlit wells outside Troy, and at the close of the book Andro-machê at her many-coloured loom, the servants busy over the hot water, the Baby Astyanax asleep in his cot (details as realistic as Burns' own) so that, in this frame, that terrific pursuit, like Tam's ride, stands out in high and vivid relief. It is the ordinary here, as in Burns' poem, that lights up and accentuates the extraordinary—and so gives to it, its own reality. And the slow tempo of the domestic scenes changing into the lightning pace of Achilles, Homer's immortal 'fleet of foot'—that variety of pace too is part of Burns' secret in 'Tam o' Shanter'. While the Devil, in the heart of Burns' poem bringing the unseen world in its mystery and magic into contact with the seen—even as do Apollo, Athene, Zeus himself by interesting themselves in the Homeric pursuit—these tremendous unseen Powers give thus a cosmic importance to what otherwise, in each case, might be an every-day episode. 'Tam o' Shanter' may be short—it is in no sense 'small'. Indeed, alone of Burns' works, it possesses a breadth and a scope—the Aristotelian 'magnitude' that is necessary for a master-piece. And—as to its shortness—the poetry of rapid motion, by its nature, can never be long. The twenty-second (the pursuit of Hector) is one of the shortest books of the *Iliad*. Macaulay's 'Armada'—perhaps the best example in English, as distinct from Scots, literature, of this genre—has but seventy-four lines in all, about one-third of 'Tam o' Shanter'. In Shakespeare's *Henry V*, the war-speeches of the King (those fiery, moving speeches 'Once more into the breach, dear friends' Act III, Scene 1, and the glorious St. Crispin's Day one Act IV, Scene 3) at respectively thirty-four and fifty lines, are notably shorter than those allocated to prelates and statesmen. The poetry of rapid motion, to be successful, must be short. . . . It is only in 'Tam o' Shanter' too that Burns shows any awareness of the mystery of life. Something happens to Tam that logic can't explain. There is, after all, an element of strangeness in life which neither the Cottar nor the Beggars, nor anyone else in Burns has run up against. . . . But recognition of this element is a distinguishing mark of—if not an essential for—all great poetry. 'Ah! but a man's reach should exceed his grasp', cries Browning in 'Andrea del Sarto', 'or what's a Heaven for?' And there is certainly no Heaven without it, for the poetry that has the clarity of the multiplication table—like so much, alas! of Burns—will never scale Elysium. 'Tam o' Shanter' alone reaches out—the poem that in technique, in vision and in range, is superior to anything else he wrote. If Burns is to enter the ranks of great poets, it is on 'Tam o' Shanter' he will do it. . . . And why not, it may be asked, as a satirist? For, as a satirist, he is indubitably, in the first rank. That scathing tongue—that wit—that concentration—line after line flailing out like the lash of a whip—that rich, unquenchable humour—above all, his unerring and phenomenal gift of seizing on the universal and not the particular, to satirise—where else, among English satirists, will you find these gifts in equal measure? Here, beyond question, is satire as well done as it ever can be. . . . And yet, a more funda-mental difficulty now interposes—over the genre itself. Can satire, however well done, however brilliant, ever be regarded as great poetry? Horace, one of its first and ablest practitioners, thought not. 'Sermoni propiora' (*Satires*, I. 4) 'nearer common talk', 'this more colloquial stuff' he called it, disclaiming for himself, as a satirist, the title of poet. For poetry you needed 'ingenium' (imaginative genius)—'mens divinior' (thought with a touch of heavenly fire about it) 'os magna sonaturum' (nobility of diction). And for these requirements of poetry he has here behind him the impressive authority of both Plato and Aristotle, on this for once in unison. You can't be a poet, argues classical thought, without these three qualities, none of which are to be found in satire. Poetry, in fine, has to be something out of the common. Whereas satire both had and has to speak the language of the street. And while the language of the street can undoubtedly at times make high poetry—Shakespeare's great *Henry V* speeches use little else 'We few, we happy few, we band of brothers', or Wordsworth's Westminster Bridge' sonnet 'Earth hath not anything to show more fair'—that language, to produce the poetry, must be shot through and transmuted by high, romantic thought, and not, as in satire, be permeated by thought as pedestrian as the words. And if Horace's view—the view of the entire classical world—be correct, satire, as great poetry, is ruled out. And indeed there is something soul-stirring, something quickening, about imaginative poetry, that is never found in satire. A line or two from *Paradise Lost*

'sage he stood
'With Atlantean shoulders fit to bear
'The weight of mightiest monarchies'—

or a line from Shakespeare 'How sweet the moonlight sleeps upon this bank' can stir a pulse that 'Holy Willie's Prayer', for all its brilliance, leaves unmoved,—can open doors, to which satire holds no key. If Burns is to be named as a poet of the first rank, it will not be by the help of satire.

But maybe, by his songs? For it is over his love-songs Burns has been most extravagantly praised. Chiefly, however, by his own countrymen who seldom look at any others. Does not Burns say it all? All, anyhow, you'd think of saying—and every word respectable (the 'Merry Muses' is conveniently left out). Warm too, if not hot. (And no Scotsman wants it hotter.) Warm all through. What more could any woman ask? And Burns' love-songs, good or bad—good, alas! *and* bad—have been flung with equal ardour at every Scots girl's head, ever since he wrote them. 'The best love-songs in the world' avers her swain roundly. 'And', with some surprise, 'for you!' . . . But are they the best? For Scotland has never been much of a love-making country. The great historic lovers belong to other lands, like Dante and Beatrice to Italy, Abelard and Eloïse to France, the romantic Antony and Cleopatra to hard-headed Rome—and in legend too, there are Troy's magical Helen and Paris, Brittany's sad Tristan and Iseult, Greece with her young Hero and Leander, and a mort of others—and, on a family plane, England's comfortable Darby and Joan. Lovers everywhere, it would seem, but no pair, on any plane at all, from Scotland. Neither in history nor in legend— not to speak of fireside talk. Didn't they ever make love in Scotland? . . .

A glance at old Scots literature and history—the background conditioning Burns' view both of women and of love—might make the position clearer. Love-making certainly didn't come first in Scotland. Fighting came first—in Barbour's 'Bruce' and Blind Harry's 'Wallace', derring-do both of them, from end to end. But in the lull after that, in some quiet corner of the fifteenth century, there was laughter over 'Cockelbie's Sow'. Cockelbie was a 'merry man' who sold his sow for three pennies.

> 'The first penny of the thre
> 'For a girle gaif he'—

And low life and rough house notwithstanding (and 'Cockelbie's Sow' is mostly both) the poem had a wide vogue in Scotland. It showed one kind of love. But there is another, close after it, from the other extreme of society, from the King himself. Here is King James I, in his 'Kingis Quair', looking out from his prison window in Windsor Castle (round about 1406 it would be) to see a girl walking down below,

> 'The fairest and the freschest yonge flower
>   'That ever I saw—'

and at that,

'Anon astert (started)
'The blude of all my body to my hert'.

And then

'Only through letting of myn eyen fall
'That suddenly my hert became her thrall
'For ever, of free will. . . .'

Here is Scotland's classic instance of love at first sight. . . . Then, at the turn of the century (c. 1500) a rather surprising person, the learned schoolmaster of Dunfermline, the poet Henryson, looks up from his melancholy 'Testament of Cresseid' and his aureate 'Orpheus and Eurydice' (the sort of stories Scotsmen liked in the fifteenth century) to write that gay, light-hearted pastoral 'Robin and Makyn' of 'boy and girl' love.

'Merry Makyn said him till
'Robin, thou rue on me (pity me)
'I have thee luvit loud and still
'Thir yearis two or three—'

to which the ungallant

'Robin answerit 'By the rude (cross)
'Naething of luve I know'—

and sternly holds to it till, of a sudden, the atmosphere changes

'Abide, abide, thou fair Makyn
'A word for onything
'For all my luve it sall be thine
'Withouten depairting'—

But it's Makyn's turn to toss her head now, and she has the famous couplet

'The man that will nocht when he may
'sall have nocht when he wald'—

and the poem ends with a situation entirely novel for Scotland

'Makyn went hame blyth eneuch
'Attour the holtis hair
        (over the grey moorlands)

'Robin murnit and Makyn lewche
          mourned   laughed
'Scho sang, he sichit sair'—
    She   sighed

with Robin, incredibly enough, left to it! No later Scot—
assuredly not Robert Burns, who liked a girl to come to his
whistle and no bother—would have left it like that. 'Scho sang
—he sichit sair.' What a reprehensible ending, to be sure! . . .
Henryson had an eye to the pretty clothes around him too. He
made an allegory 'The Garmont of Gude Ladies'. Her gown 'weill
ribbon'd with renoun', richly embroidered and 'furrit in fine
fassoun' (fashion), 'her mantill of humilitie, to thole both wind
and weit', so that you can see, as from a Dunfermline window,
this fifteenth-century girl in all her finery. . . . And then Dunbar
—1513—on the eve of Flodden, no recluse like Henryson, but
the Court poet at Holyrood in King James IV's brilliant Renaissance Edinburgh,—Dunbar knew all sorts, but women—it
would appear—better than men. His 'In Prais of Women' (a
topic unique in Scots literature!) and the richly ornate 'Ane
Ballat of Our Lady' show him in serious mood. But he has others
—and better known—as when he wrote that magnificent 'Twa
Mariit Wemen and the Wedo' (also alas! unique in Scots literature) that has so shocked the Victorian critics. (Dunbar not being
printed in full until 1824 and the first critical edition, and that a
foreign one, not till 1896, the critics into whose hands he unfortunately first fell, to his lasting detriment, were necessarily
Victorian.) It is, however, one way of love too. 'Thre gay ladies'
—dazzling blondes all of them—'sa glitterit as the gold war their
glorious gilt tressis'—their lovely faces 'of ferliful fine favour' (of
fairylike beauty)—with their veils and cloaks and fragrant
bouquets—on Midsummer Eve 'mirriest of nichts'—at a table in a
'grene arbour', sit birling the rich wine—with Dunbar himself
listening through the tall scented hawthorn bushes outside. The
setting is superb—beauty and sophistication in every detail. And
it's the beauty of the setting that carries—as it does—the sophistication of their frank Renaissance talk. That 'mirriest of nichts'
is not thrown in for nothing. The whole thing is not meant to be
taken as seriously as it sometimes is. But the questions the lovelies

N

ask, are burning questions still—the sort the B.B.C. themselves might ask in one of their more interesting 'Quiz'es. 'Quhat mirth ye fand in marryage', or 'Gif (if) ye think, had ye chois, that ye wald chois better'. Tho' both horrify the Victorians, there is nothing shocking in either. It is the answers, though, in their unsparing Renaissance detail (as they naturally would be in 1513) that raise the critics' hair. The first one rings like a cri-de-coeur—

'God! gif (if) matrimony were made to mell (last) for ane yeir!'

You can't expect any man to like that, from a girl. But worse is to come.

    'Christ! gif sic ane consuetude war in *this kith haldin*'

(amongst humans, as it is, they point out, among birds) goes on the fair one, warming to it,

      'Then weill war us wemen that ever we war free'

      ·   ·   ·   ·   ·

        'Myself suld be full seemlie in silkis arrayit

      ·   ·   ·   ·   ·

      'I suld at fairis be found new faces to see
      'At playis and at prechingis and pilgrimages great
      (the social occasions, but note the 'playis' first)

      ·   ·   ·   ·   ·

'That I micht chois and be chosen and change quhen me likit'.

She has it all thought out, it seems—the total upsetting of the holy estate of matrimony—and this from a girl of the sixteenth century. Such a thing was never heard of, in Scotland, before or since. But the second girl goes even further.

'Had I that plesand prevelage to part quhen me likit
'To change and aye to choose agane, then, chastite, adieu!

      ·   ·   ·   ·   ·

      'Upon sic materis I muse, at midnicht, full oft.'

And to them both, the experienced 'Wedo' (twice wed) shows a way out—her way out, anyway. With, perhaps, her tongue in her cheek? For Dunbar had a sense of humour.

'Now am I a wedo, I wise and weill am at ease
'I weep as I were woeful, but well is me for ever'

and she goes on to paint a graphic picture, alluring to make their
mouths water, of the ardent throng of suitors that chase after her
now.

'But yet methinks the best bourd (fun) quhen barons and knichtis
'And other bachelours, blithe blooming in youth
'And all my lovers leal,—my lodging pursues
'And fills me wyne wantonly with weilfare and joy.

.   .   .   .   .

'Sum plenis (complains) and sum prayis: sum praisis my beaute
'Sum kisses me—sum clappis me—

.   .   .   .   .

'But with my fair calling, I comfort thaim all

.   .   .   .   .

'To every man in speciall speke I sum wordis
'So wisely and so womanly'—

The 'Wedo' knows her way about. 'This is the legend of my lif'
she concludes, 'tho' Latyne it be nane'. 'Latyne' the poem certainly
is not, in the sense of the conventional—Latin the language of the
formal scholar. But as a diabolically clever skit, wickedly amusing
and light as a soap-bubble, Scotland never saw its like again—
even to the final, mocking question flung at the men, on which
the poem ends

'Of thir thre wanton wiffis, that I haif writtin heir
'Quhilk wald ye waill to your wif, gif ye suld wed ane?'
(choose)

which leaves the critics speechless. And indeed, satire tho' the
poem is, it pre-supposes a freedom of speech and thought (otherwise the satire would have no point) without parallel for Scotswomen in later ages. For these talkers are not outcasts like Burns'
Jolly Beggars (with the morals of outcasts) but rich and beautiful
young women of the very highest rank and sophisticated to the
last degree. And under the guise of satire, there falls a good deal of

social criticism. Dunbar indeed calls his poem a 'Tretis' (treatise).
Is the holy estate of matrimony, that

> 'blist band that bindis so fast
> 'That none undo it a deill (at all) may, bot the deith ane (until one
>   dies)

—as perfect as all that? Here is love as the girls have had it.
And there—is love as they want it. And the torrent of lively
thought—with Dunbar's graphic character-drawing, so that the
'lovelies' stand out clear as if they were caught in amber,—the
brilliance and beauty of the background with its gay flowers, its
Midsummer scents in the green garth—the splendour of the girls'
rich clothes—the sparkle of the wine—all these combine with the
speech and originality of the poem (for the 'Twa', unlike 'The
Jolly Beggars' has no predecessor) to carry the outspoken detail
of their talk, as an integral part of an amazing Renaissance picture.
Furthermore, this kind of love hasn't the heavy atmosphere of
those shadowy corners of Poosie Nansie's, lurid with sensuality.
This is love in the open—Dunbar's open-air setting is not for
nothing. And the words, if the frankest in Scots literature, haven't
a single undertone. There isn't a 'double entendre' (as there is in
so much of Burns) from first to last. 'Free love' then, makes its
appearance in Dunbar—as one of the things high-placed Scotswomen argued about. They were the sort of Scotswomen known
to Don Pedro de Ayala, that observant old Spanish Ambassador
at that very same Court of King James IV at Holyrood of which
Dunbar was the ornament. Writing home to his sovereigns
Ferdinand and Isabella, at their express request for information
about Scotland, this is what Don Pedro has to say of Scotswomen,
'The women are courteous in the extreme. I mention this because
they are *really honest, though very bold. They are absolute mistresses
of their houses* and even of their husbands in all things concerning
the administration of their property, income as well as expendi-
ture. They are very graceful and handsome. They dress much
better than here (in England) and especially as regards the head-
dress (Dunbar's 'curch' which his 'lovelies' wear) which is, I
think, the handsomest in the world!' Fearless, frank and outspoken, dominating their households by their beauty and their
intelligence—these were the Edinburgh women that Dunbar

knew too. And—an extraordinary pendant to it all—a corrobora-
tion, indeed, of women's high status is that, when in 1563, divorce
was first legally given in Scotland (it had been obtainable by round-
about methods in the Church Courts earlier), women achieved it
on the same terms as men—a height not yet reached by most
Continental countries and not by England until Mr. A. P.
Herbert's Act of the 1930's. There is thus a background of solid,
historical truth to Dunbar's talk of 'Free Love'. It was not an
arrow thrown at a venture, a poet's whim. It was, clearly enough,
contemporary talk among the women of his Edinburgh. . . . And
Dunbar knew other sorts of women too, like the rollicking ale-
wife 'Kynde Kittok'

'They threipit that scho (she) deid of thirst and made a gud end

.   .   .   .   .

'And by Sanct Petir, in at the yett, scho stall (stole) privily
'God lukit and saw hir lattin in, and lewche (laughed) his hert
    sair.'

But Heaven, the unattainable—once you have attained it—loses,
alas! its flavour.

'Scho lukit out on a day, and thocht richt lang

.   .   .   .   .

'And out of hevin the hie gait cought the wif gang
'For to get hir ane fresch drink—the aill of hevin wes sour.'

How like a woman, Dunbar thought, to want out of Paradise!
Wasn't it a woman who, even in Paradise, couldn't leave the
Forbidden Tree alone? And it is remarkable how constantly and
with what acute observation of character Dunbar writes of
women. From 'Ane Ballat of Our Lady', and 'In Prais of
Women', to his 'The Twa Mariit Wemen and the Wedo' and
'Kynde Kittok' he ranges from the highest to the lowest, and in
all sorts of moods, from adoration to satire and fun. His men, by
comparison, are the merest shadows. It is his women who have the
individuality, the daring, the charm. For Dunbar, as for Ayala, all
the colour, life, variety of old-time Edinburgh derived from its
women. Yet he didn't write a love-song to one of them. . . . But,

after Dunbar, a change comes over Scots life—a change per-
ceptible even in Lyndesay's *Pleasant Satyre of the Thrie Estates*
(date *c.* 1539). Here women still play an important part, but in
the low-life scenes between the Souter's wife and the Tailor's,
rather than in the high-life scenes. There Dame Chastitie and
Dame Sensualitie, obviously representing women of high degree,
still are people whose word is to be listened to, and who talk, on
an equal footing at least, with men. But they are on the defensive
now. Dunbar's easy naturalness is gone. It isn't only that Lyndesay
is a poorer poet (which he is). His women, both high and low,
are coarser. And the men, like Rex Humanitas and John the
Common Weal are coming to the foreground, to play a much
greater part. For the shadow of the debasing Reformation, to
which so much of the country's artistic poverty is due, was
already hanging over Lyndesay. And there is no surer index to the
health of a community than the status of its women. Any lowering of that status reflects instantly a lowering of the whole tone
of the community. . . . Yet there were still two poets who continued the old Renaissance pre-occupation with women or with
love.—One of them, Alexander Scott (*fl.* 1550 *circa*) is of interest
as Scotland's first lyric poet on love. And indeed, of his 36 poems,
all preserved in the Bannatyne MSS. of 1568, all but four deal with
love only. Subjective love—but not personal. 'To luve unluvit,
it is ane pane', or 'Quha likis to luve', or a longer poem 'The
Roundel of Luve', where one verse goes

> 'Lufe is ane fervent fyre
> 'Kindlet without desyre
> 'Schort plesour, lang displesour'—

Of this reflective, meditative kind of love—a kind only possible in
an ancient and well-established society—Alexander Scott is the
only example in Scots literature. He was interested in women
too, apart from love. One poem is 'Ladies Fair' and here is
another—

> 'I muse and merveillis in my mynd
> 'Quhat way to wryt and put in verss
> 'The quaint conceits of wemenkind'—

Of this old Scotland interested in women that were captivating,

free and elegant, without the remotest shadow of subjection—
Scott is almost the last voice. Last of all is that wise old Scots
judge, Sir Richard Maitland (father of Queen Mary's minister,
Maitland of Lethington) who, in his long life of 90 years (1496-
1586) saw, as he laments, Scotland change from 'mirriness' to
gloom. Here is his delightful 'Satyre on the Toun Ladyes', mocking them for their fine clothes 'And all for newfangilness of
geir'—their 'woven hois of silk, with garteris of ane new maneir',
their gay petticoats 'broderit richt braid', their collars and neck-
laces, their 'velvet hats heich on their heidis', with gold ribbons
and 'coirdit with gold', their 'shoon of velvet' too—and here
they are in Church

'In kirk they are not content of stuillis (stools)
'The sermon when they sit to hear.
'But caryis cuschingis, lyke vain fuillis (fools) (cushions)
'And all for newfangilness of geir'.

And that is the very last glimpse of the gay Edinburgh Renaissance woman. . . . And the last time any notice is taken of
what a Scotswoman wore—until, by an interesting sign of the
times, and of the resurgence of the Scotswoman, the *Scotsman*,
that staid national newspaper of Scotland, has actually, in defer-
ence to public opinion, now begun to print articles on the latest
designs of the great Parisian fashion-houses, side by side with its
articles on politics. Women's dress is once again front-page news
in Scotland! . . . And Sir Richard, well aware, despite his blind-
ness, of all that was happening around him, went on to write
'The Folye of Ane Auld Man's Marryand Ane Young Woman',
—which may well serve to introduce the great Reformer, John
Knox who, at the ripe age of sixty,—for all his thunderings at
Catholic priests for lechery—married a young girl of sixteen, thus
giving point and piquancy to the old French proverb 'Plus ça
change, plus c'est la même chose', or, as Milton phrased it, 'New
presbyter is but old priest writ large'. And with John Knox, the
whole Renaissance view of women crashed to the ground. It is
with John Knox's attack on women, indeed, that Reformation
literature begins. Gone now was the gay light-heartedness of
Henryson's 'Robin and Makyn', the idyllic love at first sight of
the chivalrous King James I, Dunbar's veneration for womanhood

in his 'Ane Ballat of Our Lady', or, at the other extreme, the
sophisticated Free Love of his 'Twa Mariit Wemen and the
Wedo'—a sophistication only possible when the status of women
is at its most assured.[1] For, with the grisly Reformation, sophistication and veneration alike faded out,—and for ever—from Scots
literature. While Scotland's early poets had known all sorts of
love, her writers now were to know but one. For the first thing
the Reformation did, was to degrade and brutalise the position of
women. 'Marriage', gave out the Reformer in his *First Book of
Discipline*, 1561, was 'God's remedy for sin'. Just that! And on that
elevated level of thought Scotland had now to regard it. And then
those luxurious stools and cushions old Sir Richard Maitland had
noticed in the churches.—Stools and cushions indeed! In the
Reformed Kirk women were to sit on the floor, and by themselves (separate, as in a synagogue), while, enthroned over the
way, their lords and masters—and they alone—sat on forms.
You could see at a glance, who mattered now. . . . On the spiritual
side, the declension was just as steep. By the seventeenth-century
Scotland had lost her Magnificat, that most ancient of all the
Church's hymns and sung for over a thousand years in every
church in Christendom, and—what mattered much more now
—every word of it in Holy Writ. But—a Woman sang it. And
what was Holy Writ (the Reformers' professed sole guide!)
against that? The Magnificat had to go. And to this day it has
never returned to any Presbyterian Kirk in Scotland. Its going
was, of course, only a symbol, but the cutting out of all mention
of the Blessed Virgin in a Kirk that still called itself Christian, and
the total suppression of Christmas (the feast of the Mother and the
Babe) could not but have the gravest consequences for the
national life—leaving, as they did, no pure ideal for the nation to
cherish. And however little the Renaissance Scot may have
regarded the ideal, he knew that it was there. The measure of his
misconduct was the measure of his falling off from it. But now

[1] Like Noel Coward's 'Fallen Angels' of our own day, which, of a sophistication equal to Dunbar's 'Twa', is possible now, but would have been quite
unthinkable in the reign of Queen Victoria, when Tennyson was writing—
and with acceptance—in Locksley Hall—

'Woman is the lesser man and all thy passions, matched with mine
'Are as moonlight unto sunlight, and as water unto wine.'

there was no such standard—nothing in womanhood to revere. The ideal was gone. . . . And not the ideal only. For the new Kirk, unlike the Old Church, banished women altogether from any share in her offices. No learned Abbesses, like St. Hilda at Whitby, no administrative Prioresses, no nuns to be 'Little Sisters of the Poor'—no religious outlet whatever for a woman, was visualised by the new order. Henceforward woman's sole duty, was—listening to the men! And tho' this spiritual loss is not at first the most obvious, its roots struck the deepest. In its ultimate effect on Scots life and art it proved, without a doubt, the most calamitous, as it was the most enduring. . . . Materially, however, the degradation was at once obvious enough. John Knox saw to that,—tho', by an irony of fate, it is not to the dull age he inaugurated that, in literature, he belongs, but to the brilliant age he ruined. For the qualities that 'make' him in his famous *History of the Reformation*—the vivid, pictorial style, the interest in women, the eye for graphic detail (native to Scots literature since 'Cockelbie's Sow') the rich humour—these are all Renaissance, and not 'Reformed' qualities. To the Reformation belong only the Reformer's scurrilous tongue, and the filthy imagination that inspired it—qualities apparent throughout his work, and personal, it would seem, to himself. . . . But in his *History* it is the Queen who, like many Renaissance women, for wit and intelligence—not to speak of tolerance—far outshines the men. What is still more odd, it is round the Queen—and not the theology!—Knox weaves his whole story, spotlighting the interviews with her, the unforgettable picture of her, robed and crowned, riding down the Canongate on those May mornings in 1563 'Such stinking pride of women, as was seen at that Parliament, was never seen before in Scotland. Three sundry days the Queen rode to the Tolbooth',—and his glimpse of the four Maries in the antechamber in Holyrood, 'all this gay gear . . . gold, garnishing and targetting (tassels), pearls and precious stones'—. The whole mise-en-scène, in fine, of the History, derives from the full tradition of the Renaissance ever alive to beauty and wit, to graphic incident and to lively humour. It is not at all in the tradition of the sour and sulky Reformation, blind to all of it. No Reformer after Knox ever spoke of a woman as an equal—let alone, a possible superior. And none ever deigned to notice so much as a ribbon she wore. . . . But it was with his notorious *First Blast of the Trumpet Against the Monstrous Regiment of Women* that Knox in 1551 opened the attack. Ostensibly only against queens, the *Blast* in reality signposted the whole Reformation attitude to women. Nature, fulminated the Reformer, had 'intended the female sex for subjection'. And not only Nature, but Moses— a conjunction almost irresistible. And when you add to that, what St. Paul thought about it all, it became 'a law divine'. Further-more, Calvin—and what Pope as infallible as Calvin now?— Calvin was on Knox's side too. Women to rule? 'A deviation' Calvin called it, 'from the original and proper order of nature, and to be ranked, no less than slavery, among the punishments consequent on the fall of man'. Knox, thus fortified, in the shattering opening sentence of his *Blast*, put it with some vehem-ence, 'That a woman should bear rule, superiority, dominion or empire, above any realm, nation or city, is repugnant to Nature, contumely to God,—a thing most contrarious to His revealed will and approved ordinance; and finally it is the subversion of all equity and justice'. . . . Of Knox's own conception of justice, Scotland was soon to have startling evidence, for, as early as 1563 (the Reformation was but in 1560!) 'The Scottish Parlia-ment, by statute, for which John Knox was a chief agitator, formally constituted witchcraft and dealing with witches, a capital offence'. Did not Moses enjoin it? 'Thou shalt not suffer a witch to live' (Exod. xxii.18). What could be more explicit? And the Kirk, Moses' faithful disciple, went to it with a will. Knox's statute, as quoted in Erskine's *Institutes*, p. 706, is, if anything, more comprehensive than Moses. 'That all who used witchcraft, sorcery, necromancy, or pretended skill therein, and all consulters of witches and sorcerers should be punished capitally'. So the fires were lit—from Caithness to the Solway—those fires that raged for close on 200 years—as the *Diurnal of Occurrents* and Pitcairn's *Criminal Trials* monotonously record. You could burn any woman now—preferably the clever ones, whom Knox hated most. But also the beautiful ones, like Lady Glamis presently on the Castle Esplanade. And the poor, insignificant ones—that Andrew Lang, surveying the scene with open horror, says were the vast majority—anywhere and everywhere. 'For 10 lodds coal to burn the witches'—'for a tar barrel'—'for towes' (ropes) 'for

20 lodds peats to burn the witches'—'Brunt in Edinbruche for a witch'—so the Kirk Session records passim. And there were the torturers to pay before that. The men 'six to watch everie nicht and twa everie day, tyme aboot in order', to keep the witches awake, night after night, until they should confess,—and the expert 'prickers', like the infamous John Kincaid, to prick them continually the while, in those parts of the body (Kincaid knew) which hurt the most—or to 'hing them up' by the thumbs—or the toes—. Had Moses thought of all that? It was all very expensive. But the Kirk indefatigably went on with her holy work —until, in the first forty years of her supremacy, she established the triumphant record, unequalled in Europe, of having burnt alive at the stake, after excruciating torture, no fewer than 8,000 souls—a total never even approached by the cooler fires of the Inquisition. And that was only as yet the year 1600. The fires went on, illuminating all Scotland—the only light there was!—from Caithness to the Solway all through the ghastly seventeenth century and the first half of the eighteenth. And it was not till 1736 that a humane Parliament at Westminster—not, be it noted, in 'reformed' Edinburgh which, so long as there was a Scots Parliament, wouldn't hear of it—revoked at long last the penal statutes against the witches. Not, however, without the accompaniment of howls of Scottish protest reverberating until 1743 when the Original Seceders—one of the narrower Presbyterian sects—put it on record that 'The penal statutes against witches have been repealed by the Parliament, contrary to the express law of God'. So that the Kirk well earned the scathing, but not unjustified tribute of Mr. Buckle, the brilliant author of the *History of Civilisation*, that the world had only 'seen the Inquisition in its full glory, twice, once in Spain and once in Scotland'. Though the Inquisition in Spain was braver—It, at least, burned men. . . . Against this atrocious and horrifying behaviour, there had been, of course, protests. A German Jesuit 'nearly a century before Calvinist Scotland ceased to burn witches', so Mr. David Ogg points out, the learned Oxford historian of the Reformation (p. 69) 'had already written an eloquent plea for the suppression of the practice'. As if a Jesuit could have anything to teach John Knox's Scotland! The fires only flamed the hotter. . . . But even in primitive Scotland there were critical voices raised. Cromwell's

hard-bitten troopers, for example, occupying the country in
1652, shrank back appalled, from what they saw. Was it right to
hang women up by the heels, whip them, and place lighted
candles beneath their toes and in their mouths? 'These', explains
Mr. Andrew Lang drily, 'appear to have been the usual methods of
extorting confessions'. But the English judges to whom the
troopers appealed, did not think it right. They, indeed, 'ordered
the minister, sheriff and tormentors to be found out, and to have
an account of the ground of their cruelty'. And, ten years later,
even the Scots Privy Council was moved to intervene. It orders
the arrest of one John Ramsay 'an ordinary pricker of witches,
to answer for the pricking of Margaret Tait, who immediately
thereafter died'. (*P.C. Reg.*, p. 198). And went on to issue an Act
(April 10, 1662) 'We, being certainly informed that a great many
persons have been apprehended and hurried to prison, pricked,
tortured and abused, under suspicion of witchcraft, forbid any
man, without legal warrant, to arrest anyone on this charge'.
Furthermore, persons legally arrested are to be tried 'without any
pricking or torture, but by order'. But what cared the Kirk for
the Privy Council? Erastianism this was! Didn't all Scotland
know the Kirk was above the State? The fires went on,—and
the torture too. Then even Bluidy Mackenzie, the King's Advocate (and no soft heart, as the Covenanters knew), appointed
now to try the so-called witches, had more than he could thole.
Denouncing the Kirk's 'prickers' as 'villainous cheats' and the
'confessions' as 'worthless', 'I know for certain' he says 'that most
of all that were ever taken, were tormented, and this usage the
ground of all their confessions'. Whereupon the Kirk, in the
person of that great Covenanter, the blessed Mr. Cargill, forth-
with excommunicated him. 'For pitying witches'—one of the
many counts they found against him. Tho' Fergusson, interest-
ingly enough, at the dawn of the New Age, takes the opposite
view—

> 'Yonder's the tomb of wise Mackenzie fam'd,
> 'Whase laws rebellious bigotry reclaim'd
> 'Freed the hail land frae Covenanting fools
> 'Wha erst hae fash'd us wi' unnumber'd dools'—
>   (Fergusson, 'The Ghaists'.)

And the fires went on. And as late as 1727—little more that thirty years before Burns was born—they burnt a poor old woman in a pitch barrel at Dornoch, Sutherland, 'a witch'— and in Mauchline, Burns' own parish, three years after his death, delated another. Delated, but—— The ministers were baulked of their prey. The Kirk had now—it was 1799—been forbidden to light her fires. . . . So that, for close on 200 years of 'Reformed' Scotland, there can hardly have been a woman who did not, in imagination, at one time or another, feel the hot breath of the flames steal up her neck. Over any sickbed, it might be, with someone at death's door—and you—could you cure him? But that was as dangerous as if he died. For that elder watching you, 'Healing by the Black Art' he'd cry, or 'Consorting with the Devil', and that dread, final shriek 'A witch'! The fires were near. . . . And then there was fornication—the Kirk's well-known and favourite charge—of which no woman was ever adjudged innocent. What was innocence? The Kirk had never heard of it. In her Session Records, teeming with fornications, the word does not occur. 'Contumacious in not avowing guilt', that's what you were. So, the jougs, the pillory, or—best of all—the cutty-stool in front of the crowded Sabbath congregation. That's where all the men could see you! . . . In 'Reformed' Scotland, John Knox's wish had been carried out to the letter. The women were fully degraded now. But, as even an all-powerful Kirk couldn't kill love, it sprang up in an unlooked-for place—not, of course, in a printed book, which the Kirk could, and would, have burnt— but on the lips of the Borderers, where the ministers would never hear it. Here—from the sixteenth century on, just after the Reformation—rose Scotland's famous ballad-poetry, with gems like 'Clerk Saunders', or the poignant 'Lowlands of Holland'. For here, in the wild Borders, as poor Thomas Boston, the minister of Ettrick, later testified, the Kirk's writ did not run. In 1709 'I have been most discouraged', mourns Thomas, 'with respect to my parish a long time'. In 1711 it was worse, 'I have a weary task of my work in this parish'. And by 1727 Ettrick had got out-of-hand altogether. 'A horse-race'—to think of it! 'appointed to be just on the Monday before (Sacrament)'.— a horse-race 'to which many were invited (it was May). I . . . told them the surprising indecency of it . . . got no answer but that

they knew not if it could be got diverted.' But, with a spirit like
that, and to the thrill of the galloping horses, the love-songs
flourished so that there grew up that splendid harvest of 'Border
minstrelsy' that awaited the garnering in the next century by
Sir Walter Scott. . . . And in these Border love-songs one salient
fact emerges. There were no downtrodden women here.

> 'Bell, my wife, she lo'es na strife
> 'But she would guide me if she can!
> 'And to maintain an easy life
> 'I aft maun yield, tho' I'm guidman'—

The sprightly author of that ballad 'Tak' your auld cloak about
ye' does not seem to have heard of John Knox. Nor has an even
earlier one, of Charles I's time (from a MS. in the British Museum,
published in Ritson's *Scottish Songs*, 1794) where, to his irate
'Dame, do the thing whilk I desire', the dame, no whit abashed,
retorts

> 'Nay, lo you luik sae like a gowke
> 'I'll do but what I list mysell'—

In Ettrick and the Borders it would not appear that the women,
as in Reformed Edinburgh, sat on the floor. No woman, doomed
to the floor, would answer back like that. And so the richest
ballad-poetry the world has ever known, derives from the un-
conquered Borders. As do the old Highland love-songs from the
only other part of Scotland that escaped the Reformation—
from Uist and Barra in the Outer Isles and such pockets of the
Western Highlands as the Kirk's fell power did not reach. Here
the Gaelic folk-songs survived, secure and safe. . . . But elsewhere,
in Reformed Edinburgh for instance, a citizen who might want,
as had done the old poet Henryson, to 'beik' him over the fire
with a book on a chilly night, need never turn now to things like
'Orpheus and Eurydice' to waft him away from everyday affairs
—(Who were these people anyway? This new Scotland had never
heard of them.) It would be to sorry stuff like *A Comfortable
Treatise on Justification*—that masterpiece of Knox's friend, Master
Henry Balnaves of Halhill—he'd have to hie him now—and make
what he could out of that!

So, by the mid-eighteenth century, when the iron grip of the

Kirk was beginning to relax, and the old pre-Reformation love-songs beginning to be published in the many collections like *The Lark*, no one could remember a time when woman had been independent, or indeed anything but a chattel. And the only kind of love-song you could write to a woman like that, was the kind Burns wrote—for most of his life—for a kiss and an embrace, and then off to someone else to-morrow. With no spiritual ideal to inform it, the Calvinist ideology of women had penetrated too deep. It ran now in the very life-blood of the nation. So that Scott, brought up in a strict Presbyterian household could no more write a love-scene than fly. What did one say in it? Something perhaps like the great Lord Braxfield, on the historic occasion when his Lordship knocked at his chosen one's door, 'I'm lookin' for a wife, Lizzie. An' I think ye'll dae. Let me ken —aff or on—the morn.' To the point, certainly. Yet it didn't sound right for a love-scene either? Not, perhaps, as Shakespeare would have done it, in those scenes with Benedick and Beatrice —or Rosalind—. And Scott left the love-scenes out. As did Stevenson, brought up in an even stricter Presbyterian household. If love there was, it should be off-stage. As it was in real life. Nobody had ever seen a Calvinist husband making love to his own wife—still less, to anybody else's. Tho' they did both, no doubt, in heathen France or even in easy-going England. The love-motif was strong there. Thackeray's Becky Sharp—his Beatrix Esmond too—Later, Thomas Hardy's Tess. English literature—even modern English literature—was full of out-standing women. But not Scots. It was only on the stable-level— the love-level Calvinism knew—that Scots literature now could do it at all, as in Grassic Gibbon's *Sunset Song* full of little else. Even to-day the 'dead hand' holds. Love on the gay level—the 'Robin and Makyn' level, has not come back. That delicious 'Tea for Two' light as lemonade, in *No, No, Nanette* was written by an Englishman—and an Oxford don at that. There is no parallel in Scotland. . . . And a glance at the sister-art of portraiture, that so faithfully reflects the social life of a country, tells the same melancholy tale. The superb elegance of Margaret of Denmark —James III's Queen—in that Trinity College altar-piece now in the National Gallery in Edinburgh—strikes the eye at once. The cut and line of her magnificent dress, as of the finest Parisian 'haute couture', with not an otiose ornament anywhere—the poise and bearing of the Queen herself, completely unself-conscious and alive with intelligence—these show the pre-Reformation Scotswoman at her splendid best. And in the next room sit Raeburn's women—the women Scott knew—cluttered up with clothes—shapeless masses of shawls and hoods and scarves and voluminous heavy skirts—clothes everywhere and with no line, no cut,—and no intelligence! Not the sort of women to endow a College, like the enlightened Lady Devorgilla, John Balliol's famous wife—and foundress, as early as the fourteenth century, of the still more famous Balliol College, Oxford. Or to found a Hospital, as did Mary of Gueldres, James II's Queen, the beneficent foundress of that fifteenth-century Trinity College Hospital in Edinburgh, that the boorish Victorians pulled down. College or Hospital—what did Raeburn's women know of either? Not the sort of women that Scott or anybody else, would write a love-scene about.

It is against that national background that one must consider Burns' love-songs. For the main fact about Burns himself is that, hate Calvinism as he undoubtedly did, he was himself the product of it—a Calvinist through and through. No man can escape from heredity and environment and both, in his case, unluckily pulled the same way. And tho' it is to intellectual Calvinism, in his satires and in 'Tam o' Shanter', that he owes his best work, yet —when it comes to his songs—it is not so. Here in large measure the influence worked against him. For Calvinism and love are contradictions in terms. 'I like a mild and lukewarm zeal in love', proclaimed Scotland's first post-Reformation poet, the bland Sir Robert Ayton (1570-1638), 'altho' I do not like it in devotion.' And 'mild and lukewarm' the zeal continued to be, even up to Allan Ramsay's time. If Burns was to be a great love-poet, he must find inspiration elsewhere. The Dionysiac element in the Highland tunes supplied it. But, at its full strength in innumerable Highland bards this had produced—at best—an extravagant meandering that evaporated as quickly as the froth of champagne —at worst—a deal of rant. Burns' best songs never meander and in his love-songs there is no rant. For the strong native streak of Calvinism in himself pruned the Highland extravagance and cut out the rant. In his best songs. But the flesh could not be held in

check for ever and the others—the vast majority—ask for but one
night of love, like the popular German music-hall ditty

'Nur eine Nacht soll'st du mir gehören
'Bis zum Morgenlicht'

and rank no higher than that. 'The mild and lukewarm zeal',
so admirable to the earth-bound eyes of the Presbyterian Kirk,
carries you no further. . . . For, to attain international standard,
a love-song must show intensity of passion. Even the sparkle of
momentary ardour Burns so often shows, will not do. Passion
here must burn white with incandescent flame. And not physical
passion only. Mind too is involved. And up to the hilt. For it is
this intellectual element which transmutes and colours the baser
sensual one, so that the whole song glows and radiates with the
perennial beauty of a fine-cut gem. But, in the love Burns heard
of, Sunday after Sunday—the love he saw at the Holy Fairs—
in the fumes of Poosie Nansie's—there was nothing perennial at
all. He saw it somewhere, nevertheless—at a fireside in Ayrshire
—a love that burned clear and deep, with the grossness burnt out
of it. And it is somewhat odd that love like that should have
inspired him, hot-blooded as he was. But it did. It was the artist
in him that responded to it. For there is nothing out-of-tune in
'John Anderson, my jo', but a depth of real feeling (the quality
which, above all others, he found hardest to get) throbbing in
every line. And, matching the emotion, are the words, simple and
noble—no horrors here like that prosaic 'sever' of 'Ae Fond Kiss'.
The verses, alight with simile and metaphor 'like the raven'
'like the snaw', 'clomb the hill' 'totter down' stir the imagination,
as these figures invariably do, at every step. And then, what skill
in the presentation! It is the wife who sings it. And not the
husband, with his Scots incapacity for emotional speech. But the
wife, with a studied restraint. Just a touch, about the hair gone
grey—one look-back at life, the hill and soon the foot of it—
no endearments but one, that simple and recurrent 'my jo' beat-
ing the thought in, and to be the last thought she leaves with you.
In a touch or two like these—Burns is never more Impressionist
than here—the whole song is across. Its subtle simplicity,—the
reserves of emotion—fun, pathos, love—it holds in leash; its
power to suggest so much more than it says,—its masterly brevity

o

—these all mark it with the authentic quality of a masterpiece. Here Burns has written, at any level, one of the great love-songs of the world. . . . As perhaps he has in 'My Love is like a Red Red Rose'. A man's song this and one of actual, contemporary passion. In this sphere Burns has more competition. Others, of premier rank, have blazed the trail here. But, as in 'John Anderson' it is the similes and metaphors—those glorious figures which, in his ordinary writing, are so rare—that lift and carry the song, as on wings of fire. The direct avowals 'Sae deep in luve am I', and 'I will luve thee still, my luve' occur, significantly enough, both in the second verse and after a build-up, and again in one line of the third. But the main emphasis is thrown on the similes. All the colour of the song derives from them. But perhaps there is just enough passion to suggest sincerity? The poet is not too much interested in his lovely similes? The fact that not one single line of this song is of the poet's original composition and that everything is taken from old songs, marks it out only as the more consummate achievement. He has, indeed, interposed a word here and there—altered this or that—but the result is something wholly new,—a song absolutely and entirely his own. Nothing Burns ever wrote, gives more convincing testimony to his genius. But —has he then produced a burning love-song? To be set alongside things like Catullus' 'Odi et Amo', or Sappho's φαίνεταί μοι κῆνος. Like all Scots of his day, Burns hedges at passion. Animal feeling? Yes, as much as you like—but lifelong, burning passion such as Antony felt for Cleopatra, that 'serpent of old Nile', or Catullus for Lesbia, or Sappho for her lover? Passion of that quality was unknown to him. So, if he could not feel it, he borrowed it here from those who could—those old anonymous love-songs that were Scotland's lost heritage. And whether the patchwork is cleverly enough done in 'The Red Red Rose' so that, with the words, he has carried the passion over too, is a moot point. His countrymen have thought it was. . . . But, if you can only regard a woman from the physical standpoint—which, thanks to Calvinism, was the only way Burns ever knew (in this, like the vast majority of his countrymen then) you are not going to be able to write love-songs to her, however great an artist you are, that will compare with the best work of those who regard her as their equal and who see in her much more than an animal.

Passion on a level like that, is the flame that illumines the best
love-songs. Maybe Burns can suggest it—for a moment—in 'The
Red Red Rose', when he is not busy distracting your attention
from it by his wealth of similes? And if it's not in 'The Red Red
Rose', it is nowhere—and M. Angellier, that acutest of French
critics is speaking the truth when he asserts flatly Burns never was
in love. As Mr. Hilton Brown too may perhaps have conjectured,
wondering why none of the fine ladies Burns met in Edinburgh
—or, for that matter, in Dumfriesshire, Maria Riddell among
them—ever fell in love with him. The only folk who did were the
barmaids and the village girls—and the servant lasses of the
Capital. The explanation is simplicity itself. The fine ladies knew
in a second (nothing is easier to sense) the valuation Robin was
putting on them, and froze at once. The barmaids, knowing no
other, liked it. Clarinda knew it too—and more than half-liked it
—and out of that affair Burns drew enough inspiration for the
last of his great love-songs, 'Ae Fond Kiss', the most personal, as it
is the most sophisticated, of them all. It is the parting in it, rather
than the love, that forms its main idea. And parting is always an
emotional business. You get the emotion ready-made here. The
poet doesn't have to work it up—which suited Burns admirably,
slow as he always was at deep feeling. Parting, moreover, was
something of which, by now, he had great experience (what with
Mary and Jean and the rest) so that, in 'Ae Fond Kiss' he distils
from it—with expert hand—the very last thrill. The rapture and
the misery—Sappho's immortal 'bitter-sweet'—everything that
can be got out of a kiss—a long, long kiss—Burns here gets. But
the love—where is it? . . . For this is a song of Farewell. And if
Farewell has to be said, it could hardly be better said—or with
more finality. Its make-up too is different. Here there are no
similes, and only two metaphors ('Star of Hope' and 'Despair
Benights') both clichés. Burns is using no imagination here. But,
more than in any other song, verbs. His head is never clearer.
Parting it is to be—parting all through—from the first line to
the last. . . . Other poets, one remembers, when faced with the
same crisis, do not acquiesce so readily. Michael Drayton's fine
sonnet, for instance, 'Since there's no help, come let us kiss
and part' (and sonnets are calmer than songs) ends on a wild note
of hope

'Now, if thou would'st, when all have given him over
'From death to life thou might'st him yet recover'.

And even the Victorian Browning's 'Last Ride Together', on a sudden dramatic cry

'What if we still ride on, we two
'With life for ever old, yet new'—

Young Lochinvar would never have sung 'Ae Fond Kiss (that 'Farewell' now—over and over! Nothing could be more definite). But then, 'Ae Fond Kiss' is not a young man's song. And Burns is firm. He does not ask for second thoughts. He does not ask at all. He just tells. 'Despair' or no, this is the end. And if Shakespeare has it that 'Love's not Time's fool' (Sonnet 116) and

'Love alters not with his brief hours and weeks
'But bears it out even to the edge of doom'

(Sonnet 116)

—well, Burns never saw it that way. He saw it, indeed, quite differently. For him the essence of love was that it did change.

'The sweetest hours that e'er I spent
'Were spent amang the lasses, O.'

Shakespeare couldn't have written that. . . . And one of these hours,—the sweetest of them all—was undoubtedly the hour of 'Ae Fond Kiss'. There was so much in that hour to delight him —all the joy of the Flesh, concentrated and held in that last, voluptuous kiss,—and then (what Burns could never be really happy without) that sense of moral rectitude (Clarinda after all was a married woman) he got from leaving her. As in 'Tam o' Shanter', here the two worlds meet. And Burns is on the right road again—or will be, soon—. Was there not parting in every line? In every breath?—to-morrow. But now—this heavenly now—(Burns' Heaven was always now) here was this complete and utter bliss. 'Ae fond kiss—and then we sever'. The two worlds meet. Of this mood—and it is a common human mood—Burns is surely the most brilliant of all interpreters. But it is a mood merely. Not love, as the great poets know it. . . . For it is actual and life-long passion the great love-songs of the world set out to convey.

Like Catullus' magnificent 'Vivamus, mea Lesbia atque amemus', where life and love are, on this high plane, equated. Burns never goes as far as that. Life at all times held for him, as for most Scots, a great deal more than love. And even if one makes allowance here for nationality,—admitting that an Italian song would naturally be hotter than Scots—yet Catullus gets something into his brief love-song (briefer than any of Burns') that Burns never does—a poignant sense of the mystery of life—

> 'Soles occidere et redire possunt,
> 'Nobis cum semel occidit brevis lux.
> 'Nox est perpetua una dormienda'[1]

lifting the thought from what happens to just two people, into the context of all humanity, and setting human love, as it were, in relief against mortality. Burns, even in 'The Red Red Rose' never sees love in this way. He isn't even present with her in 'The Red Red Rose', when passion might be heightened. She is in the next room, or somewhere else. She is just a thought in his mind. Yet Tennyson, who chooses the same setting (Maud off-stage) for his exquisite 'Come into the garden, Maud', gets far more excitement into it than Burns.

> 'She is coming, my dove, my dear
> 'She is coming, my life, my fate—'

Burns never gets worked up like that. And Sappho, into the most vivid of her love-songs weaves a sense of the unattainable—the apple in the highest bough that the reapers couldn't reach. But Burns had no sense of the unattainable—in love or in life. He could always get the girl—or a girl—he wanted. His songs, like all his other work, hold fast to the common earth. . . . So that, in the light of those,—Sappho, Catullus, the English Donne—who have written what are among the greatest love-songs in the world, there is something lacking in Burns. It is not merely the lack of true passion, in which all these surpass him,—altho' heat of passion would seem to be a prime necessity and of the first importance, for a love-song. And in ardour and flame of passion

[1] Suns that set, can rise again
But we,—once our brief light is out
It's night for us—one long, unbroken night for sleep.

it is undoubtedly true that Burns falls short of all these. Yet Scotland, since the Reformation, is not a country that finds passion easy of utterance, nor approves of it much when heard. As far as passion goes, Burns satisfies and has always satisfied, his countrymen. . . . But it is on a graver count, more vital to his quality as an artist that he definitely takes lower rank. The very greatest love-songs, as of these, reach out to something more than passion—to something higher, nobler, more divine. Catullus, to the mysterious terms on which mortal life is held,—Sappho to the infinite heights one can only look up to, but never reach,—the intellectual Donne to the subtle analysis of the 'why's' and 'wherefore's' of it, of the ecstasy and the depths. There is a fullness and a completeness of outlook, an integrating of passion at its very height, with the rest of human life—that is absent from Burns, and that makes his love-songs, good as they are, shallow in comparison with the others. Like the texture of his other work, they are too superficial. They do not see enough in love. Originality and sweep of thought are as necessary to the great love-song, as profundity of feeling. And in his view of love, Burns' intellect was never involved. As a poet of love, that is his final condemnation.

Tho' this derives, not so much from any personal defect in Burns himself, as from the heredity and environment to which he was subjected. Calvinism, by its rigidly authoritarian outlook (was not John Knox 'of the Privy Council of God'?) is not a faith that tolerates, far less encourages, freedom of thought. And Calvinism it was that for the last two centuries had dominated Scotland. To her, all knowledge was static, and all was hers alone. Full and final revelation had been made to Calvin only. Her textbook, therefore, the Shorter Catechism, in all its theological intransigeance, she drummed into the youth of Scotland by a process of parrot-like repetition—the only process, given her premises, open to her—like the multiplication table that Catechism usually bore on its cover, and of precisely the same order of validity. Did not both fall into the same category of unquestionables? But parrot-like repetition, alas! is the very antithesis of the true Socratic method of quickening the mind—that vivifying 'Question and Cross-Question' that roused into scintillating life, every intellect in fifth-century Athens, and put civilisation for

all time in Athens' debt. Parrot-like repetition, far from quickening, only deadens the mind. Even as Socrates himself, 'the
master of them that teach',—in Dante's vibrant phrase—is the
antithesis of Calvin. And—most fatal of all—Ayrshire and the
West Country, into which Burns was born and bred, were and
for long had been, the very heart and hotbed of Scottish Calvinism. Over in Edinburgh—a liberal-minded Capital—the air blew
freer, so that a minister like the bold 'Jupiter' Carlyle could even,
in defiance of his Presbytery, applaud a play in the Canongate
theatre—and that, as early as 1756, three years before Burns was
born. While up in chilly Aberdeen, a century before that,—
as that notable Calvinist, Samuel Rutherfurd testified, banished
there in 1636—the air blew positively cold. 'The Lord hath
brought me to Aberdeen', mourned Mr. Samuel, 'where I see
God in few'. You could think in Aberdeen. . . . But it was into
narrow Ayrshire Burns was born, into an air fetid with Calvinism. Over his porridge he heard of a God—defined in the *Shorter
Catechism*, as not in the Fourth Evangelist—without one word of
His property of love. On the contrary, it was 'the wrath and curse
of God'—a phrase unknown to the New Testament—that was
sown broadcast in the Shorter Catechism. It was not in such an
atmosphere of shackled thought and horrifying dogma that songs
of love to either God or man, could well be written. . . . For a
love-song divine or human, as all history goes to show, demands,
as a prerequisite for its writing, a certain liberty of the human
spirit. In the Great Age of Greece, it is from Athens and the
Ionian Isles, where intellect ranged sun-free, that the great love-
songs rise. Sappho's songs front Lesbos, the dithyrambs of
Simonides from Athens. From Sparta, the State-controlled, rise
none. At Rome, again, it is the uncensored freedom of the
Republic produced the love-songs of Catullus,—not the later
Imperial Rome of the 'delatores'. Nearer at hand, the sonnets of
Shakespeare and the love-songs of the Cavaliers, like the noble
hymns of George Herbert, rise from an England rejoicing in a
humane Anglicanism that had never known the constraint of
Calvin. Love and Liberty go together. . . . Even on a lower level,
the same rule holds. That Bohemianism that connotes freedom
from all convention, connotes in the same breath the gaiety of
love-songs light as gossamer, the seductive music of a Strauss

waltz under the blue Vienna sky, things like the fascination of Franz Lehar's

> 'Velia, Velia, witch of the wood,
> 'Would I not die for you, dear, if I could'—

the splendour of Paris nights in the Bois, with echoes of *Mignon* or *La Bohême*. Love and Liberty go together. . . . Or again, on the divine level, the great Mediaeval hymns of rapt devotion like Abelard's 'O Quanta Qualia' or St. Thomas Aquinas 'Lauda, Sion, Salvatorem' spring from the Catholic tradition of Divine Love, free to all. Calvinism, with its emphasis on 'wrath and curse' has produced none. Or in painting, the love of Mother and Child, on any level, derives from that old tradition too. All the Madonnas —the great Raphaels and Bellini's that have so enriched Art— are by Catholics. Tho' here, in the freedom of a new Scots Renaissance untrammelled by the Kirk, the Glasgow School in Scotland is, at long last, painting mother-love now. Archibald McGlashan's studies of Mother and Child hang in Scots galleries to-day. Love and Liberty go together.

Looking back, then, it seems inescapably true that the hand that framed the *First Book of Discipline* in 1561, enchaining the mind, signed the death-warrant of great art in Scotland. For great art has never been merely a question of personal gifts. Of these Burns had his full share. But there must also be the right atmosphere in which these gifts may grow and flower—an atmosphere where everything under the sun may be freely talked of and discussed, instead of the closed shop prescribed by the Reformer. 'All interpretation disagreeing from the principles of our faith . . . is to be rejected' (*First Book of Discipline*). 'Lest, of a profitable exercise (*sc.* reading the Scriptures) might arise debate and strife, curious, peregrine and unprofitable questions are to be avoided' (*First Book of Discipline*). But debate and strife, and not less, discussion of these same 'curious, peregrine and unprofitable questions' so hateful to the Reformer, are the very soil on which great art is nurtured. By opening the windows of the soul wide to new thought, they provide pabulum for the intellect— means by which it can grow and develop—and thereafter, an informed audience to demand and appreciate the work of the artist. Like the audience which uniquely (for it has never happened

again) at the brilliant close of the free eighteenth century, de-
manded and achieved the *Edinburgh Review*. But the Kirk, alas!
recovered, and the *Edinburgh Review* and its audience alike faded
out. . . . 'Curious, peregrine and unprofitable questions'—had
Burns been trained to use his mind on these, he might well have
climbed that Parnassus, at whose foot he was destined always to
remain. . . . And not only the right atmosphere is necessary.
There is the further requisite of the right audience. No man can
play to an empty house. And if the theatre asks only for low
comedy, the Shakespearian actor will not emerge. And that 'mild
and lukewarm zeal in love', the viewing of marriage as 'God's
remedy for sin'—base ideals like these inculcated into a nation—
rule out inevitably any appearance of the starry love-song that is
to set the world on fire. Nor—with these, the accepted ideals of
Calvinism and received throughout the land—will there arise any
of those glowing Epithalamia, like Spenser's proud poem—in
Saintsbury's phrase 'that union of intellectual and sensual rapture'[1]
—which is the glory of Elizabethan literature, or like Catullus'
'On the Marriage of Vinia and Manlius' which is, equally, the
glory of Rome. There are no Epithalamia in Scotland. For if it is
true that a country gets the government it deserves, it is most
certainly true that it gets the art. And in Burns' time there was no
audience in Scotland—there is probably not much of an audience
now—that asks for anything better than what Burns gives them.
'The best love-songs in the world', so, roundly, any Scotsman
still to any girl. And—for Scotland is still in large measure John
Knox's country—who is she to say that a man doesn't know?

[1] Saintsbury, *History of English Literature*, p. 268.

CHAPTER II

IS BURNS A NATIONAL POET?

AND HOW FAR DO his songs—or his work in general—speak for all Scotland? Is Burns really a national poet? Here the acute observation of Oscar Wilde on what happened in France, comes into mind, 'You may have noticed' said he, 'how for some time Nature has set herself to resemble the landscapes of Corot'. In the woods about the Seine there were sunlit green glades everywhere now, where before Corot no one had seen them. And in the same way Scotland, ever since Burns, has become more and more the country of 'The Cottar' and of the political songs and of 'Auld Lang Syne'. The master has stamped himself on the imagination of the people so that they see in each other—and to that extent, reproduce in each other—the qualities he ascribes to them. It is a phenomenon well-known in literature as in painting, when the personality of the master is strong enough. And Burns, like Corot, marks a turning-point in the history of his art.

The picture of a Scotland geared to Burns, if something of a caricature, has yet a basis of truth. Burns did indeed seize on some basic features of the Scots character, and spotlight them—its interest in religion, with the corollary, hypocrisy,—its national aggressiveness as in the political songs—its facile sentimentality as in 'Auld Lang Syne'. But these are only *some* basic features— not all. And in spotlighting them, he has isolated them from others equally fundamental—as ambition, love of scholarship, love of roaming—to which the illustrious list of Scots abroad from the thirteenth century onwards, bears ample and glowing testimony. For that side of Scotland—and many would hold it to be the nobler side—he does not speak at all. Yet in any true picture of Scotland, alongside his Cottar and Holy Willie—common enough types both of them—must be set the equally familiar figure of Neil Munro's John o' Lorn, that homesick exile that Burns had never met,—of the myriads of wandering scholars that wrote Scotland's name large in every university in Europe—of the pioneers in Canada and Australia and the wilds beyond—of the sailors from Lewis or the Shetlands. In any true picture these have their place. Burns' Scotland—by contrast—, the Scotland he has put across, is a limited one. Even in his own day it fell far short of the whole truth. And to-day it is living on its reputation.

Take the City of Glasgow, for example, on a festive night, when the huge mixed crowds pack the St. Andrew's Halls to the very door. What are the songs that stir them, as the wind stirs the sea,—the songs they all know by heart? No song of Burns's. But whisper a line of 'Cruachan Beann' or of 'Eilean Muile'— those Gaelic songs with their passion of longing for the Highlands and Islands—and they'll raise the roof for you in a moment. Or if you want it in English, 'The Bonnie Banks o' Loch Lomond' will do the same. You can sweep any Scots crowd anywhere off its feet with that. And tho' none of the three may stand comparison with Burns at his best, yet they answer a need he fails to meet. They do express, in Gaelic or in English, that ache of yearning for the home-places (An Gleann 'san Robh mi òg) which is a key-instinct of Scots character. But Burns never wrote a single word to give an outlet to that emotion. . . . And what of his love-songs, the greatest songs he wrote? They certainly should speak for Scotland, for they are sung universally by Scotsmen, wherever English is spoken. But in the Highlands it is not always spoken. And in Gaelic there are those hundred words for 'darling'. A language that possesses a vocabulary like that, is likely to have some love-songs of its own. If not very good ones. For if you keep all your hundred words in use, you must scatter them indis-criminately—which does not make for a good love-song. A gay one 'Ho Ro Mo Nighean Donn Bhoidheach', rather than a deep one. Or again, there is no word in Gaelic—or only an imported one—for 'kiss' (pòg). Love is a lighter thing without that. So that Burns' best love-songs—like the piano to which they are sung, and which is out of tune with the Highland musical scale—are ever so little out of tune with the Highland temperament. They take things too hard—that 'Ae Fond Kiss'—as if love mattered as much as fighting—and they go too far. The 'Red Red Rose' with its

> 'An' I will love thee still, my dear
> 'Till a' the seas gang dry'—

As to that, you never know what is round the corner, and John o' Lorn is always on the road. The only thing he would love like that, is Ben More itself, for God made many women, but only one Highlands. Burns' love-songs have a foreign air in the Clanranald country, or up by the Crask. You would not put them on with an Oran Mòr—the 'great music' of the Highlands, with its beat of the sea and the storm and fighting and death. It is in the Oran Mòr—and not in Burns—that speaks the soul of the Highlands.

His political songs, in popular thought, are always associated with Scotland. Do not all Scotsmen sing 'Scots Wha Hae', or, in more assertive mood, 'A Man's A Man for a' that'?—Scotland's signature tune, the one or the other. And these may well reflect, in great measure, a Scotsman's picture of himself, as Burns impressed it on him. But,—to find his champions of national independence, Burns, writing for the eighteenth century with the flames of the French Revolution before him ('Scots Wha Hae' is 1794) had to go back to the fourteenth. Only there could he find national champions at all. Later on, they were all sectional, for their own particular pigeon—as, for the King or, like the Douglasses, against him, for the Reformation or agin it, for this or that Covenant, for the Union or against it—. Only Bruce and Wallace (Ayrshiremen both, like Burns himself) cared altruistically for Scotland as a whole,—for Scotland's liberty

'Wha for Scotland's King and Law
'Freedom's sword will strongly draw?'

But in the intervening centuries Freedom's sword hadn't been drawn at all. Scots poets after Barbour had never mentioned it. And after the now famous 'Declaration of Arbroath' (1320) —significantly enough, the work of prelates of the Roman Church, those doughtiest champions of Scottish independence —Scottish statesmen, and the Scots Estates with them, said no more about it. For centuries the thought lay dormant. Liberty, if not independence, lapsed. And naturally so, for after 1560 (the date of the Reformation) only the Kirk possessed either and wild horses wouldn't have made her share the one or the other. But with 'Scots Wha Hae' and the gleaming past of Bannockburn, Burns swept all that shabby self-seeking away and made Southern

Scotland at least liberty-conscious. The Scots who lived in it became to a man the 'Scots wham Bruce has aften led'—as, perhaps? they still are to-day, tho' Liberty as a slogan is again in the doldrums. What Scots miner would allow it, in action or in thought, to a fellow-member of his Trade Union? For the truth is that Scotland, as a country, has never been distinguished either for pursuit of liberty or for toleration of it. One has only to look at Athens, that native-land of liberty, where speech and act and thought were free as the sun, or at England where Magna Carta ran from 1215, to see how little, in respect of freedom, Scotland measures up to either. But 'Scots Wha Hae' came at a time when Freedom was dawning anew over Europe and the masses, in France and in Scotland, were seeing it, for the first time, within their grasp. Burns had caught the psychological moment. His 'Scots Wha Hae' spoke for (Southern) Scotland then. And the illusion that it still does, lingers on, when the reality is gone. For the Welfare State, determining, controlling, circumscribing, every act, is the enemy, par excellence, of liberty. The Welfare State, as omnipotent to-day as the Kirk ever was, and potentially as tyrannical—the Welfare State, in ideals and in principle like Sparta of the old days. And in Sparta, as every Athenian knew, there was no liberty. . . . But, with the Highlands, 'Scots Wha Hae' even on its first appearance, made little contact. Bruce and Wallace were but names up there, and 'sons in servile chains' of whom the song spoke, a thing unheard-of. Then 'Freedom's sword' was altogether too abstract to have any appeal at all. If you wanted to rouse the Highlands, it would have to be the 'Camerons'' sword, or the 'Macgregors'' or the like. What was Freedom anyway? And, as for 'Scotland's Law'

> (Wha for Scotland's King and Law
> Freedom's sword wad strongly draw?)

a less alluring argument of war could hardly be devised by the mind of man. 'Scotland's Law' indeed!—North of the Highland line! Who was going to fight for that? . . . In fine, as a brilliant concert-piece 'Scots Wha Hae' may be admired, in Scotland as elsewhere, but to-day it no more speaks for Scotland, North or South, than does Ossian. Even, perhaps, less. . . . What has happened to 'A Man's A Man' is more curious. This song is of a wider application, the challenge of the poor man anywhere to the privileged, and magnificently flung down, in a way that makes the blood tingle yet. As such, it has become a European, or even a New World manifesto, popular in ever-widening circles. But no longer, in any true sense, national. For in Scotland, since Burns' day, the poor and the privileged have changed places. It is the wearer of the 'hodden grey'—the manual worker—who is privileged now and, ironically enough, with every symptom of that same arrogance and stupidity once characteristic of My Lord, and that are pilloried in the song. And it is 'the birkie ca'd a lord', 'the marquis, duke, an' a' that' who is now poor, and striving, in his turn, to point out to an incredulous 'worker' that

> 'The rank is but the guinea's stamp
> 'The man's the gowd for a' that'—

No 'worker' is going to believe that, of an employer. And then the 'new poor' do not make a song of poverty. So 'A Man's A Man' is out. You can hear it at Scots concerts, or on glamorous 'Burns' nights' sung by a 'patriot'—but more and more rarely. For it has no obvious relevance to modern Scotland. The cast of its thought—its whole terminology—is against it now—'honest poverty', 'The honest man, tho' e'er so poor', 'the man o' independent mind'. But where, in the national or local Press, will you hear these words to-day? Poverty is 'the lower income class' now —the word itself is obsolete. 'Honest'? But the talk is all of 'delinquency' now. And for 'independence' read subsidy. Time has moved on. The national ideals and the practice have both changed. And when a word goes out of use, the idea it stands for —as any linguist knows—infallibly goes too. 'A Man's A Man' has become a period-piece, like those beautiful old eighteenth-century mansions (its contemporaries) we are all so busy pulling down to-day. They and it no longer fit in with our way of life. The only verse with any semblance of real meaning for to-day, is the last one,

> 'It's comin' yet for a' that
> 'That man to man, the warld o'er
> 'Shall brithers be, for a' that.'

And, as a hope, that is not specifically Scotch. . . . The impact of the song on the North is different. Nothing that Burns ever wrote, runs so counter to the Highland spirit. Here poverty, honest or not, is and always has been, a commonplace. But—to make a song about it, when there's war and the mist on the hill and the cattle at the shieling and so much else that is interesting, to sing about—who would do that? Not a Highlander, least class-conscious of mortals. And then, this business of 'hingin' his head'!

'Is there for honest poverty,
'That hings his head, an' a' that?'

But who that has ever seen the lad in the kilt, has seen him hing his head? 'Fier comme un Écossais', they'd say on the Continent, watching the tartan swing by, in the proud way they knew. Without a bawbee, maybe, but—'hingin' his head'? No fear! The 'hodden grey', if you like, for that—but John o' Lorn? Never! . . . And the song went on,—to the Highlands, more incomprehensibly than ever—

'The pith o' sense, an' pride o' worth
'Are higher rank than a' that.'

But neither the one nor the other has the status here that you might wish. It wasn't 'pith o' sense', for instance, took the Seven Men o' Moidart, out with the Prince in the '45. Seven men—to conquer England, the unconquerable! Not much 'sense' there! And yet, if they hadn't come out—what the world would have missed! The wealth of romance, the chivalry, the breathless daredevil gallantry like the brilliance of a falling star. No— it's the lost cause for the Highlands,—the one odd chance that may never come off—behind the ranges, a voice calling—the tattered flag—as her whole tempestuous history testifies. And to each and all of these high incentives Robert Burns was tone-deaf. His blood never beat the faster for one of them. . . . The end of the song strikes an even gloomier note, with its prayer

'That Sense and Worth o'er a' the earth
'Shall bear the gree an' a' that.'

A thought of the devious, but delightful Simon Lovat (like whom there are many in the Highlands) flashes across the mind. Old Lovat the Fox. Not much 'Worth' there. And yet it was his rich, if quite unprincipled humanity charmed Hogarth's pencil, as no one else's did. And what colour he brought to the Stratherrick country! Down in London, though, with 'Sense and Worth bearing the gree' they beheaded him straight away, for all the snows of his eighty years. A dull world, if that's to be the way of it. . . . Even the idealistic hope at the end that

> 'Man to man the world o'er
> 'Shall brithers be for a' that'

leaves the Highlands cold. Had Burns the realist ever read his history? In what Nirvana are Campbells and Macdonalds to be brothers, with Glencoe red between them? . . .

The drinking-songs, with Glenlivet, Talisker, Ferintosh—all the distilleries being up in the North—do have a more general appeal. And yet the Highlands are not—or were not—a hard-drinking country. Of the 4,000 odd Gaelic proverbs in Sheriff Nicolson's comprehensive collection, only one, as has been pointed out, mentions whisky. And in Boswell's own (eighteenth century) Tour of the Hebrides, while he saw whisky punch, as a matter of course, in nearly every house from Skye to Inveraray, the only one to get drunk on it was Boswell himself, at that unfortunate Corriechatachin. The great topers who could drink you under the table were the eighteenth-century Law Lords, of the Parliament House in Edinburgh,—folk like Raeburn's Lord Newton, or the incredible Lord Hermand—Lowlanders to a man. Tho' it is possible the distinction on this score between North and South no longer holds. . . .

But, with 'Auld Lang Syne', as with none of his other work, Burns speaks for all. Here—and here alone—by some magic, he touches the springs that move any Scot. That past we both know, 'we twa' and no others—for Scots, Highland and Lowland, keep themselves to themselves—the roaming, not particularised, 'we've wandered mony a weary fit' and that's all about it—the austere emotional reserve 'Then here's a han', my trusty frien' and no more than that—say it with whisky 'we'll tak' a richt gude willie-waught'—a steady look back, with the final thought that lingers, 'For Auld Lang Syne'. There's not a false note anywhere here. It's the authentic voice of the North, as of the South. By his economy of language, as of emotion, by the power to suggest so much more than he says, Burns carries this song straight to Scotland's heart. Its qualities of reserve, rigid discipline of thought and word, of passion held in leash, of warm-heartedness—are, in fine, the nation's qualities and expressed as the nation would have them. How then did Burns manage to speak here for all? The answer is not in accordance with the general picture of him, but from the 'Epistles' and the drinking-songs, as from his drawing of the cronies in 'Tam o' Shanter' it would seem to be the truth, that Burns understood friendship better than he did love. And 'Auld Lang Syne' is the apotheosis of friendship.

But if Burns leaves out so much of Scotland in his work, it is still true, paradoxically enough, that it took all Scotland— Highlands as well as Lowlands—to make him what he is. What lifted him from the prosaic rut of his Ayrshire ploughed fields into a rainbow world of high excitement and vivid experiences? What transformed the solemn author of 'The Cottar' (that poem 'Ayrshire' from start to finish and so respectable as almost to be the product of an elder of the Kirk!) into the Bohemian poet of 'O Whistle an' I'll come to you, my lad', or 'Green grow the rashes, O'—songs with all the carefree abandon of the wildest Gaelic puirt-a-bheul? It was the Highland tunes did it. They and nothing else. To them Burns, for all his Lowland ancestry, responded like the thoroughbred to the race-course, responded as if he'd been John o' Lorn himself, from the back of the Bealach nam Bò, where there's nothing but a fiddle-string and mist. Unlike any other Scots poet, he vibrated alike to the emotion of the North and the intellect of the South. Tone-deaf as he was to much (and that, not the least important part) of what Scotsmen feel, he yet was alive and tingling to the way they feel it. It is his way of saying things that carries him over the Highland line—and not what he says. With the Highland tunes knocking the 'sense' out of him, and his Lowland head ruthlessly cutting out the Highland rant, Burns is, in that light, and uniquely, Scotland's national poet.

P

BIBLIOGRAPHY

1. *The Centenary Edition of Burns' Works.* 4 vols. ed. Henley and Henderson, 1896. T. & C. Jack, London.
2. *The Works of Robert Burns.* 6 vols. ed. W. Scott Douglas, 1879. W. Paterson, Edinburgh.
3. *The Letters of Robert Burns.* ed. De Lancey Fergusson. O.U.P.
4. *The Songs of Burns,* by James C. Dick. O.U.P., 1908
5. *Notes on Scottish Song,* by Robert Burns, by James C. Dick. O.U.P. 1908.
6. *The Merry Muses of Caledonia.* Burns Federation, 1911.
7. *A Primer of Burns,* by A. W. Craigie. Methuen, 1896.
8. *Robert Burns,* Vol. I, *La Vie,* Vol. II. *Les Oeuvres,* by Auguste Angellier, 1893. Hachette, Paris.
9. *Life of Robert Burns,* by Hecht, trans. by Lymburn, 1936. Hodge.
10. *Life of Robert Burns,* by F. B. Snyder, 1932. Macmillan, New York.
11. *Burns' Life and Works,* by Daiches. Columbia University— New York. 1952.
12. *Life of Burns,* by J. G. Lockhart, 1890. Ward Lock, London.
13. *Life of Burns,* by Catherine Carswell. Chatto & Windus, London, 1930.
14. *Essay on Burns,* by Thomas Carlyle, 1904. Blackie & Son, London.
15. *Men and Books (Essay on Burns),* by R. L. Stevenson. Chatto & Windus, London, 1898.
16. *Essays from the Edinburgh Review* (Jeffrey's Essay on Burns). Routledge, London.
17. *The Story of the Kilmarnock Burns,* by John Ross. Aeneas Mackay, Stirling, 1933.
18. *Fergusson's Poems,* Fullarton, 1879, London.
19. *Tea-Table Miscellany,* by Allan Ramsay, 2 vols., 1876. Robert Forrester, Glasgow.

20. *The Gentle Shepherd*, by Allan Ramsay, 1899. A. & C. Black, London.

21. David Herd's *Ancient and Modern Songs*, 1769.

22. Joseph Ritson's *Scottish Songs*, 2 vols, 1794. London.

23. *The Poems of Dunbar*. Scottish Text Society. ed. H. Small. 5 vols.

24. *Satyre of the Three Estates*, by Sir David Lyndesay, 1871. Wm. Paterson, London.

25. *History of the Reformation*, by John Knox. 2 vols. ed. Dickinson, 1953. Edin. Univ. Press.

26. *Letters of Samuel Rutherfurd*. Oliphant, Anderson & Ferrier, Edinburgh.

27. *The Memoirs of Thomas Boston.*

28. *The Autobiography of Jupiter Carlyle*. T. & N. Foulis, 1906.

29. *Memorabilia Domestica*, by the Rev. D. Sage. Wm. Rae, Wick.

30. *Ministers and Men in the Far North*, by Rev. A. Auld. John Menzies, Edinburgh.

31. *Source-book of Scottish History*. ed. Dickinson. Edin. Univ. Press.

32. *A Literary History of Scotland*, by J. Hepburn Millar.

33. *History of English Literature*, by G. Saintsbury. Macmillan.

34. *Scottish Men of Letters in the Eighteenth Century*, by Gray Graham. A. & C. Black, 1901.

35. *The Bible in Scots Literature*, by James Moffat. Hodder & Stoughton.

36. *The Reformation*, by David Ogg. Ernest Benn, London, 1927.

37. *Bygone Church Life in Scotland*, by Wm. Andrews, 1893. London.

38. *The Scot in the Eighteenth Century*, by John Watson. Hodder & Stoughton.

39. *The Scottish Jacobite Movement*, by George Pratt Insh. The Moray Press.

40. *Edinburgh Essays on Scots Literature*. Oliver & Boyd, 1933.

41. *Scots Vernacular Literature*, by T. F. Henderson.

42. *The Presbyterian Tradition*, by C. Warr, 1933. Maclehose.

43. *Scottish Life and Character*, by Dean Ramsay, 1911. T. & N. Foulis.

44. *Law in the Making*, by Lord Constable, 1924. Wm. Hodge, Edinburgh.

45. *Scotch Marriages Regular and Irregular*, by F. P. Walton, 1893. Edinburgh.

46. *The Literature of the Highlanders*, by Nigel MacNeill. Aeneas Mackay, Stirling.

47. *Literature of the Highlands*, by Magnus Maclean. Blackie & Son, London, 1903.

48. *Transactions of the Gaelic Society of Inverness.*

49. *Life of Sir George Mackenzie*, by Andrew Lang. Longmans, Green, London, 1909.

50. *The Northern Muse*, by John Buchan, 1924. Nelson.

51. *Edinburgh Life in the Eighteenth Century* (from Captain Topham's Letters). Wm. Brown, Edinburgh.

52. *Scottish Literature*, by Gregory Smith, 1919.

53. *The History and Character of Calvinism*, by Macneill. O.U.P., 1954.

54. *The Making of the Scottish Prayer Book*, 1637, by Gordon Donaldson. Edin. Univ. Press, 1954.

ACKNOWLEDGMENTS

ACKNOWLEDGMENTS are due to the following for permission to quote from copyright works: to Professor Sir W. A. Craigie (from a paper read to the Cambridge Philological Society), to Mr. David Ogg and Messrs Benn (from Mr. Ogg's *History of the Reformation*), to Mrs. Flecker (from Flecker's *Hassan*); also to Messrs Macmillan (from Saintsbury's *History of English Literature*), and to Messrs Hodge (from a pamphlet by the late Lord Constable), and to Messrs Hodder and Stoughton (for the use of material from Moffat's *Bible in Scotland*); also to the Scottish National Portrait Gallery for permission to use the Nasmyth portrait of Burns. And my best thanks go to the Edinburgh Central Library and the Glasgow Mitchell Library for their kindly and valuable help.

INDEX